TEACHING PHILOSOPHY TODAY

SECOND EDITION

EDITED BY

TERRELL WARD BYNUM

AND

ARNOLD WILSON

PUBLISHED BY
THE PHILOSOPHY DOCUMENTATION CENTER
CHARLOTTESVILLE, VIRGINIA, USA

The first edition of *Teaching Philosophy Today* was edited by Terrell Ward Bynum and Sidney Reisberg. It was published in 1977 by the Philosophy Documentation Center, in cooperation with the National Information and Resource Center for the Teaching of Philosophy. This edition has been edited by Terrell Ward Bynum and Arnold Wilson, and is being republished by the Philosophy Documentation Center as a service to everyone who teaches philosophy.

The Philosophy Documentation Center provides online access to this volume for members of the American Association of Philosophy Teachers and the Philosophy Learning and Teaching Organization.

ISBN-13: 978-1-889680-91-0
ISBN-10: 1-889680-91-5

Philosophy Documentation Center
P.O. Box 7147, Charlottesville, Virginia 22906-7147
E-mail: order@pdcnet.org;
Tel.: (434) 220-3300;
Fax: (434) 220-3301

©2012 Philosophy Documentation Center

TEACHING PHILOSOPHY TODAY

Table of Contents

Editors' Introduction to the Second Edition v
Editors' Introduction to the First Edition vii

I. CRITICISM OF THE LATE SIXTIES: "PHILOSOPHY IS IRRELEVANT"

The Travesty of the Philosophers
    Abraham Kaplan 1

Professional Philosophy and the Layman
    Ed Helbig. 15

II. MAKING PHILOSOPHY "RELEVANT" AGAIN

Applied Philosophy
    Leslie Stevenson. 21

Two Kinds of Teaching
    Huston Smith. 29

Philosophy as Psychoanalysis
    Marcia Cavell 39

The Inevitability of Holding Philosophical Beliefs,
or Le Bourgeois Undergraduate Gentilhomme
    David Nyberg. 49

III. NEW CLASSROOM ACTIVITIES

Teaching and Learning Philosophy in a Classroom
    Mark Levensky 61

Is There an Innovative Pedagogy for the Teaching of Philosophy?
    Karl F. Hein. 73

A Hierarchy of Values: An Approach to the Teaching of Philosophy
    Ronald H. Epp. 83

A New Medium for Teaching Philosophy
David West 89

Teaching Philosophy by the Guided Design Method
Gene D'Amour.. 103

Using Computers to Make Logic Relevant
Frederick Suppe 111

IV. RETURN TO THE TRADITION

Dare to Be Wise
Richard Taylor... 125

Philosophy Today
Paul Feyerabend.. 137

A Way to Philosophy
Eva Brann... 147

V. A VIEW FROM THE LEFT

Philosophy as a Profession
Alison Jaggar 161

Institutional Obstacles to the Teaching of Philosophy
Michael Goldman... 177

Beyond the Eleventh Thesis: Philosophy and Social Change
Robert Atkins.. 185

Teaching Alienation
Richard Schmitt.. 197

Editors' Introduction
(Second Edition—2012)

The present volume is a republication of *Teaching Philosophy Today* edited by Terrell Ward Bynum and Sidney Reisberg, published in 1977 in response to many requests from attendees of the 1976 [First] National Workshop-Conference on Teaching Philosophy, and in anticipation of the forthcoming 1978 Second National Workshop-Conference on Teaching Philosophy. (Both conferences took place on the campus of Union College in Schenectady, New York.)

Those two conferences were important events in the so-called "philosophy teaching movement" which arose in the late 1960s and early 1970s because of a flood of "non-traditional" students entering American higher education—students who, previously, would not have gone to college. In the 1960s and 1970s, a military draft was still in effect in the United States and the Viet Nam War was very unpopular. As a result, an enormous number of young men chose to go to college rather than to be drafted into the Army and sent to fight the unpopular Viet Nam War. Many of those young men had little or no interest in—as they would say—the "very dry, abstract, and irrelevant" kinds of courses, including philosophy courses, being taught in American colleges and universities at the time. Most philosophy courses, for example, were aimed at *philosophy majors* expected, eventually, to become *philosophy teachers*. The new, non-traditional philosophy students were not impressed by the symbolic logic, meta-ethics, and history of philosophy courses being taught then. The students demanded, instead, to have courses that were "relevant to real-world problems," such as war and peace, racism, women's rights, medical ethics, and many more "applied philosophy" topics.

As a result of student demands for "relevance," as well as the many social changes and controversies occurring at the time (for example, an unpopular war, the civil rights movement, the feminist movement, affirmative action, abortion, organ transplants, the computer revolution, and on and on) the so-called "philosophy teaching movement" was very exciting and productive in the 1970s and beyond. The American Philosophical Association established a Committee on Teaching Philosophy, the journal *Metaphilosophy* created a section entitled "The Philosopher as Teacher," and the new journal *Teaching Philosophy* was launched. New "applied ethics" subjects (for example, medical ethics, computer ethics, caring ethics) generated courses, textbooks, conferences, research centers, journals, and teaching methods. A variety of non-lecture teaching methods in philosophy were tried and refined; and an important re-examination of the nature of philosophy arose. Is philosophy *a set of traditional ideas* about which to lecture and write books, or *an activity* that one must learn *how to do*? Should the teaching of philosophy occur primarily in colleges and universities, or should it also be taught in elementary schools, high schools, old folks' homes, even prisons?

The present volume was first published at a crucial time during the "teaching philosophy movement" and it had a significant impact upon that movement. It emerged as one of the influential consequences of the first two National Workshop Conferences on Teaching Philosophy. Those conferences, in turn, led to the founding of the American Association of Philosophy Teachers (AAPT) whose national and international conferences have occurred every two years since then with significant impacts upon the teaching of philosophy in America and a number of other countries.

This volume is being republished by the Philosophy Documentation Center as a service to everyone who teaches philosophy. The collection contains all of the papers oringally published in *Teaching Philosophy Today*, including the original introduction. Arnold Wilson went through the volume and made minor corrections to remove blemishes in the original edition. We both agree that many of the ideas and teaching methods discussed here are still relevant and helpful, more than three decades after they were originally published. The most dated part of the book is clearly the Marxist critique of philosophy teaching presented at the end, though this still has historical interest.

New Haven, Connecticut
September 2012

Editors' Introduction
(First Edition—1977)

In the late 1960s, during the era of "campus unrest," professional philosophy (like many other disciplines) was severely criticized by students and others as "irrelevant and arcane." Philosophers responded in a variety of ways. Some, of course, simply ignored the accusations; but many others advocated changes in the *kind* of philosophy that is done and in the *way* it was taught. The two articles in chapter one below provide strong examples of the kind of criticism that was leveled against philosophy.

In chapter two it is argued that philosophy should become, as it used to be, more practical and more concerned with the whole person. Thus, it should deal with affect and emotion, and with serious human problems such as abortion, euthanasia, and racism; and not merely with its own internal "meta" issues in logic and semantics. Some new teaching methods are suggested to help move in that direction.

In chapter three philosophy is viewed more as an *activity* than a set of facts or theories to be described in a lecture or a textbook. Being an activity, philosophy is best learned, it is argued, by *doing* it in mock trials, in team projects, in panel discussion, etc., rather than passively taking notes from lectures. In keeping with this conception of philosophy, these articles describe a variety of alternative classroom activities.

The authors in chapter four propose a return to "the good old days," when philosophy was a broad and learned pursuit of wisdom. One must engage in it for the love of learning and wisdom rather than for practical consequences or "relevance." Yet, there *is* a practical result: the philosophy classroom becomes again a *community* of persons engaged in a common and rewarding enterprise.

Taken together, the articles in chapter five provide a broad "leftist" critique of traditional philosophy teaching. Thus, it is argued that professional philosophers have a vested interest in mystification, in setting themselves up as "experts" and keeping the public philosophically ignorant. The current educational structure, it is claimed, has built-in biases—moral, political, and epistemological doctrines—which force students to be nonautonomous, noncooperative, and alienated from learning. Educational institutions, including the philosophers within them, have become tools of government and business which help "depoliticize" the people, making them easier to mold and command.

* * *

The editors wish to express their sincere thanks to Alice McDermott for the excellent job she did in preparing the camera ready copy for this volume.

PART I:

Criticism of the Late Sixties: "Philosophy Is Irrelevant"

The Travesty of the Philosophers

ABRAHAM KAPLAN

A few years ago an article appeared in one of the philosophical journals with the provocative title, "The Dreariness of Modern Aesthetics." That title could have been used just as well for most of the other fields of philosophy. In America today philosophy may not be altogether an intellectual wasteland, but it *is* dreary.

As an academic discipline, to be sure, it is booming. Philosophy departments with fifteen or twenty full-time faculty and perhaps an equal number of graduate assistants are commonplace; undergraduate courses attract hundreds of students; graduate schools often count fifty or a hundred candidates for the Ph.D. in philosophy. But all this activity remains academic. There is little excitement, little thrill of discovery, little evangelical fervor, very little sense of what Alfred North Whitehead called the adventure of ideas. So it appears, at any rate, in contrast with the condition of philosophy at other times and in other places.

Only a generation or two separates us from such influential American philosophers as William James, George Santayana and John Dewey; Whitehead did much of his work in America; Bertrand Russell spent several eventful years here. Now the men of the highest standing in the profession—like Rudolf Carnap and the late Hans Reichenbach and C. I. Lewis—have little impact on the culture at large; their very names are comparatively unknown. For the most part philosophical ideas in America are of no particular interest outside the profession.

Perhaps the only men in America today widely known and listened to as philosophers are Eric Hoffer and Herbert Marcuse. Hoffer has no professional standing. Marcuse, however, is not only the idol of the student activists; he has also been honored with the presidency of the American Philosophical Association's Pacific Division (there are no national officers). Yet it is hard to escape the impression that it was primarily a political gesture; his views have had little impact on other philosophers.

On most campuses departments of philosophy decidedly make their presence felt. Student leaders from Mario Savio on are often majors in philosophy; the faculty of philosophy often plays a leading part in campus demonstrations for peace, for student power or for academic freedom. The free speech that is still possible at UCLA, for instance, is likely to be spoken in Meyerhoff Park, named for a philosopher (an old friend and colleague) who studied and taught there and was active on behalf of many causes. Such activities by students and teachers of philosophy, though, usually have nothing to do with their concerns in the classroom or the study. Hans Meyerhoff himself was an exception. But more typical is Donald Kalish of UCLA, a dedicated worker for peace in Vietnam and a professor of formal logic and semantics. The impact, in brief, is not made by philosophy but rather by professors of philosophy, not by ideas but by personal commitments.

Personally, I honor those commitments, and professionally I endorse them. To encapsulate the mind is to emasculate it. If we do not use our reason on the great problems, it makes no sense to exercise reason on the little problems. Yet it is one thing for us intellectuals to insist on our right to action—indeed, our duty to act. It is quite another for us to suspend the intellect or set it aside for the sake of action. Still, the gap is widening in our time between *professed* philosophies and the philosophies men live by. If what is important in life does not appear in professional work, or is brought in only to be negated, the work cannot have any place in the important contexts of life. Philosophy then becomes only an occupation, something incidental, while the life itself remains unexamined, and thereby, as Socrates had it, not worth living. The gap between professed and lived philosophy makes action thoughtless and thought pointless.

The new treason of the intellectuals is that we have shared and even contributed to the current loss of faith in the power of the human mind to cope with human problems, faith in the worth of reasoned discussion, faith even in the possibility of objective truth. That philosophy has been set apart from our most basic concerns is a mark of this new failure of philosophic nerve. If we ourselves cannot in good faith profess the love of wisdom, we might at least reaffirm the significance of its continued pursuit.

What I question, in a word, is the *relevance* of philosophy. I am quite aware of the shoddy thinking which the demand for relevance can rationalize. Too often there is a vulgar pragmatism in what is taken to define relevance—the most immediate problems posed by what is happening in Vietnam, in the ghetto or on the campus. Often, too, there is a sophomoric dogmatism—far from childish in import—in the unyielding assumption made by those who demand relevance that they already know what is relevant and what is not. In the life of the mind an abstract theory for reflection may be far more relevant than a concrete program for action; and openness to a new truth is a necessary condition for any intellectual growth.

Nevertheless it makes sense to ask for the bearings of philosophy on what Charles Sanders Peirce, the founder of pragmatism, characterized as the "vitally significant topics." In spite of his pragmatism (or maybe because of it), Peirce held that philosophy has nothing to say about such topics. That certainly seems to be true of contemporary philosophy. And if it remains true, philosophy itself will scarcely have any vital significance. What *does* philosophy have to say to us today about the problems of war, of racial inequality, of poverty, of a dehumanized technology? About the achievements in nuclear physics, in the exploration of space, in molecular biology, in behavioral science? About the new directions in religion, in morality, in art? Even the most defensive professional would have to concede that the answer is "not very much."

Perhaps the answer need not be a concession. The satisfaction of intellectual curiosity does not call for any apology. "All men by nature desire to know," said Aristotle. That desire surely—for philosophers, at any rate—is its own justification, whatever the knowledge which is desired. We need not seek to know only what matters to other people. The disinterested pursuit of understanding for its own sake is surely the very essence of the philosophical quest. But though the motivation is admirable, the subject matters in which it finds expression often reduce philosophy to what is at best a harmless pastime and at worst a trivial mental exercise.

It might be urged that the human significance of philosophy is indirect, like that of pure science. But if the philosopher is not chained to the wall of Plato's cave, neither can he indefinitely remain at ease in the sunlight of pure ideas. The work of philosophy is as much to assess the practical import of theory as it is to disclose the theoretical presuppositions of practice. If philosophy becomes a purely theoretical discipline, a new enterprise will be needed to explore the relations between such a discipline and other human concerns, in both theory and practice. What else should this new enterprise be called if not "philosophy"?

A certain indirectness of relevance, to be sure, is an inevitable characteristic of any fundamental approach. The more profound a philosopher—like Plato, Spinoza or Kant—the greater the distance between his abstract thought and the concrete problems of action from which he takes his departure. Yet the relevance is there, and thought remains significant for action. But in much contemporary philosophy, what is thought has relevance only to the thought of other philosophers. We dig so far down into the foundations that we come to see life only in terms of our own subterranean existence. What we term philosophical analysis often might better be called "notes from underground."

Philosophers today are still occupied, for instance, with the so-called problem of "free will." This problem is usually discussed, with great technical subtlety and ingenuity, in terms of quantum indeterminacy, computability and decidability in formal systems, or the grammar of subjunctive modalities. Such considerations may be fundamental in some sense, I suppose. Yet I think most of us would like to see someone trace their implications for what we experience as the significant problems of freedom—the problems posed by political authority, economic necessity, psychological compulsion or social pressure. I once spoke on Spinoza's metaphysics of human bondage to an audience of former drug addicts struggling to regain their freedom; I learned as much as I taught. When philosophy is truly fundamental, as with Spinoza, there is no doubt of its relevance.

Similarly, the so-called problem of our knowledge of "other minds" does not necessarily become more fundamental when formulated in terms of the epistemology of sense-data. The substantive problems of knowing other minds are those posed by our efforts to reach out to others across the gaps of generations, races, cultures and power structures. When we turn away from the things that are important on the face of it, we are not necessarily approaching fundamental matters; it might simply be that we are coming to occupy ourselves with trivialities.

Whatever in contemporary philosophy is not irrelevant is still likely to be *remote*. It is likely to deal only with what we say about significant problems rather than with the problems themselves, which it assigns to science or to practice. Philosophical discourse is said by formalists to lie in the so-called metalanguage, that language in which we talk about talk rather than about things. Non-formal analysts share the "meta" perspective, if not its technical locutions. Thus, ethics is concerned with good and evil, right and wrong. But what we usually find in American philosophy today is *metaethics*, an analysis of when and why people might *say* that something is "good" or "evil," or that an action is "right" or "wrong." I recall a brilliant dissertation dealing with moral obligation done by a doctoral candidate. At his oral examination the dean of the School of Social Welfare invited the candidate to point to some bearings of his analysis on the sorts of ethical issues involved in the administration of the welfare programs. The question was well-meant, but the candidate—now one of the ablest ethical theorists in the country—was quite at a loss for reply. The trouble was not that he knew nothing about such issues but that his philosophical preoccupations were so remote from them, or from any like them. Alas, there is much force to Henry Aiken's plaint that we need not "meta" ethics but "betta" ethics.

If metaethics wants concrete cases as examples, it is as likely to discuss schoolboy pranks and domestic peccadillos as to discuss the moral dilemmas of selective conscientious objection, legalized abortion or ethnic separatism. When philosophical analysis is sufficiently remote, its ultimate subject no longer matters; the proximate subject is always the same—language. Only words count. I sometimes feel that the resources called for by philosophy today are neither knowledge nor wisdom but a sensitivity to usage, a good dictionary and pedantic doggedness. This feeling is not wholly justified, to be sure; but it is far from being altogether groundless.

To take another instance of remoteness, many philosophers today are occupied with what has come to be called the "theory of action." They are concerned with the analysis of such phenomena (idioms?) as having an intention of making up one's mind. But the psychodynamics of character and personality often falls outside the philosopher's purview, being assigned to psychology or psychiatry. Such matters as the paradox of organization—that organizations develop their own interests which qualify and even subvert the original goals to have been served by organizing—are even less likely to find a place in the philosophical "theory." Yet most significant action today is carried out by collective agents—such as states, political parties and corporations—rather than by individuals. Empirical hypotheses concerning legal practices, political institutions, the dynamics of small groups, or the techniques of psychotherapy have, in my judgment, far greater import for the understanding of action than do purportedly philosophical analyses of what a man means when he pleads that he did something "unintentionally."

There is in philosophy today an unmistakable trend toward formalism and scholasticism. From a lively awareness of the problems of men we are moving to merely academic concerns, and these in turn are couched more and more often in the jargon of remote technicalities. This is a trend not only in philosophy. The humanities and the human sciences increasingly incorporate what they see as the style of physics. What Morton White once called the "hup-two-three" schools of thought are everywhere in the ascendancy. Like him, I wish to dissociate myself from antiscientific obscurantism and from the attacks on technology which disguise self-interest and fear as devotion to the human spirit. Yet technicality is no substitute for content, and as was proclaimed by H. H. Price in a famous paper, clarity is not enough.[1]

At various times in the history of philosophy, it was nature, rather than God or man, which served as the focus of speculation. That philosophy in our time has been much influenced by science and mathematics is not in the least responsible for its irrelevance or remoteness. On the contrary, wherever that influence has been most marked, philosophy has been furthest from empty scholasticism. Nor is the emphasis on analysis in itself unphilosophical. Here again I must insist on the contrary; one of the basic tasks of philosophy is undeniably the clarification of our ideas and the explicit formulation of basic assumptions. What I do protest is that the analysis practiced is so often almost hopelessly remote in both form and content from any significant ideas or assumptions outside certain narrow branches of mathematics. Students elect courses in logic, and curriculum committees require such courses, in the expectation that in them one can learn something of scientific method and rational decision making. Disappointment is bitter and widespread.

I do not appeal to the values of a vulgar pragmatism. Courses in logic need not teach us how to think, any more than courses in economics should teach us how to make profitable investments, or courses in chemistry teach us how to improve on Molotov cocktails. But it is not unreasonable to expect that courses in logic will help us to *understand* what is involved in thinking straight. One might reasonably expect logic to have *something* to do—if only by contrast—with legal argument and political debate, with the rationality or irrationality of our emotional life, with cultural patterns of thought and personal styles, with such matters as the distinction Marxists draw between dialectical and mechanical thinking, and at the very least, with what science recognizes as sound inference and reliable evidence. What most logic courses present instead are the foundations of set theory and related mathematical formalities.

Such matters may be of considerable importance to computer technology and to certain other special disciplines. In any case, they are worthy of being prized for their own sake, even if they were to have no applications whatever. The work of logicians like Alfred Tarski and Willard Van Quine is justly famous and is intrinsically philosophical. But I venture to say that these logicians themselves would recognize how far removed their work is from the ideas that dominate our minds and the affairs that populate our lives.

Even what is called "philosophy of science" often has very little to do with any actual science except certain parts of mathematics, and possibly certain reconstructions of parts of physics. A study of the history of science itself contributes more to an understanding of the spirit and method of science than does a study of contemporary philosophy of science. Not only is the philosophy of science irrelevant to almost all scientific practice; often it is also distressingly remote from any significant scientific content. The paradigm of a scientific law, which has been subjected to endless analysis, is "All crows are black." Distinguished philosophers of science like Ernest Nagel and Carl G. Hempel are well acquainted with both the method and the content of several sciences, but today this is far from true of many specialists in the philosophy of science. Larger issues relating to the place of science in society and the impact of science on other cultural domains are left entirely untouched. In short, logic and the philosophy of science are by and large as remote from their ostensible subject matter as metaethics is from the issues and ambiguities of moral practice.

This is the contemporary fashion in American philosophy. The form of the philosophy is analytic, its content is logico-linguistic—sometimes with greater emphasis on formal logic, more often with greater emphasis on ordinary language. American philosophy is hardheaded and tough-minded, down-to-earth even about its abstractions, matter-of-fact even about its remote generalizations. There is little human folly in it, but even less divine madness.

A fashion is not just a matter of frequencies. It is not a merely superficial trend but an underlying tendency. The statistic is not accidental but is produced by the steady thrust of overt social forces or more subtle cultural pressures. In the domain of thought, prevailing fashions are indistinguishable from orthodoxies.

Philosophic orthodoxy is reinforced by many practices. To start with, Ph.D. requirements today make it virtually impossible to get the degree without considerable work in logic, philosophy of language, and epistemology; but it is quite usual to complete the requirements without any graduate studies in the philosophy of politics, art or religion, and often without philosophy of science as well. Hiring practices also inevitably reflect prevailing fashions of thought: it is hard to distinguish a man's philosophical capacity from the "soundness" of his views. (Of course, someone with unconventional interests or attitudes may be hired in a gesture of token integration, or—more probably—to provide service courses for other departments.) Granting agencies, too, are understandably guided by reputable judgment. Editors, like Gilbert Ryle of the British journal *Mind*, can exert enormous influence on the style of thought itself, and not only on the style of its presentation.

It is not surprising, therefore, that philosophy today is so academic, in the sense in which we speak of academic art. It is mechanical, cold and uninspired—as it must be when the man himself, whether artist or thinker, has no place in his work; when, indeed, all human concerns give way to a preoccupation with "professional standards." In such an epoch, creation is a labor without love, governed only by occupational anxieties or by the unfeeling application of established formulas. In philosophy such formulas can be identified not only in the sameness of the problems which fill the journals (to say nothing of dissertation files), but also in the sameness even of their very titles. Creative imagination, I suppose, is always in short supply, but in philosophy today what little there is seems to exceed the demand.

There are, of course, fashions in all fields, and quite possibly orthodoxy is no more prevalent in philosophy than elsewhere. But there is something peculiarly unphilosophical about fashions in philosophy. One of the major tasks of philosophy—as Socrates saw it in the ancient world and Kant in modern times—must surely be to question all conventional patterns of thought, to examine critically every received doctrine, to affirm the rights of reason and experience against every claim of established truth. Today we philosophers are freethinkers about everything except our own orthodoxies.

Fashions are nowhere easier to discern than in unusual settings—there is a truth expressed, after all, in the fiction of the Englishman who dresses for dinner in the jungle. One might expect to find the logico-linguistic style in, say, the theory of knowledge or the philosophy of science. But it is even more markedly characteristic today of fields like aesthetics and the philosophy of religion. A typical problem, for example, of contemporary American aesthetics concerns what is called "the status of the aesthetic object"—the ontology of poems, plays and symphonies which cannot be identified with specific physical objects or events nor yet be given a purely mentalistic locus. How remote such a problem is from the aesthetic presuppositions and implications of the new styles in art and the new media for their expression! Philosophers of art have never seemed so uninterested in waiting even a little for Godot.

Comparable tendencies can be discerned in contemporary philosophy of religion. Typical problems focus on religious knowledge and religious language—on the analysis, say, of prayer as poetry; that is, as "emotive," "noncognitive" in content. Yet today we are involved in religious changes which may be as momentous as those of the Reformation and the Counter-Reformation: changes in the structure of religious authority, both individual and institutional, and changes in the responsiveness of religious practices to crises of action, both personal and social. On these matters philosophers of religion (as distinguished from religionists of philosophical bent) have not been very articulate or very illuminating.

I do not say that the questions which *are* being discussed by philosophers of religion are of no philosophical import. On the contrary: there are important changes today in ritual, changes, for instance, which make quite relevant studies of the role of symbolism in religion, and of the nature of religious language. Still, the tendency is to allow a certain narrow class of questions to preponderate, indeed to make their discussion the very standard of acceptable philosophical discourse.

When a man feels that the times are out of joint, he is well advised to consider carefully whether it might be his perception of the times which is distorted. I cannot persuade myself, however, that I am nostalgic for a supposedly golden past. In fact, my impression is that in my youth philosophical orthodoxy was, if anything, even more firmly entrenched than it is today, though it was a different doctrine, to be sure. I had the privilege then of being a student of Rudolf Carnap, Bertrand Russell and Hans Reichenbach. Recently I found occasion to confide to Carnap that these days I sometimes feel like a Trotskyite. As a student I was associated with the philosophical revolutionaries. In due course the revolution triumphed, or at least *a* revolution did. But the dictatorship of the proletariat is as repressive in its way as was that of the czars, and now to proclaim anew the ideals of freedom is to risk being thought counter-revolutionary.

No doubt many of the shortcomings of the profession are due precisely to its professionalism. Graduate schools of philosophy are devoted almost exclusively to training teachers of philosophy. The whole program is thus largely self-contained. It is important for the autonomy of philosophy to be persevered—philosophy should not become a handmaiden to politics, art or religion any more than to science, mathematics or linguistics. Yet what masquerades as the preservation of autonomy may in fact be an inward turning which progressively loses contact with the ambient reality.

Even the tasks of education in philosophy suffer from this involuted preoccupation of the discipline with its own practitioners. On the one hand, textbooks (to say nothing of "popularizations") have at best a dubious professional standing. On the other hand, little guidance in cultivating the arts of teaching is provided for our graduate students. Their training is almost wholly a matter of inculcating them in certain professional skills—in what is called philosophical analysis—and in transmitting to them a certain body of information: the history, ancient and contemporary, not of ideas in their broad cultural setting, but of the work of other practitioners of our own professional skills.

Students of philosophy enter their training with most admirable philosophical motives. They come with intellectual curiosity, puzzled about the foundations of science, disturbed by religious questions, agonized over politics, captivated by literature and art. All that nonsense is knocked out of them. Studies of medical schools have shown that first-year students have high ideals of devoting themselves to healing suffering humanity, ideals which become progressively less important to them in successive years of their training. When they have abandoned such notions altogether I suppose they are judged ready for membership in the American Medical Association. I am fearful that, like the medical profession, the profession of philosophy may be its own worst enemy; the training we give to our students may have the side effect of producing a progressive degradation of their philosophic impulse.

How could it be otherwise, in view of our introversion? As professionals we speak only to each other; our students acquire the gloss of professionalism by entering into that circumscribed dialogue, not by persisting in their involvements with the larger world, save avocationally, in their personal lives. As Emerson said, if in our philosophy we meet no gods, it is because we harbor none.

There is a philosophic function to be performed in every culture. That function is not to be confused with the activities of what is identified as the profession of philosophy in the division of labor prevailing at any given time. (It may be that much of the work of philosophy is in fact done by men who are not professional philosophers.) Philosophic activity takes place chiefly at the interface between the life of the mind and the arts of practice, on the frontiers of every domain of knowledge and action. Philosophy thus must look outward for its very life; it grows only at the edges. As the profession turns inward, more and more of its work must be done by outsiders—in our day by such people as Margaret Mead, Erich Fromm, Noam Chomsky, even Marshall McLuhan. A half-century has gone by since John Dewey analyzed the philosophic function in his *Reconstruction in Philosophy*; it may be that, as Dewey has said of democracy, such a reconstruction must be carried out anew by each generation.

The problem is much deeper than that posed by the superficial tasks of keeping up with the times. Nietzsche once remarked that a married philosopher belongs to comedy; could it be that the notion of a professional philosopher is equally absurd? If philosophy is taken seriously as the pursuit of wisdom it is surely a calling rather than a profession, a vocation, not an occupation. Those who undeniably had the vocation—men like Socrates, Epictetus, Spinoza—were truly philosophers, not professors of philosophy. To be sure, philosophy, like religion, needs its priests as well as its prophets. But the voice of prophecy seems to have been stilled, and only the priesthood flourishes. Our dilemma is that subservience to the priests may better serve the spirit than does whoring after false gods.

A department of philosophy is, after all, an academic department, not an enclave dedicated to personal salvation or to social revolution, and as an academic department it may be expected to share the problems of the academy. On the whole, departments of philosophy are better off than many others—and not only the fields notorious for their intellectual slackness. Students of philosophy continue to be of very high quality, as are philosophy faculties in general. The ambivalent myth of the philosopher as profound in intellect but laughably incapable of grasping realities is no less a myth today—in both respects—than in the time of Aristophanes' *Clouds*. There are, I suppose, professors of philosophy who are basically fools, but they are proportionately no more numerous, I dare say, than the asses laden with books who plod through other domains of scholarship. Philosophy, though, does suffer more than other fields from the usual academic overemphasis of publication. The number of books and journals of philosophy increases steadily; publication is by far the broadest avenue to professional advancement for both the graduate student and the non-tenured faculty. How old-fashioned it seems to suggest that philosophy may demand calm reflection, the slow growth of ideas, the mature fruits of a lifetime, perhaps, of deliberation.

Academic competitiveness also seems quite unphilosophic in spirit. The conduct of our seminars, the proceedings of our societies, the tone of the reviews published in our journals, the controversies with which the journals abound—all combine to promulgate a caustic and corrosive spirit. It is very rare in philosophy today, outside the technical advances in mathematical logic, for one man to build on the work of another, for ideas to be welcomed because of the further ideas they generate, or for a viewpoint to be accepted as understandable and perhaps reasonable even though it is not shared by the commentator. Hostilities seem to be limited only by the proliferation of regional defense systems, coteries of cross-reference among the members of particular philosophic schools and their subordinate sects. In striking parallel to what holds true in society-at-large, we have become quite practiced in the techniques of destruction, while allocating only a small part of our resources to the peaceful uses of our energies.

Like other academicians, too, we exaggerate the importance to philosophic training of what we teach. (Yet quite often philosophers do most of their work in fields other than those reflecting the special interests of their student days.) It is difficult, I suppose, for any graduate or professional school to recognize that on-the-job training may be as important as what the schools can teach. The result is that requirements tend to become too severe, and too rigidly imposed. The tacit assumption is that if graduate students, in philosophy at any rate, are allowed to pursue their own bent, they will be poorly prepared for their subsequent work. I suspect that such an assumption serves only self-interest, rationalizing the all-too-human impulse to impose on those in our charge our own values and perspectives. This must surely be unhealthy in the teaching of the arts or the sciences; in the teaching of philosophy it is fatal.

Of course standards must be maintained, especially in the face of the accelerating demands for trained personnel to staff the new colleges and universities springing up everywhere. But standards are not high merely because they are rigid. On the contrary, they might be effectively higher if they were not mechanically imposed without regard to differences in skills, interests, capacities—in everything that makes up the cognitive style of the individual. I have known aestheticians required to devote several years to acquiring a modicum of skill in the manipulations of symbolic logic, philosophers of science required to spend time on the study of Greek philosophy which they might have better spent on the history of Greek science (or Greek art, for that matter), ethical theorists required to become caught up in the intricacies of English idioms rather than in the convolutions of unconscious desires or political maneuvers. However radical the philosophic ideas, departments of philosophy are not conspicuous for their leadership in freeing academic life from its traditions and conventional constraints.

The mission of philosophy, in the university as in the society-at-large, is to provide the perspective in which we can see the world steady and see it whole. The task of philosophy is synoptic; analysis has its intrinsic worth, but it comes to fruition in the synthesis it makes possible. This task is more difficult today than it has ever been, made so by the increasing complexity of human affairs, and especially by the explosion of knowledge in our time. Yet the need remains, and, indeed, is greater than it ever was. However multifarious the world has become, man still needs to be at one with himself. More than ever we desperately need principles of integration by which we can achieve a consonance of our beliefs with one another, and of belief with action. The more difficult the problem is because of its great scope and complexity, the more pressing is the need to cope with it somehow.

We cannot fulfill our philosophic responsibilities by always emulating the sciences and attacking our problems piecemeal. Specialization within philosophy is almost a contradiction in terms. Today such specialization has proceeded so far that one is tempted to call for a supra-philosophy to unite the philosophical specialties and interpret them to one another, were it not that such synthesis is undeniably the task of philosophy itself. A philosopher is inevitably a generalist. In an age of specialization a high price must be paid by the generalist for unavoidably being somewhat superficial and out of touch with the very latest developments. Why should its own profession exact a stiff penalty over and above this price?

Philosophy must reach out to the boundaries of knowledge and experience in every direction. Parochialism is a grievous fault anywhere in today's world; it is especially shocking in philosophy. We *are* parochial, even in the most literal sense. Geographically speaking, American philosophy today might as well be in the eighteenth century. The philosophy in other parts of the world which our own philosophy takes into account—as measured by discussions or even mentions in our work—is distributed, I venture to guess, in very roughly the following proportions: England (analytic philosophy), about 70 percent; Western Europe (existentialism, phenomenology and neo-orthodox theologies), 15 percent; Eastern Europe (Marxism, both classical and humanistic), 10 percent; the whole of Asia (Indian, traditional Chinese, and Japanese), 5 percent; and South America, Africa, and the rest of the world (except for British elements of Australian culture), less than 1 percent. Hardly an expression of philosophic breadth of vision!

The time may have come to declare that the emperor (or should I say, the philosopher-king?) has no new clothes. I do not intend a palace revolution or any other kind. On the philosophical scene, at any rate, there is little to be gained by initiating controversy and inviting confrontation. But a heightened self-awareness of the aims and methods of the philosophic enterprise in America today is surely worth attaining, even if we were to conclude that no changes at all are called for.

A separate department outside philosophy should be established for mathematical logic, formalistic philosophy of science, the communication and computer sciences, and related disciplines. (What exactly should be included would vary from place to place, according to the skills and resources already available or sought.) Psychology is only the most recent of the disciplines to split off from philosophy; there is no reason why it should be the last. In many universities such departments, or at least formal programs of study, have already been established; it is time to give these new domains *de jure* as well as *de facto* recognition. The happiness and growth of both mother and child are thwarted when their separation is too long protracted.

For the Ph.D. in philosophy, we should strongly encourage the earning of the master's degree, or at the very least, an undergraduate major in some other field. Subsequent work in philosophy is to be related to that field, rather than representing a complete shift of interests. How better to restore to philosophy it substantive content when we know we must seek nourishment in some more effective way than by chewing our own entrails? It is especially ironic that while professional modesty impels us to disclaim competence in other fields outside our own, we hesitate so little to commit ourselves on such matters, in both belief and action, so long as we can do so without professional responsibility.

The requirements of Ph.D. examinations and dissertations should be radically liberalized or even abolished. This is not to say that standards should be lowered; but I question the measure by which they are now declared to be high. What are called "professional standards" are, to a great degree, standards of professionalism, not significant performance. They are to a considerable extent initiation rites rather than realistic assessments of the capacity to contribute to the philosophic function of our time. Such assessments might better be made with some sort of apprentice system in which examinations are seen by both teacher and student as guides to further study, and not as hurdles to be overcome. Instead of a full-scale, pedantic dissertation, would we not all be better off with a stimulating though short paper, or even a penetrating oral discussion of some philosophical problem?

What is important is that we face the realities of our condition, see to what favor we have come. Philosophy is and will remain part of the academy. Our task nevertheless reaches out beyond: it is to mediate between the academy, as embodying the whole life of the mind, and the larger world of affairs, which gives to mind its place purpose. Our challenge today is what it always was—to bring to bear the works of the mind on the great issues and concerns of our time. "When skies are hanged and oceans drowned, the single secret will still be man."

Note

Originally published in *Change* magazine, January 1970. Reprinted here by permission of the editor and the author.

1. "Clarity is Not Enough," *Proceedings of the Aristotelian Society*, 1945

Professional Philosophy and the Layman

Ed Helbig

Philosophy as a distinguishable body of problems and talk about problems makes but little impact outside the narrow world of professional philosophers. The fact that this lack of impact is accepted by philosophers indicates a certain view of philosophy held by professional philosophers. I would like to describe and challenge this view because it is ill-founded and because it portends bad days. I would like to also offer an alternative view of philosophy.

That philosophy does not have an impact on the world outside our classrooms and conference halls is fairly obvious. I have yet to see a philosopher interviewed on television or a living philosopher quoted in an editorial. It does not occur to the news media to seek help in solving political and moral problems from philosophers. One finds psychologists, religious leaders and politicians on the radio, on television, in the newspaper, giving learned information on relevant issues, but no philosophers.

It may be argued that philosophy does not make its impact through news media, that it can only produce its effects through the assimilation of philosophic content by more and more people and that this is necessarily slow. But the evidence is that no assimilation is occurring, not even slowly. People simply do not look to philosophy at all as a source of solutions to their problems. They look upon philosophy as abstract talk about remote matters, quite removed from problems of pollution, abortion, war, religious commitment, beliefs and values.

Surprisingly, many professional philosophers share this popular view. They agree that the content of philosophy is far removed from common problems. If they take positions on some current issue, they do not do so as professional philosophers. As professionals they will take positions on nominalism, material implication, analyticity, deontology; as professionals they will tell you about Quine's quarrel with Carnap over intentionalism, about Hume's arguments against induction and Harre's response to Hume. But, as professionals, they won't take a stand on the value of punishment, the war, religion, or even about rational belief. They will not, as professionals, point out the inconsistencies in current thoughts about education, the vagueness in popular ethical discussion, the lack of good reason for some psychological advice.

It has not always been thus. In the past philosophers viewed their profession as eminently practical. Plato thought philosophy so important to the practical guidance of human activity that he considered it essential for political leaders to be philosophers. Maimonides wrote philosophy to guide the perplexed out of real perplexities about the relation of secular to sacred beliefs. Aquinas produced his theology-philosophy to provide answers to everyday problems of medieval man. Descartes addressed himself to all readers who suffer from doubt. But our modern philosophers only address each other, because no one else understands them, and no one else is interested in the kinds of things they discuss.

What has happened is that the philosophic discussion has taken an extremely technical turn. The turn began, I opine, with Kant, but received its greatest push from symbolic logic and from the attendant hope that the seemingly endless problems of philosophy could be settled or at least clarified with new tools for regimenting language. The attempts to sharpen the tools led to new problems, and to new formulations of old problems. But the new problems and the new formulations were tied to the technical vocabulary that had to be developed to carry on the conversation. By now the old hope of using the tools to solve or eliminate old problems has all but disappeared and philosophers are now content to carry on a private discussion about minute matters relevant to the development of the new tools of logic and analysis. Graduate schools of philosophy train their students to take part in that highly sophisticated technical conversation.

Philosophy, viewed thus by professional philosophers, has little impact outside the little world of philosophers. I find this unfortunate, because the basic problems of mankind are philosophic, and it is unlikely that solutions can be found that ignore philosophy. The basic problems include these: Of what can I be justifiably certain? How can I in practice distinguish a warranted belief from an unwarranted one? How should I act? Is such an action good, bad, or indifferent? Is there anything real that is not spatial? And of course many more. The person who has not faced these problems and who is unaware of the development of the discussion is simply not equipped to solve problems about war, abortion, politics, religion, personal adjustment, child rearing: the problems of everyday life. The view of philosophy as a sophisticated technical dialogue *inter nos* cuts off people from the possibility of valuable enlightenment.

It may be argued that it would be either intellectually dishonest for a professional philosopher to pretend to respond to the questions given above, or else a betrayal of ignorance. Given the last century of philosophy (it may be argued) one must realize that any hope for solving the practical problems lies in the technical dialogue that sharpens the modern tools of analysis and logic, that attempted responses to the practical problems which ignore these sophisticated developments is sure to be over-simplified and naïve at best, and at worst stupid.

Of course, it will be argued, a philosopher might teach history of philosophy, i.e., he might tell people what various philosophers have responded to these questions. But it is fairly obvious that none of these historical responses are adequate. When the historical presentation is over, the problems remain. The philosopher simply has no answer to those problems (it may be argued) and our hope for solutions such as it is, lies in the increasingly technical development of the tools of analysis and logic. So, although the current view that philosophers take of their subject may be unfortunate, it is the only honest, intelligent view possible.

I want to argue that this current view of philosophy is partially erroneous, that we philosophers need not limit our professional life to either a scholarly review of historic philosophies or else to the modern dialogues, that there is a role for substantive philosophizing that is neither analytic nor extremely technical, and that this role need not eschew devotion to clarity and disciplined reasoning.

It is important to emphasize that last clause. The foremost truth of methodology is this: the problems of philosophy cannot be solved in undisciplined, unregimented layman's language. That belief is basic to logic and Western thought. Any attempt to reduce philosophy to bull-sessions, to popular discussions (no matter how relevant the issue) will only produce confusion, error, and dishonesty. If we must choose between a highly technical elite philosophy and discussion-parading-as-philosophy, we should unhesitatingly choose the former, because it is philosophy, it is honest, it does further the intellectual endeavor, while the latter is through and through a farce and a lie.

We advocate philosophizing that is disciplined, but does not talk about the tools of a particular regimentation; viz., those of the analytic schools. After all, Aristotle reasoned as carefully as Quine; Aquinas achieves as much clarity as Carnap. It isn't as if Plato argues sloppily because he lacked the tools of analysis, or that Scheffler argues better because he argues in the symbols of *Principia Mathematica*. As a matter of fact, no one argues in the symbols of *Principia Mathematica*. The difference between preceding philosophy and the modern technical dialogue is not in method, but in content. The modern dialogue is pursuing esoteric minutiae relative to certain analytic tools, but is using the same methods of defining, dividing, assuming, observing, and reasoning that philosophers have always used. I advocate only that philosophers return to the old problems and to the real problems of people and speak out as professional philosophers on those problems. I advocate only that professional philosophers recognize that one can be a bona fide philosopher without being concerned with analytic talk, and that such a bona fide philosopher need not reject clarity and disciplined method.

Besides the reasons alluded to, I have selfish reasons for advocating this giant step sideways, a selfish reason shared by many professional philosophers, I think. It is this: I want to keep my job. Very few students take courses in philosophy because of this view that philosophy is a pursuit of abstractions and minutiae. Since no one looks to philosophy for practical help in life's problems, the students see no value in our courses. And too often when they do take a course in philosophy, their views are confirmed: it *is* a pursuit of abstraction and minutiae. Or—God help us—it is another meandering discussion of "relevancies"! In which case philosophy is no more useful than an evening at the local bar.

Not that students are not interested in philosophic questions. Very many are interested in the perennial questions, but they don't look to courses in philosophy for help with those problems. And this is because, may I repeat, professional philosophers have a view of their subject that limits its serious content to the elite-initiate, and leaves only a pseudo-philosophizing for the undergraduate. This view leads most students (and most people) to ignore philosophy and that means fewer teaching positions for philosophers.

The ignoring of philosophy is even more noticeable in the junior college. At a recent conference of the Missouri Association of Junior Colleges not a single section, not a single speech was devoted to philosophy although twenty-two other departments were given time and space. It was as if we were non-existent. Many junior colleges do not have even one full-time teacher of philosophy. A teacher in some other department may offer a philosophy course twice a year. This slighting of philosophy in junior colleges is not traceable to the career orientation of junior colleges. In spite of that orientation, other academic departments are alive and well: English, music, social science, psychology. The slighting is due to this persistent view of philosophy about which we have been speaking. Junior college people, students, teachers, administrators, see English, psychology, etc., as addressing real needs of people. They view philosophy as an elite game pleasant enough for those so inclined, but not for the kind of student who goes to junior college. This view is costing philosophers hundreds of teaching positions.

Those who agree that this view of philosophy is both unfortunate and unnecessary face a serious problem: How to present philosophy in a way that is professionally competent and honest, and which also addresses the inchoate philosophic interests of non-specialists. As an initial response to that question let me only suggest that there is no reason to think that most students need to be bored by a professionally competent and honest presentation of philosophy. There is admittedly some tension between carefully reasoned philosophic reasoning and popular discussion methods. It is suicide to drop the discipline in favor of popularity, because to do so is to encourage the belief that everyone can handle philosophic problems, and in that case professionals are frauds. But it is also suicide to pretend that careful disciplined reasoning required the tools of symbolic logic or analysis, that it required the niceties of current discussions. Disciplined method requires skill in defining, in making distinctions, in observing; it requires a sensitivity for inconsistencies, a penchant for clarity, and primarily a devotion to warranted belief.

Philosophy is unique in its subjection to this discipline. It therefore has a unique role to play in the intellectual endeavor. It is the critic and guardian of method, and consequently the arch-critic of all intellectual endeavorings. If philosophers would enlarge their view of their profession to include this role, which they alone can play, philosophers would be in demand. Both the layman and we would be better off for it.

Note

Originally published in *Metaphilosophy* 4 (1973).

PART 2:

MAKING PHILOSOPHY "RELEVANT" AGAIN

Applied Philosophy

LESLIE STEVENSON

> *What is the use of studying philosophy if all that it does for you is to enable you to talk with some plausibility about some abstruse question of logic, etc., and if it does not improve your thinking about the important questions of everyday life?*[1]—Ludwig Wittgenstein

It is common for non-philosophers to demand of philosophy that is should be "relevant," which seems to mean that it should provide answers to "the important questions of everyday life," in morals, politics, religion, etc. It is also common, at least in recent years, for professional philosophers to reject this demand as misconceived, saying that they have their own specialized concerns in which they are more interested, and there is no reason to expect these concerns to be of any wider relevance than those of the physicist, the philologist, or any other academic specialist.[2] I want to suggest that, although any popular demand for quick or simple answers is misconceived, there is a clear and important sense in which philosophy can be relevant to "the important questions of everyday life." I also want to suggest, how, in these days of expanding higher education, the vital need for the application of philosophy to those questions can be better met.

That phrase, 'the *application* of philosophy,' already suggests the basis of my approach, namely a distinction between pure philosophy and applied philosophy, analogous in some ways to that between pure and applied mathematics, and in other ways to that between science and technology. Before attempting to define criteria for the distinction, I shall simply list what I intend to go on each side. Under pure philosophy I intend to include most of what is now studied as philosophy in the universities, *viz.*, mathematical and philosophical logic, metaphysics, epistemology, philosophy of mind, philosophy of science, *and* most of the questions now discussed by professional philosophers about ethics, politics, and aesthetics (e.g., the validity of the fact-value distinction). As examples of applied philosophy I suggest the rational discussion of particular controversial moral questions such as sexual morality, the Catholic ban on contraception, the use of hallucinogenic drugs, abortion, euthanasia, eugenics, the definition of death, and many other medico-ethical legal problems raised or soon to be raised by the coming "biological revolution"; also certain aspects of various difficult social and political problems, such as educational policy (comprehensive schools? religious education?), the need for public participation in planning (do people know what they want twenty years from now, and is it identical with what they need?), world economic development (do the richer countries have a *duty* to help the poorer? Should Indian peasants be *forced* to change agricultural methods?); also the critical examination of various political and religious ideologies in the forms they take now (e.g., Marxism, and the various denominations of Christianity); also the discussion of methodological problems in particular scientific or supposedly scientific theories (e.g., Freudian psycho-analysis, and various sociological theories).

Is there any general criterion for making the distinction thus suggested by lists? It might be suggested that pure philosophy is the discussion of general questions, whereas applied philosophy is the discussion of more particular ones; but such a distinction is only a matter of degree, and some of the "applied" questions, e.g., those about educational policy, might be counted as more "general" than some of the "pure" ones, e.g., on logic. I suggest that the distinction is rather one of motivation, that pure philosophy is the scholarly pursuit of truth for its own intrinsic interest, whereas applied philosophy is the seeking of answers which make a difference to what we do (Shall we seek an abortion? ... press for comprehensive schools? ... join the Communist Party? ... pay for psychoanalytic treatment?). Applied philosophy is thus essentially connected with *action*, whether that action is a matter of private morality or of public policy. So in applied philosophy, we are, like Socrates,[3] "discussing no trivial matter, but how we ought to live."

There are various objections and difficulties which may be raised about this notion of applied philosophy. First, are issues such as those I have mentioned as examples rationally discussable at all—are they not in the last resort a matter of individual ("subjective") opinion? If this objection is right, there can be no genuine applied philosophy at all; but I think it is profoundly wrong. For one thing, it is begging a very big question of pure philosophy to say of all questions of value that they are not rationally discussable. This was indeed said by the "emotive theory of ethics" of A. J. Ayer and C. L. Stevenson in the 1930s, and by certain forms of existentialism, and it is still a popular view; but it is now philosophically discredited. A question as big as this should not be begged by such a counsel of despair. The only proper way of finding out whether such questions are rationally discussable is to try to discuss them rationally, i.e., to do applied philosophy. I think that some of the questions can be answered quite definitively and clearly by the application of philosophy, e.g., I think that the Catholic ban on contraception cannot be *rationally* justified.

But there are some grains of truth inside this misconceived objection. One is that as a matter of *fact*, people generally make up their own minds (or have them already made up!) about such questions, whether or not they engage in any rational discussion of them; for how often does someone change his mind significantly as a result of intellectual argument alone? The answer may be "Not very often";

although it does happen sometimes. But is there not a quasi psycho-analytic task for applied philosophy to do in such discussions—that of making explicit the presuppositions, both of fact and of value, which underlie people's expressed attitudes? To make someone aware of presuppositions of which he was not fully conscious is to change him, to put him in a position in which he can examine his presuppositions critically, and perhaps change them. But it is up to *him* to change them, and this is the second grain of truth—the "democratic" view that in the last resort, after being presented with all relevant rational considerations, people *ought* to, and ought to be free to, make up their own minds about controversial questions of morals, politics, and religion.

Another objection questions whether there is any *one* discipline which lies in between the philosophy studied at universities and the "important questions of everyday life." Agreed that we can use certain philosophical techniques (for instance the examination of arguments for validity) in many areas of everyday life, just as we use simple arithmetic, or knowledge of the properties of electricity, in many areas, but does that show that there is a single discipline of applied philosophy? In this respect, isn't applied philosophy more analogous to technology, which isn't really a single discipline but simply a vague general label for the application of science, than to applied mathematics, which is a single discipline, or is at least accepted as such in universities? Now if a "single discipline" requires a certain specifiable subject-matter reasonably clearly demarcated from other subjects, then I would not accept the main point of this objection. One cannot define a *subject* by the motivation for studying it. Applied philosophy as I have defined it is the use of philosophical methods to help decide what we should do. So it is hardly the study of a demarcated subject-matter. However, when A. J. Ayer said that philosophy is to be distinguished from other arts or sciences by its methods rather than its subject-matter,[4] he expressed a widely-held conception of pure philosophy. How can we distinguish philosophical methods from others? Negatively, we can say that any question which is answerable purely by appeal to the fact, or by mathematical calculation or proof, is not a philosophical question. More positively, we can say that whenever questions of meaning are raised, as when we distinguish between definitions, statements of fact and value-judgments, and when we ask whether an argument is logically valid, we are applying philosophical methods. But this does entail that there is no *sharp* distinction between applied philosophy and persistent common sense, for in everyday life we often raise questions of meaning to clarify our thoughts, assertions, and disputes.

Connected with this second objection is a third, which asks why we should talk of applied *philosophy*, for in the kind of example we cited, are not other disciplines just as relevant, if not more so? For instance, for the problems of abortion, we need the expertise of doctors, psychiatrists, lawyers, perhaps sociologists, perhaps theologians, etc., at least as much as that of philosophers. This is perfectly true, and very important. But there is a sense in which questions about what we *ought* to do, as opposed to questions about what we *can* do, and what is likely to happen *if* we do, cannot be answered by any of the factual disciplines. (Of course, theologians may claim to answer them, but their claims raise specially controversial problems, which are themselves a wide field of applied philosophy!) And there is a sense in which the philosopher as such *is* specially qualified to deal with 'ought' questions. Not, of course, that his personal quirks and prejudices should be given any more attention than those of others. But he ought as a philosopher to be better equipped than others to do the analytic job of elucidating the meaning of such questions and making implicit presuppositions explicit, the imaginative job of thinking of all possible relevant facts and arguments, and the synthesizing job of weighing together all the relevant considerations, and thus arriving, even if only provisionally and tentatively, at the best-supported answer. Note the need for the philosophically unfashionable functions of insight, imagination, and synthesis, as well as the accepted one of conceptual analysis!

In these ways I would like to defend the notion of applied philosophy, and from the defense there emerge several important points about its nature. One is that it is essentially interdisciplinary, for the problems with which it deals are usually complex practical ones to which more than one kind of expertise is relevant. This means that in these days of necessary specialization applied philosophy will have to be a cooperative venture if it is to be done properly. Such cooperation between experts is by no means easy, and the philosopher can also make himself useful by helping each expert to interpret his discipline to the others. Thus there is a further reason for my second point about applied philosophy, that it requires insight, imagination, and synthesis, as well as analytic expertise. The third point is that there is no sharp dividing line between pure and applied philosophy—"applied" problems will raise "pure" questions (e.g., the ban on contraception raises the question of the justifiability of the concept of natural law), and "pure" principles can be applied to particular problems (e.g., a falsifiability criterion for a theory's being scientific can be applied to psycho-analytical and sociological assertions). The fourth point is that there is no sharp division on the other side either—between applied philosophy and the application of common sense to any problem of life ("every man is his own applied philosopher"). But not everyone is interested in, or capable, of pure philosophy; and not everything in pure philosophy has wider implications (e.g., I doubt whether philosophy of mathematics has any). So we can now see how it is true that although philosophy has its own specialized concerns which are not necessarily of wider interest or relevance (those of pure philosophy) it is also true that philosophical methods can, and should, be applied to "the important questions of everyday life" (applied philosophy).

That "should" leads to a fifth point—that applied philosophy is badly needed, by each of us individually, and by all of us together in matters of public policy at local, national, and international levels. And this naturally provokes the question of how the needed applied philosophy can be done, and where, and by whom? There has been a huge growth in professional pure philosophy in recent years, and this is in itself a welcome change. But I think the need for applied philosophy is not being adequately met (it's too important to be left to the journalists and TV pundits!). in the rest of the paper, I'd like to suggest how the need might be better met.

Should applied philosophy be taught in higher education, like applied mathematics? Should it be the concern of special research institutions? Should it be done by each person for himself? I don't see why the answer should not be 'Yes' to all three questions. Certainly, each person should do his own applied philosophy for himself as much as possible—this is just a restatement of the orthodox "liberal" or "democratic" belief that everyone should think for themselves on moral, political, and religious matters, with the help of the widest possible communication of fact and opinion. How to encourage the further development of society in this direction is largely a matter of educational policy. And there I think the teaching of philosophy has a vital role to play, which I'll expand on in a moment.

But not everyone has the ability to do applied philosophy very well, and because of its essentially interdisciplinary nature no one person has all the relevant expertise needed to do it properly. Because there is a very great need for applied philosophy at the level of public policy. For these reasons, it cannot be left entirely to individuals. There is a need for study groups, panels, commissions, research institutes ("think-tanks"), and publications. Of course, a good deal of these exist already. Many of the commissions and study groups set up by governments, professions and churches find themselves doing applied philosophy, for instance when they consider the problems of medical ethics or of criteria for mental disease. The American "Center for the Study of Democratic Institutions" is a permanent research institute whose studies are aimed at "discovering whether and how a free and just society may be maintained under the strikingly new political, social, economic, and technological conditions of the second half of the twentieth century."[5] Studies as wide-ranging as this must involve applied philosophy at many points. Excellent examples of publications in applied philosophy include Professor Hart's work on the concept of criminal responsibility[6] and the series "Philosophy at Work"[7] whose declared purpose is "to demonstrate, through the treatment of problems drawn from contemporary life, the practical relevance of philosophy. The aim is to show how philosophical problems can arise out of, and can exert a profound influence upon, our personal and social problems; and how philosophical analysis can enlighten our moral attitudes, aspirations, and decisions." This is exactly the conception which I am arguing for here.

Thus much good work is already being done.[8] But still, I feel, we need more. The social needs for applied philosophy are urgent. In a future of accelerating technological and social change, the needs will increase. In these days, there is a lot of trained philosophical expertise around, and I agree with Popper's view[9] that those with special knowledge have a special responsibility to use it. Therefore more of our present professional philosophers should devote some of their time to applied problems. Let me hasten to add that I am not advocating, like Plato, that philosophers should *rule* because they are qualified to know what's best for us all. But I *am* arguing that the expertise of philosophers can help to answer some of the difficult questions of practical policy which face us. One important way of encouraging the systematic and persistent study of such questions is to set up more "think-tanks," i.e., permanent interdisciplinary research institutions, whether in universities or on their own. Such institutions should be independent of direct control by government, industry, or whoever sponsors them. Their cost would be small compared with that scientific and technological research, yet it can be argued that they are just as socially necessary.

What of philosophy within the universities? They are, of course, the places for teaching and research in pure philosophy. But is there not room, and need, for applied philosophy within them too? If it is true, as I believe it is, that one of the essential functions of a university is liberal education in the widest possible sense, as well as vocational training and pure research, then there is a clear case for the teaching of applied philosophy. Furthermore, although pure philosophy is not for everyone, applied philosophy must be, for rationality is part of being human, thinking for oneself about how one is to live is part of being a citizen of any democratic society, and the encouragement of sensitive, rational, and persistent consideration of controversies in morals, politics, and religion is the way to produce such a society. As the producers of future politicians, managers, planners, civil servants, scientists and teachers, the various institutions of higher education have a special duty to encourage applied philosophy. Some form of it should be readily available for all students, not only those in traditional arts subjects.

Again, a lot is done already. It happens in debates, society meetings, and guest lectures, and of course in private discussions in the small hours. But is there not a need for academic courses to do it more formally and systematically, whether as a component of specialized courses or as a common interdisciplinary course? This is not the place to start going into details of course organization, of how far such applied philosophy should be encouraged or made compulsory, and of how it could be taught and assessed. My concern here is only to argue the general need for it, and the special responsibility of philosophers themselves to do it and encourage it. To argue this is in no way to deny the value of continuing teaching and research in pure philosophy.

There will be the usual academic scorn for "popularizing," and "journalism." I think we should not be afraid of this. The issues are, as I've said, too important to be left to the journalists. The correct reply to the taunt of "journalism" is that of "social irresponsibility." A related objection is that applied philosophy is necessarily controversial, potentially subversive of established beliefs and practices. So vested interests may well want to kill it, just as they did Socrates. "The philosopher . . . escapes derision for irrelevance only by risking doom for subversion."[10] The risk is one we must accept when we do applied philosophy. But we need not accept derision when we do pure philosophy. The familiar complaint of irrelevance is unjustified on two counts—philosophy is worth doing for its own sake even if "irrelevant," and anyway, some of it *is* highly "relevant," as I have tried to show.[11]

Notes

This is a revised version of a paper originally published in *Metaphilosophy* 2 (1971). This version is from October 1973.

1. Wittgenstein to Malcolm. From Norman Malcolm, *Ludwig Wittgenstein: A Memoir* (Oxford: Oxford University Press, 1958).

2. G. J. Warnock, *English Philosophy since 1900* (London: Oxford University Press, 1958), 168ff.

3. Plato, *Republic* 352D (quoted as a motto by R. M. Hare in *The Language of Morals* [London: Clarendon Press, 1952], 151)

4. A. J. Ayer, *The Problem of Knowledge* (London: Macmillan, 1956), 1.

5. Publications list (Summer 1967) from the Center for the Study of Democratic Institutions, Santa Barbara, California.

6. H. L. Hart, *Punishment and Responsibility: Essays in the Philosophy of Law* (Oxford: Oxford University Press, 1968).

7. Published by Hutchinson, under the general editorship of Patrick Corbett, including *Sexual Morality* by R. Atkinson; *Equality* by John Wilson; *Ideologies* by Patrick Corbett; and *War and Morality* by W. B. Gallie, etc.

8. Since I wrote the first version of this article, a lot more high-quality applied philosophy has appeared. There is a series called "New Studies in the Practical Philosophy" (published by Macmillan under the general editorship of W. D. Hudson, including *Applications of Moral Philosophy* by R. M. Hare; *Crime or Disease?* by Antony Flew, etc.). The new journal *Philosophy and Public Affairs* has started, and the old journal *Philosophy* has espoused a more "applied" policy under its new editor Renford Bambrough (see the editorial in the January, 1973 issue). Also, many books are now appearing on philosophical and methodological issues in psychology and social sciences.

9. Sir Karl Popper, "The Moral Responsibility of the Scientist," a paper presented at the International Congress of Philosophy at Vienna in 1968, and published in *Encounter* (March 1969).

10. Michael Scriven, *Primary Philosophy* (New York: McGraw-Hill, 1966), preface, viii.

11. After all this preaching, perhaps I should point out that I have tried to practice what I preach in my own *Seven Theories of Human Nature* (New York: Oxford University Press, 1974).

Two Kinds of Teaching

HUSTON SMITH

When I think back over the memorable teachers I had or have known, the fact that stands out most is the diversity of their styles. Bill Levi at Roosevelt College would sit crosslegged on the desk moving nothing during the entire class hour save his lips and his mind. Meanwhile, at nearby University of Chicago, David Greene was a pacer. Fresh from his farm at eight on wintry mornings, manure still clinging to his boots as Greek poured from his mouth, he strode with a vigor that made the advancing wall seem adversary. We felt sure that sooner or later he would slam his face into it, but he never did; invariably in the nick of time he would swirl and bounce off the wall not his head but his behind, gaining thereby momentum for the return journey. Gustav Bergmann, logical positivist at Iowa State University, was so authoritarian that when a student dared to question something he had said he thundered, "Let's get one thing straight: from ten to eleven on Mondays, Wednesdays, and Fridays, there is but one God, and his name is Bergmann!" His opposite was a teacher so non-directive on principle that students used to say he not only didn't believe in anything, he didn't even suspect anything. I had teachers who wrestled with me socratically as evangelists with the village drunkard, and teachers who simply dished it out—very well indeed!

The surprising thing is that learning occurred in all these contexts. I conclude that there is no one way to teach; in speaking here of two ways I speak only of ways that have taken shape in me. Who knows who learns, and under what conditions? The act remains essentially mysterious, like love, or sex, or life itself; more strange than familiar, less science than art, a word to which I shall return.

I

During its first twenty years my teaching followed a single pattern. Questions and discussion were encouraged and fun, but lectures were the focus. Today, lectures are on the defensive. Almost everything we would like students to know we can place in their hands *via* paperback. They can read faster than they can listen to us, and print is durable; they can go back if they miss something or forget.

All this is true, but the points don't add up to the conclusion that lectures are passé. One of my most memorable learning experiences was a course Thornton

Wilder offered, once only, at the University of Chicago. The classroom was in fact an auditorium, and it was invariably packed. If there was a single question or comment from the floor I don't remember it, yet the exhilaration of those hours! I would leave the auditorium walking on air. In those early afternoons of autumn even Chicago was beautiful.

Plays, too, can be read faster than we can sit through an evening at the theater, but reading doesn't take the place of the performance. Moreover, lectures provide the opportunity for trying out ideas while they are still in the process of formation and are thus part of the teacher's laboratory, with the advantage to the listener that he is not presented with a finished treatise but is watching a living mind at work and given an insight into its strategies.

Just as there is no one way to teach, so too there is no one way to lecture. John Dewey's lectures are said to have been rambling and dull—until the student awoke to the fact that he was witness to a powerful mind's direct involvement in the act of thinking. Minds have their own dispositions; some, like Wittgenstein's, are splitters; mine happens to be a lumper. This fact, so apparent that I suspect that it is grounded in my brain structure, makes metaphysical reticence impossible for me. And as it affects my approach to lecturing in other ways as well, before saying more about lecturing proper I propose to indicate why a holistic approach to my field is in my case the only approach possible.

Gestalt psychology has made its mark, and gestalt therapy is bidding to do so. In this age of analysis, this heyday of analytic philosophy, is there a place for holistic, gestalt philosophy as well? If the discipline takes its cues from the sciences, the answer seems clearly to be 'yes.' Gestalt psychology I have already mentioned; psychology abandoned atomism with its discovery that there is no area of experience, perceptual or otherwise, that is free from what positivists used to call non-cognitive factors. In biology, the attempts of molecular genetics "to reach the beautiful simplicity of biological principles through concepts derived from experimental systems in which the ordered structure that is the source of this simplicity has been destroyed [are proving to be] increasingly futile," and physics, in its complete experience "does not support the precept that all complex systems are explicable in terms of properties observable in their isolated parts" (Barry Commoner).

Turning to philosophy itself, epistemology has found element analysis ineffectual. Whether we approach knowing analytically or phenomenologically, reports agree: there is no datum unpatterned, no figure without ground, no fact without theory. Instead of a one-way process whereby through perceptual archeology irrefrangible primitive elements—Hume's impressions, Russell and Moore's sense data—are first spotted and *then* built into wholes, knowing (we see now) is polar. Part and whole are in dialogue from the start. No man looks at the world with pristine eyes; he sees it edited, and editorial policy is always forged in the widest field of vision available.

The same holds for ethics, for doing is vectored by overview as much as knowing is. "Deeper and more fundamental than sexuality, deeper than the craving for social power, deeper even than the desire for possessions, there is a still more generalized and more universal craving in the human make-up. It is the craving for knowledge of the right direction—for orientation" (William Shelton).

In playing the game of life-orientation, the first rule is to capture everything in sight, for the elusive might prove to be crucial; if it is and it escapes your net, you may get rich, but you won't win. The second rule is to set what has been captured in order, to array it in pattern or design. Thus the twin principles of gestalt philosophy are: (a) attention to the whole, taking care to see that nothing of importance has been omitted, and (b) attention to the pattern of the whole's parts. Complementing clarity and consistency which are the virtues of analytic philosophy, the virtues of gestalt philosophy are scope and design.

Now back to the lecturing. As a gestalt philosopher both these principles of scope and design figure in the way I approach my task. Scope enters to position the topic to be discussed within the panoply of human interests generally. Why among the myriad of things we could talk about during this hour or this semester are we giving time to this? The answer needn't take much time; indeed, no time at all if it is self-evident and acceptable. But evident and acceptable to students, not just to me; that's crucial. Answers which, however evident, are *not* acceptable to students are: "Because the professor happens to be working on a paper about the subject;" "because this is what the instructor was taught in graduate school, so knows most about—read, 'is most invulnerable with respect to'"; "because having avoided math the student needs a course in philosophy to graduate;" or "because it will help those who intend to continue in philosophy to get into graduate school."

Once the topic has been positioned in the sense of linked to an acknowledged human interest or need, the elements bearing on the topic must be positioned. Enter pattern or design.

Paintings begin with a discovery, a new and exhilarating perception. Immediately the painter faces enormous difficulties; he must force shapes and static colors to embody what he has felt and seen. The lecturer's task is analogous. He, too, must fix, articulate, and objectify what on first discovery was nebulous, fluid, and private. How within the artifice of a class hour can he make a subtle aspect of life or being evident? Every sentence calls for knowledge of his materials and their limitations and an unswerving eye on the effect intended. It is an old problem: how anything of the real can pass the gap between intuition and expression. The passage can be effected only by translation, not from one language to another, but from reception into creation. Everything at the instructor's disposal—facts, concepts, anecdotes, analogies, arguments, humor—must work to enforce the impression intended, to the end that at the hour's close the student feels 'that's true and important, or at least interesting.' It's no good if he stops with 'that's true.' As Whitehead noted, "it is more important that a proposition be interesting than it be true. The importance of truth is just that it adds interest." As irrelevancies deaden the effect, omission is of the essence.

What constitutes a masterpiece here, or (to drop the hyperbole) at least an authentic work of art? When a man for whom the topic in question is vital, who as a consequence has lived with it and pondered it, summons everything he has discerned on the problem, distills it, compresses it, pounds it into a form that *makes sense*! Thoughts emerge, but not in mere succession: architecturally, in meaningful pattern; possibly, in addition, as incarnated in a life that is being lived, his own. That's what sent me walking out of Mandel Hall on air those Chicago afternoons. And that, now that I think of it, is the way subliminally I have sensed myself as a lecturer: traveler, pilgrim, archeologist of space and time, trying with the help of a parcel here and a fragment from there to piece together the largest possible meaning for life and the world. Such meaning, though it is intelligible, exceeds the merely rational. Or if one prefers, is the highest category *of* the rational.

In characterizing lecturing as art, my model has been the painter rather than the actor. Not that lectures can't be dramatic performances too; they can be, as the adage that every good teacher is part ham attests. But the comparison means little to me—again the variety in teaching styles. Writing is as different from speaking as reading is from listening, but the feelings that infuse me while writing and lecturing are much the same. Attention is fixed on content; issues of delivery and audience contact work themselves out unconsciously.

II

It will be apparent from what I have said that I haven't lost faith in the mix of lecture and discussion that is higher education's abiding rubric. I continue to teach one course each term by this format; it involves me and, given the averages, students show symptoms of satisfaction. But there has been a change. For the last eight years I have also taught a course by almost opposite canons.

This second course roots back to the summer of 1965, when I was invited to Bethel, Maine, to observe for two weeks the work of the National Training Laboratories with small groups: T- (for Training-) Groups, Encounter Groups, or Human Interaction Laboratories as they have come to be called. By pleasant coincidence I was to bring back from Bethel what Bethel had originally drawn from my own home base, for it was from Kurt Lewin's pioneering work at M. I. T. that the National Training Laboratories evolved. Something happened to me at Bethel, but it is also the case that I was ready for it to happen. It wasn't that I had grown disillusioned with higher education, but the question of whether it might not be better had become insistent. For however one assessed its virtues, university learning struck me—and it still strikes me—as:

1. Insufficiently experimental. It scans less than does industry, say, for improved ways of doing things.
2. Too authoritarian. Persons aged seventeen to twenty-five would at other times have been launched into the world. Here they continue to be subjected overwhelmingly to directives that flow down to them instead of rising up from their own volitions.
3. Too passive in the role in which it places students. On this point clean proof is at hand. Take a word count in almost any class: who talks the most, even in discussion classes and seminars? As learning requires doing, the arrangement is ideal for teachers, but one hears that it's the students who pay tuition.
4. Too detached from students' on-going lives, their hopes and involvements, the points where their psychic energy is most invested. It is as if the curriculum's cerebral thrust connects with the top six inches of the student's frame while leaving the other sixty inches idling. "It is by living, by dying, by being damned that one becomes a theologian," Luther advises us, "not by understanding, reading, and speculating." Or perhaps by both? What is clear is that academic reading, speculating, and understanding is joined very little to students' living, dying, and damnations. The most substantial recent study of American education, Charles Silberman's *Education in the Classroom*, concludes that reformers and innovators have an obligation to lobby for more emphasis on the education of feelings and the imagination and for a slow-down in cognitive rat-racing.
5. Too impersonal. Colleges used to be communities. Universities have in our time become almost the opposite: huge anti-communities like virtually every other institution in our mass, mobile, agglomerate society where rules and regulations take precedence over persons and seasoned relationships.

What encounter groups showed me first and above all else was a way to generate involvement. I hadn't been at Bethel forty-eight hours before my entire life seemed to sink or swim in terms of my group—fifteen strangers, none of whom I had laid eyes on two days before nor was likely to see again ten days thereafter. Swiftly, almost instantly, the criss-cross of human interactions—words, feelings, glances, gestures—had enmeshed me. Thought was emphatically involved, for apart from the therapeutic hour each afternoon when I deliberately turned my mind off and flung myself into the blissfully uncritical arms of impersonal nature (a lake), every waking moment was given to trying to make sense of what was happening. But not thought only; perception, too, as I tried to see what was transpiring in nuances of gesture, tone, and silence, and to feel what was happening in me at subliminal levels. My will, too, was engaged as I wrestled with whether to speak, risk, act.

New Possibilities demanded consideration. How, precisely, encounter groups might ameliorate education's weaknesses, I had no idea; but it was inconceivable to me that, operating powerfully in precisely the areas of those weaknesses, they would have nothing to offer. For encounter groups are:

1. Experimental. This remains the case even though they have been with us in various forms since World War II. The extent to which they have caught on suggests that they tend to be useful, but they are no panacea. Their utility is not unvarying nor established by objective criteria.

2. Non-authoritarian. It is part of their definition that leaders leave them largely unstructured, let them develop in their own ways and for learning vehicles use whatever transpires. Part of the fascination of such groups derives from seeing what does develop when eight to sixteen lives are closeted for appreciable time while deprived of tasks, agenda, and assigned hierarchy.

3. Activating. Where nothing happens save by the group's initiative, boredom, anxiety, the will to power and the will to play see to it that initiative is taken.

4. Involving.

5. Personal. Attention is focused on the here and now, and in encounter groups, this means people. Again, remove tasks, to which lives tend to get subordinated, and lives change from means to ends.

I shall not here try to say what encounter groups are. Most readers will know; the few who do not or who wish further elucidation can turn to a book such as *Carl Rogers on Encounter Groups* (Harper & Row, 1970). Let me say only that since 1965, half of my pedagogical interest has been devoted to trying to discern the potential for higher education latent in what Rogers himself considers this "most rapidly spreading social invention of the century, and probably the most potent." To the end of augmenting my understanding of group processes, and effectiveness in facilitating them, I have participated in training programs conducted by The National Training Laboratory, Tavistock Institute and the Washington School of Psychiatry; and have led seminars and workshops each summer at Esalen Institute and other growth centers. To explore their relevance for formal education, I have in each of the past twelve semesters taught courses ranging in subject matter from "Introduction to Philosophy" to "Philosophical Anthropology" which combine encounter techniques with cognitive learning. Students are appraised of the intended mix during pre-registration screening interviews; registration is closed at sixteen; a balance of men and women is desirable. The course opens with an encounter weekend, which means that we spend thirteen hours together before we open a book. My object is to get the Waring Blender of human interaction churning, then feed into it eyedropper drips of cognitive content. After the opening weekend the class meets for a three-hour stretch each week. Typically the first hour goes to student-directed discussion of the week's reading assignment; the second hour is mine to either lecture or continue the first hour's discussion under my direction, and the third hour continues the weekend encounter group. In mid-semester we have a second weekend encounter, if possible off-campus and out of the city. When I can secure budget or prevail upon the good offices of my wife who works professionally with groups, I have an outside trainer conduct the weekends. This helps to reduce student-teacher distance and to get authority issues more openly onto the floor.

How has it gone? Roughly 85 percent of the 160 students who have been in these courses report on anonymous, post-course check-sheets that they were glad we used this approach and would recommend that it be continued; that compared with other humanities courses they enjoyed it more, were more interested in it, and learned more from it. I have no illusion that these statistics are clean, particularly the last one. If one includes 'learning how' as well as 'learning that'—learning how effectively to occupy a place in life as contrast with merely knowing about life; Kierkegaard's truth as subjective transformation of oneself and education as 'the curriculum one had to run through in order to catch up with oneself'—then even the last statistic could be valid, but I doubt that students have acquired as much cerebral knowledge of subject matter in these courses as they do in others. Encounter aspects of the courses seem to fill such a vacuum in students' lives and become thereby so seductive that I find I must constantly throw the weight of my office on the side of the cognitive learning to keep the course from developing into encounter group only. Being unsettled in my mind as to how cognitive learning does fare in such courses, I do not recommend casting all education in their mold. I should think it might be ideal for each university undergraduate to carry one encounter course each term, but not more. As a side benefit, a college that instituted the policy of having them do so might, I suspect, find itself reducing its psychiatric and counseling staff appreciably.

With regard to the specifics of ways in which I have tried to link group process to cognitive learning I would happily say nothing, for I am far from satisfied with my formulae and keep devising new ones constantly. But this is the nub of the matter, so lest my statement on T-group teaching, or peer-group learning as it might better be called, ends up looking like a Taoist composition around the void, I list some samples of things I have tried.

- Have students pair with partners they know least, look into one another's eyes for two minutes without speaking, then express nonverbally how they feel toward each other. For their next reading assign Martin Buber's *I and Thou*. Did the pairing exercise illumine experimentally what Buber means by an I-Thou relation?

- Ask students to take ten minutes to recall and write down their earliest childhood memory. Place the statements in the middle of the circle. Ask a student to select and read one of the statements at random. Can the group guess who wrote it? Does the discussion corroborate ontogenetic emphasis on the formative influence of early experiences as argued, say, in Erik Erikson's *Childhood and Society*?

- Read Konrad Lorenz' *On Aggression*. Do its theses shed light on the competition and hostility that have come to light within the group's own experience?

- Read Nietzsche's *Will to Power*. How much of the group's life—most obviously the struggles for leadership within it, but not these only—support its central thesis?

- The greatest anxiety I, personally, have felt in a group setting was in the initial meeting of sixty-five persons who were closeted for two and one-half hours with no agenda whatever. Watching every attempt to structure that chaos come to naught was an unnerving experience, but it was insightful too, for it showed me directly the way formlessness without produces formlessness within. Not knowing my place in the group, I didn't know where I stood in *any* context: who I was, how I should act, anything. Compare Heidegger's notion of *angst* in *Being and Time* as symptom of the collapse of 'the worldhood of the world'; also Harry Stack-Sullivan's famous essay on "The Illusion of Individuality."

- Read the first essay in Leonard Nelson's *Socratic Method and Critical Philosophy* and ask if the goal of encounter education is to complete Nelson's approach to philosophy with two emendations: the socratic method becomes the *group* socratic with the total group replacing a single individual as midwife, and feelings as well as thoughts are intentionally brought into the picture.

- A 'low' tends to settle in on groups the last few sessions before they terminate; the impending death of the group seems to awaken presentiments of individual, personal death. The experience provides concrete, shareable data relating to Heidegger's notion of being-unto-death as a criterion of authentic living.

I stress that I have not listed these projects in order to recommend them to others. I cite them only as instances of the kinds of bridges that can be thrown from group experience to cognitive learning. It appears to be of the essence of encounter teaching that no canned rubric will work for long. I wish I could report that I feel like a veteran architect of bridges of the kind described, but the fact is the opposite. I have come to suspect that how and where to throw such bridges will be my pedagogical *koan* (Zen meditational problem resolvable in life only, not in words or formulae) till I retire.

If I not only haven't solved the problem of relating group process to cognitive learning but doubt that it admits of a standardized solution, why do I make of it more than a marginal issue? Others who have ventured into these waters and stayed long enough to ask questions will probably answer as I do. A new panorama has opened before me. With it has come every variety of self-doubt, fear, and suspicion: am I simply giving students what they like, afraid to demand of them hard work and drudgery; am I playing group therapist; am I merely hungry for intimacy? But in the end I have been forced to listen to a new claim. Let me articulate that claim. We need wisdom. To this end we need knowledge, but knowledge that is established in life: connected with feelings, illuminating choices, in touch with wills. This is not exactly what we now have. As Nietzsche observed a century ago,

> We knowers are unknown to ourselves, and for a good reason: how can we ever hope to find what we have never looked for? Our treasure lies in the beehives of our knowledge. As for the rest of life's so-called 'experience'—who is serious enough for that? Or has time enough?
>
> What we need, in Kierkegaard's word, is edification.
>
> The law for the development of the self with respect to knowledge is this, that the increasing degree of knowledge corresponds with the degree of self-knowledge increases, the more it becomes a kind of inhuman knowing for the production of which man's self is squandered, pretty much as men were squandered for the building of the pyramids, or as men were squandered in the Russian horn-bands to produce one note, neither more nor less.

Since this new educational vista opened I have been looking for comrades in arms. To say I am still looking would be to overstate the case, but in view of the size of the task, not to overstate it much, at least not as concerns philosophy.

Note

This article originally appeared in *The Key Reporter*, Summer 1973, and was later published in *Principles of Quality Teaching at the University Level*, ed. Thomas H. Burton and Keith W. Prichard (Columbia, SC: University of South Carolina Press, 1973). Reprinted here by permission of the author and the University of South Carolina Press.

Philosophy as Psychoanalysis

Marcia Cavell

The model of philosophy by which most Americans of my generation were taught, and which we learned to identify simply *as* philosophy, is a model which values above all clarity, critical acumen, tough mindedness and taught argument. Our style was lucid, if often dull and unreadable to the uninitiated. Our posture was defensive (on guard against undeclared assumptions) and aggressive (we were to attack conclusions which "didn't go through"). Our goals were more the unmasking of a shoddy argument than the discovery of a new philosophical perspective. I don't want to say that this model should be rejected; though these are no longer my own posture or goals, many of the values—particularly clarity—I still share. But I do think that we also need—and to some extent have already found—other models. As most of us have come to know—perhaps through the study of post-Kantian European philosophy which simply was not offered in many graduate schools fifteen years ago—the reigning Anglo-American conception of philosophy as analysis does not define philosophy, but only one kind of philosophy. Furthermore, I think it provides a fairly poor model for the undergraduate teaching of philosophy, where to my mind even those students who will eventually go on to become professional philosophers need to be encouraged to see philosophical problems and questions in a larger perspective and in terms of other sensibilities than the analytic model provides.

There are two ways of amplifying this model that I have to suggest. The first is that, where appropriate, we think of philosophy more as psychoanalysis than as analysis. I don't mean here what Wittgenstein meant when he spoke of philosophy as therapy. Nor do I mean a lot of other things that might come to one's mind: that we should be psychoanalyzing Plato or Spinoza or each other, or that we should be treating philosophical systems as symptomatic of our favorite psychological mechanisms. What I mean has to do primarily with a way of thinking about thinking, about knowledge and insight, which emerges from familiarity with the psychoanalytic process.

The second way relies on the current questioning of masculinity and femininity. Here I want to say that philosophy needs to be "feminized." As a matter of fact, I don't think these suggestions are really different, but only two ways of getting at the same thing. In claiming that philosophy needs to be "feminized," I am of course playing on the stereotypes of masculine and feminine. To be masculine is to be logical, aggressive and objective; to be feminine is to be intuitive, guided by feeling, concerned less with the grand order than the life of the day and the body. As we continue to free ourselves from these stereotypes, the woman who thinks clearly and the man who thinks passionately will no longer be regarded as the exceptions that prove the rule, but simply as human beings who function well. Many years ago a man said to me that women didn't have it in them to be important philosophers, because they weren't equipped for building intellectual systems. As a description of women's achievements so far, what he said was true. Though changes in cultural attitudes and in the conditions which make for the survival of the species may reveal this aspect of women also to be historically determined. It doesn't matter to me whether he was right or not. Because it is in itself a masculine value judgment which locates the nature of philosophy in the large design. In our century, of course, Anglo-American philosophy has committed itself instead to the small clarity. But that isn't the alternative I have in mind; rather, both a style and a subject which is more personal, more tuned to feeling, than the professional journals usually allow; in short, a philosophy that by the standards of the stereotype is feminine, and that by those of psychoanalysis is less "dissociated." Obviously this won't be appropriate to all philosophical areas or problems. But it is to many. And it should open to philosophical investigation, furthermore, questions which have for the most part been relegated to other disciplines such as literature and psychology.

The dilemma that many of us feel about our profession now confronts us most poignantly when we are writing philosophy. For in general we have to choose on the one hand between the most highly respected journals and a rigor of argument which takes nothing but its own point of departure for granted; and on the other, the second-string journals, or non-philosophical publications like *Harper's* or *The New York Review of Books* or *The New Yorker*, where the transitions from paragraph to paragraph may be less in the mode of deduction than of analogy, less analysis than synthesis; and which encourage us to strive for the provocative rather than the ineluctable connection. It *is* a dilemma because, schooled as we were by the analytic model, we still value lucidity and discipline; we are still suspicious of language which cannot be cashed into specific experiences. Yet these are values which often severely restrict us. To begin an article by announcing one's thesis and the three or four tacks which the article will take to support it is the sign of certain intellectual virtues. But there are others—spontaneity, imagination, felicity, the ability to forge odd but revealing connections between widely differing parts of one's experience—which often one has had to sacrifice or discourage in the process.

I have put it as if we were faced with a choice foisted upon us by the differing notions of philosophy of the journals for which we write or which we hope will publish us. But it isn't that simple. It's more that it is difficult to find a way of talking philosophy which avoids a choice that strikes me as unfortunate and false. We would like to be clear without being obsessive, readable without being fuzzy or sentimental. In terms of philosophical content, existentialism has provided us with a model for how to be philosophically concerned with questions closer to the bone of our daily lives (so, by the way, did our own Pragmatists). Yet many of us who are moving away from analytic philosophy are unhappy with what strikes us often as both the inflatedness and the dogmatism of existentialism. As for style, I can think of only a handful of books and articles which manage to avoid simultaneously jargon and sloppiness, insularity and a cogency whose price is grace. In our century, Nietzsche and Wittgenstein have perhaps come the closest to calling into question the previous models of philosophy. And for both, style was as inseparable from content as it is in Henry James or Robe-Grillet. But neither provides quite the model I have in mind.

Philosophy always has been and always will be that order of discourse which questions the seemingly unquestionable, finds problems where we had thought there weren't any, and seeks support for those beliefs that, without knowing it, we had been taking on faith. The subject of philosophy is thought, and in pursuing that subject it will always seek to provide at the same time a paradigm of rational investigation. Here is where I think there may be a certain conflict; for while the aim of philosophy on the undergraduate level is to make people more thoughtful, rationality—as we usually think of it—and thoughtfulness are not the same. And if one hopes to encourage the latter, I am not sure that showing students the errors in theirs or others' arguments, or the implications of their beliefs, is the best way. The trouble with reason is that it is so easily misused, as it is, in my opinion, when it is divorced from the feeling which in a particular case would be appropriate. Were feeling accorded its rightful place in philosophical thinking, questions which have been little dealt with in traditional philosophy would begin to occupy us more—like the relations between sex and love, the peculiar kind of knowledge of children, the relationship itself between thinking and feeling in certain kinds of experience, for example in self-discovery and guilt. And we might begin to think of traditional philosophical questions in a new way. A change in the way we think and encourage our students to think—a change in style—would inevitably entail a change in content and conclusion.

Again, it is not that the old way is wrong, but that it needs to be supplemented. For example, the Kantian insistence on principle as the heart of moral thinking leaves out what seems to me an equally important point about moral response—the fact that often, if not typically, it addresses itself to a particular act or situation. Sometimes one's judgment is a consequence of one's having accepted beforehand a principle which applies to actions of that sort. But often it arises immediately out of a response to this particular situation. The passion and the recognition behind "You betrayed me" or "You lied to me" does not usually derive from one's prior decision that treachery and deceit are morally wrong. Though one may after the fact begin thinking in terms of such generalizations.

Hume saw the place of passion in moral judgment. But unfortunately he did not go on to discover that sometimes the process of reasoning itself necessarily includes feeling. By "necessarily" I am suggesting that sometimes the having of certain feelings, or the familiarity with them, is a precondition for one's being able to say sensibly that he or she has thought about something. For example, could someone with a very limited capacity for imagining and empathizing with the suffering of others really think about the decision to use a particularly painful weapon against a group of people? Does someone who, for whatever reason, never consciously feels guilt or remorse, really know what he's saying when he says to someone he presumably cares for, "I know that I hurt you, and I'm sorry!"?

The psychoanalytic view of human thinking (though of course it is not only the psychoanalyst's) is that it is never a process completely divorced from affect and from primary human needs; that about some subjects—one's own life, one's relation to others and to his own behavior, to his body and his intentions to do acts or harm—it is a process very much informed by feeling if it is genuinely "thought" and not such gestures of thought as rationalization and intellectualization; that so-called rational processes are only one of the ways that the mind works and not always the most important nor even the most productive. It is a way of thinking about thinking that leads me along a fine line. A psychoanalyst once remarked to me that Descartes' doubt was nothing but the symptom of an obsessional neurosis. It was the "nothing but" that I objected to. The man Descartes may have been unconsciously worried about something quite other than the existence of the external world. But the philosopher Descartes was responding to the scientific challenges to the mediaeval cosmology, to St. Augustine and St. Thomas, to Galileo and to the current skepticism, and so on. On the other hand, philosophical thinking as most of us in England and America have been trained to do it does encourage an obsessive focusing on a single discursive line, whereas creativity of any sort requires the ability to let go, to free-associate, to tolerate a while of chaos. The great philosophers, like the great composers and scientists, have had this ability to alternate easily between what psychoanalysts call primary and secondary process thinking. My point is that the conception of philosophy which guides us now, the standards implicit in the important philosophical journals and probably in most teaching, inhibits rather than encourages philosophical creativity. Furthermore, I suspect that in the classroom it is conducive to an idea of rationality which doesn't discriminate between the subjects to which one's feelings may be irrelevant and inappropriate and those to which they are vital.

Students need to learn that there are different ways of being "objective," different meanings of 'objectivity.' Here is both another subject for philosophical thought, and a clue to how philosophical style, in writing and in our teaching, should reflect and shape content. When one is looking through a microscope, 'objectivity' means one thing; listening to another person talk about his life, it means something else. If we are setting up an experiment to check out a hypothesis about the behavior of certain gases under certain conditions, the injunction to be objective is a reminder that the nature of scientific experiment is such that it must be repeatable, observable by others, and so on. It asks us to do nothing about our feelings one way or the other—unless for the moment to forget about them. When a court puts together a jury, it tries to weed out people whose preconceptions may prevent them from giving the defendant a fair trial. Here objectivity does have to do specifically with attitudes and feelings; not that it requires us to be impassive, but capable of a relatively spontaneous response to the data upon which we will be asked to decide. The judge is not looking for someone who will have no feelings about an act of rape or homicide. Potential jurists are disqualified only if their feelings are so intense that they will be unable to see the act in question in its particular context, or when for other reasons they are likely to prejudge the defendant. For a psychoanalyst, 'objectivity' means, among other things, the ability to use his feelings in a special way. What is asked of him—insofar as is possible—is to be able to distinguish between those feelings arising from within him, as expressions of his own fears, conflicts, and fantasies, and feelings that are being expressed by the patient. The hope is that his own analysis will have greatly diminished the extent to which he defends himself from perceptions of his own behavior and that of others which would make him uncomfortable. It can be put more positively: for the psychoanalyst, objectivity requires being able to perceive, and empathize with, what the patient is feeling.

To summarize the implications of what I have said so far for the undergraduate teaching of philosophy: it needs to encourage creativity as well as clarity, a sense for psychological relevance as well as for logical relevance, the capacity for synthesis as well as for analysis, as sensitivity to where feeling is appropriate and even a prerequisite for thinking philosophically, some comprehension of the complexity of reason itself and an understanding that there are different models of both rationality and objectivity, none of which is dispensable.

One of the things this may mean is that from some of our students, anyway, we should ask for clarity only later on in their study of philosophy. I spent years unlearning the first lesson I had learned as a philosophy student: to ask at the hint of ambiguity, "What do you mean?" There are times, of course, when it is the only question to ask. But for me, at least, the ritual of asking that question served the dubious function of allowing me to wait to be told what somebody meant rather than trying to figure it out myself; and it encouraged a tendency which was no doubt already present: to dismiss any impulse, thought or feeling which couldn't be cleanly articulated and furthermore defended.

At the height of my anxiety about the impending preliminary examinations for the Ph.D., I remember expressing dismay to a fellow graduate student that I had not yet had an original philosophical thought. He said to me, "But you can read an article and find the weak spots, can't you?" I agreed that often I could do that. "But that's all philosophy is," he replied. I suspect that something like that is the conception of philosophical activity which prevails in many classrooms. How to get around it? Certainly the easiest thing to do with Descartes is to show where he was untrue to his own intentions to being at the beginning; with Hume, that he couldn't account for our experience of an object, let alone for our beliefs in the continuous existence of our objects; with Kant, that his reasons for thinking there must be a noumenal world don't hold. But what one really wants to do in making these points is to get a student to see the profundity of the philosophical problems involved, to make them "real" for him—whatever that requires—and to be able to ask himself the kinds of questions that will lead him to discover problems and invent solutions.

Seeing problems and asking questions are related activities, but they are not quite the same. To ask a question is to recognize a problem. In fact, one cannot see a problem unless he has first asked the right question. Yet unlike questions, problems exist whether we acknowledge them or not; they are not invented, but seen. Questions, on the other hand, must be actively asked, which is sometimes a matter of locating words for the worry one discovers he already has. The relationships between problem and solution, question and answer, are also dissimilar in interesting ways. Problems disappear in the face of a genuine solution. But while questions may be answered, what counts as an answer for one person and in one context may not do so for another, and an answer doesn't necessarily make its question go away. As students of philosophy discover if they last beyond their initial dismay, an answer may be a good one without being conclusive.

One of the ways to get students to ask philosophical questions, to think with feeling and to develop a capacity for synthesizing elements of their experience in new ways, is to have them alternate their readings of philosophical works with works of literature. Kafka's *The Trial* is a marvelous way of getting at the question, "What does it mean to be guilty?" Sophocles' *Oedipus Rex* is a good dramatization of the difference between insight and the kind of knowledge that takes place, let's say, in the learning of chemistry. And though every undergraduate philosophy program should have courses in metaphysics, epistemology and ethics, and the traditional sequence of courses in the history of philosophy, it should provide as well courses which tackle philosophical questions in an interdisciplinary context. As I have already implied, philosophy and psychology or psychoanalysis is an obvious combination; but so are philosophy and anthropology, science, and history, among others. To elaborate on the relations between philosophy and psychoanalysis: anyone interested in the nature of reason and its role in human affairs needs to know, for example, that little children's phantasies about how sexual reproduction takes place have little to do with whether they have been told the truth; and that while it may not seem reasonable to worry—despite the evidence of our senses—about the integrity of our own bodies, both children and grownups quite normally do. What strikes us often as illogical may yet be psychological; and committed as they are to a belief in their own rationality, philosophers as a group may be peculiarly insensitive to this fact. I would argue that not only as teachers but also as professional philosophers, we cannot really continue to talk about the mind-body problem, our knowledge of other minds, knowledge itself, without some awareness at least of what has been claimed by psychoanalysts about the relationship between body-image and self-consciousness, about what is involved in coming to recognize one's self as being separate from others, about the phenomena they refer to when they speak of thought processes and of feelings which are in some sense "unconscious."

Another way is to encourage students to find in themselves the phantasies which are the counterpart of a number of traditional philosophical problems, Descartes' questions about the reality of his body, the connection between his body and his mind, the existence of the external world and of other minds, grab students who like puzzles and who have a natural philosophical bent. But others simply think him silly, or mad. His worries are indeed the worries of madmen. But they are also the worries of all of us, in some moments. The question about the existence of other minds can be expressed in the language of feeling as the sense of abandonment, of being utterly alone. My guess is that precisely Descartes' question—How do I know that all the others aren't only automata, who look and act like me, but who don't think and feel like me—has occurred to most children when they were feeling separation anxiety, or when they were being misunderstood. And there isn't anyone who hasn't had an experience so puzzling, so seemingly unlike the experiences of those around him, that for a moment, at least, he wondered if he was insane. In philosophical terms, that worry is expressed by all the questions philosophers have raised about the relationship between perception and reality. Finally, the questions about the relationship between body and mind and about the reality of one's own body can be expressed—as Husserl, Heidegger and Sartre, among others, later saw—as the disturbing recognition that is an object of perception, my body is more available to others than it is to myself. In fact, one begins to be a person, to have "a self," as one becomes self-conscious; and self-consciousness implies a duality. What I am for others I am not necessarily for myself. What others think of me may be mistaken. What is out of my view—my own backside as well, often, as the consequences of what I do—may be plain to someone else.

Here again the use of literary works may help to give emotional embodiment to philosophical problems that otherwise can strike students as irrelevant even to their intellectual lives. For example, Tolstoy's *The Death of Ivan Ilytch* is a dramatic rendering of the relationship between what it is to have a self, and self-consciousness. At the point at which he has begun to question his own life and whether or not he was even as content as he had always thought he was, Ivan engages, for the first time, in a dialogue with himself. In the context of the story, the problem of explaining how someone can be deceived about his own well-being is solved by saying that it happens when one hasn't begun to question one's self in the first place.

The kinds of written work that we assign students tell them as much about the model we have in mind as the comments we make on their papers when we return them. Beyond the standard essays and dialogues which we were assigned and which we continue to assign, it seems to me perfectly within our province to ask as well for original stories, including fairy stories (the brothers Grimm are a gold-mine of disturbing illustrations of both psychoanalytic insights and philosophical worries), narrative writing of all sorts, and the keeping of a "philosophical" diary. (Sartre's *Nausea* is one kind of philosophical diary; Descartes' *Meditations* is another.) The point of such a diary would be to sensitize students to the philosophical puzzles and assumptions lurking in our most ordinary experiences; for example, the shock of surprise that we sometimes feel when we catch ourselves unexpectedly in the mirror calls to our attention how profoundly we take the continuity of our bodies and of ourselves for granted.

Such suggestions as I have made will certainly not solve the following problem, but they may attenuate it: Every teacher of philosophy is familiar with the disappointed student who thought that philosophy was going to change his life in some unspeakable way, and whose first philosophical yields seem instead to be a handful of technical terms. In fact, we ourselves, many of us, were once those disappointed students. And then we readjusted our goals, and now advise our students to readjust theirs. It will be a long time, if ever, we warn them, before philosophy will provide the enlightenment they are seeking. We may even go on to say, cynically, that the etymology of 'philosophy' is misleading, and philosophy doesn't in any case, or any longer, have to do with wisdom.

But it can. And though it's true that students will not usually find the *kind* of answers they are seeking, I think that even from the beginning, philosophy can be more enlightening than it is. Students will not, must not, emerge from a course in ethics with the sense that all present and future ethical dilemmas have been solved. But they can have come to face the massiveness of their own confusions; to recognize, perhaps, the lure for them of general, exceptionless principles, or on the other hand, of an ethical position which seems to justify their own lack of principles. And here I think the first and not the least important values of philosophy and of psychoanalytic therapy are quite comparable. It is a long while before an analytic patient will really have resolved the conflicts which, whether he recognized them or not, first made him seek help. But he will never resolve them until he has faced them without qualification, and unless he is willing to give up some of the control which reason represents for most of us.

Both psychoanalysis and philosophy are disruptive of old orders and certainties; and therefore, unless one's feelings are disengaged, both are painful. As philosophers

I think we have to avoid here the temptation to make things easier for beginning students by providing them with what we think are the answers, or by trying to disguise genuine philosophical perplexities behind the delusive clarity of diagrams, definitions, and paradoxes too easily resolved. Philosophy can help students to feel and tolerate anxiety for a while; to settle for the moment with half answers, or none at all; to be suspicious, at least, of all absolutes, including absolute relativism. And if philosophy succeeds in these ways, its success will have encouraged and required a fusion of thought and feeling, mind and body.

Recently I attended a conference to which primarily philosophers were invited. Under discussion were the sorts of ethical questions that confront doctors in this era of unprecedented medical technology. The opening paper presented the following situation: Suppose that someone, a philosopher, had carefully thought out all the pros and cons of euthanasia and had finally decided on the basis of reasons which he could fully articulate and defend, that it was always wrong. Suppose further that he were then taken to visit the terminal ward of a hospital where patients were being kept alive under conditions of enormous suffering. If the philosopher then found that all his previous arguments still held but that his new experiences were beginning to pull him in another direction, what should he make of this tension and how should he deal with it? The final thesis of the paper was that experience, including the experience of feeling, is simply irrelevant, and categorically so, to moral reasoning. To a man (I was the only woman present at the conference) the philosophers found this thesis interesting, if not actually plausible or true. I and the one psychoanalyst were appalled that it could be taken seriously even for a moment. This means, I assume, that the philosophical approach I am suggesting here will not be sympathetic to a great many philosophers. I don't expect it to be. For one thing, I am well aware that psychoanalysis is anathema to many people, and perhaps to most philosophical people. But perhaps there will be some others who share my anxiety about the kind of sterility toward which contemporary philosophical thinking tends, and who are trying to avoid perpetuating what they may see as the misdirections of their own philosophical education.

The discovery that rationality is a process involving emotion, and meaning different things in different contexts, is not original to psychoanalysis. But the guiding notion of rationality fostered by the majority of Anglo-American philosophers and by our society in general is one which does not make such syntheses and distinctions. This is one of the reasons why reason is currently out of fashion, and why many students believe that the only alternative to a rationality which they find wedded to a technological view of the human being is irrationality; why, knowing nothing or next-to-nothing about "traditional" psychoanalysis, they are nevertheless convinced that there cannot be in any sense a science of human behavior; and why they are predisposed to believe that if psychoanalysis is to be practiced in any form, only that of the existentialists, with their emphasis on encounter and the uniqueness of the person will do. For students are familiar with the notion of objectivity appropriate to the natural sciences, and unfamiliar with the quite different notion of objectivity which is one of the ideals of every psychoanalyst, whether Freudian, neo-Freudian or existentialist. The counter-culture's celebration of miracle and mystery, its attack on reason, must and can be answered; not by calling reason to account, but our own denatured conception of it.

Note

This article originally appeared in *Metaphilosophy* 6 (1975).

The Inevitability of Holding Philosophical Beliefs, or Le Bourgeois Undergraduate Gentilhomme

DAVID NYBERG

The title of this paper comes from Moliere's comedy, *Le Bourgeois Gentilhomme*, in which M. Jourdain is taught by the philosophy master that he has in fact been speaking "prose" all his life without knowing that it was "prose" he was speaking. The philosophy master, being in M. Jourdain's employ, was tactfully laconic in his witness of this revelation, while le monsieur fell agape in pride and wonder.

Whether philosophy masters of modern universities are similarly in service of the bourgeoisie is presently at least debatable. In any case, they rarely have the luxury of such tutorial arrangements with their students. Many of us who teach philosophy find ourselves dealing with groups of undergraduates, young and old, whose diverse motivations *vis-à-vis* philosophy make it difficult to know just how best to begin teaching a given class, and make it nearly impossible to get satisfaction from teaching in the lecture/text fashion. The problems that concern me here are those of instructing philosophy, (1) to undergraduate students who may be motivated to take the course only by a college or program requirement and therefore may hold a skeptical reluctance toward philosophy as a whole, and (2) to students who may indeed be curious to know more about philosophy but who also feel intimidated by its erudite and esoteric reputation. My attempt to deal with these problems has led me to develop a "Belief Profile" concept, a sample section of which is to be found in Appendix 1, and the justification for which follows here directly.

In these first years of my career as a university teacher I have noticed two things that *must* affect my teaching style. First, the number of students who come to university because they want to study something particular is quite small compared to the number of students who come because they do not know what else to do for the moment. Second, from under this motley student mantle comes a demand of me to explain what philosophy of all things has to do with anything important, such as getting a job.

I have accepted the sundry character of our university student bodies, and I have accepted the burden of explanation demanded of me. I have spent hours, too many hours, trying to justify the calamity of "having to take philosophy," because philosophy is perceived as something of a pointless discipline which now ridicules the poets of our culture instead of inspiring them as it once did, in *some* cultures anyway, if not in an earlier version of the American culture. As philosophy is perceived more as a discipline than as a disposition, as "knowledge" is seen to be more of a function of "proof" than of "belief," as the literature of the field becomes more mechanically numerable and symbolic, to this extent it becomes onerous to entice students into the study of philosophy, to amuse students with its charm, or to make the case that philosophy is for people generally and not for professionals only.

I am not so much interested to cant a new slogan of "Philosophy to the People" as I am interested to demonstrate that philosophy, or at least some philosophical belief, is inevitably present in the lives of thinking persons, that the primary problems of philosophy can be stated in such a way as to show that they are also the primary problems of living. As Michael Scriven[1] puts it: "We cannot choose whether to answer (these problems), for to live requires that we answer them in our lives. We can only choose whether to think about them."

Philosophy and Personality

Socrates learned that knowing oneself was the foundation of philosophy, and he expanded this learning into a claim that has survived as "The unexamined life is not worth living." Oedipus led some of us to believe that the well-examined life is often unlivable. And not too long ago John Barth suggested that self-knowledge is almost always bad news. These three, together, give us a way to think about neophyte philosophizing: whatever one knows about oneself is at least part of what one knows about philosophy. Fichte put it this way: the kind of philosophy a man chooses depends upon the kind of man he is; suggesting that philosophy does not really change the man so much as the man's living changes his philosophy. Nietzsche, as usual, put it more fetchingly: "Gradually it has become clear to me that what every great philosophy so far has been: namely, the personal confession of its author and a kind of involuntary and unconscious memoir (autobiography)."[2]

Each of us has a biography, that much is clear. That one's biography has in it a philosophy of sorts is not so clear. It is, however, at least plausible that if one were to learn a certain manner of expressing certain aspects of one's biography, one could come to see to what extent one had been developing philosophical positions on philosophical issues.

If attempting such expression, as my Belief profile (see sample in Appendix 1) is meant to facilitate, we are bound to find out a good deal about beliefs that we have held, with or without conscious awareness, and about some of the implicit difficulties we have in justifying such beliefs, and in expressing them clearly enough to be understood by another person who may or may not share them. Such a focus on one's held beliefs is intrinsically interesting: there is no more favorite topic of conversation than oneself.

Now some may object that although this exercise may be of value to philosophers, it simply is not appropriate to expect undergraduate students to express their own philosophical beliefs and their own justifications for these beliefs. To begin with, goes this argument, they lack the skills necessary for philosophical analysis of beliefs and their justifications; and what's more, we should remember that such philosophizing often involves more sophistication and more ability to cope with grand-scale conceptual reorientations than we can or even ought to expect of undergraduates.

There surely is a point to this objection, but not a clearly productive one. If we sustain the objection we have no alternative than to introduce our students to philosophy through the beliefs held by *others*. And we are then led, by their usefulness for such purposes, to texts of the he-said-this-and-she-said-that variety, which, in their second-hand (often *third*-hand) and compendious character, are not immediately compelling to the fundamentally unmotivated reader. We remain obliged to *provide* such motivation where it does not exist, and that has been the baleful, boring bane of textbook teachers everywhere.

If, however, we choose not to sustain the objection, we might appeal to G. E. Moore's way of doing philosophy as a model for our point of view. As G. J. Warnock[3] puts it:

> Part of the great interest and importance of [the way Moore did philosophy] is that this is something anyone can do—to practice philosophy in the manner of Moore, it is not necessary to have (as most of us doubtless have not) nor pretend to have (as some of us at least would be unwilling to do) large-scale metaphysical anxieties. It is necessary only to want to get things clear.

Now getting clear on where our living has led us, in terms of the beliefs we have come to hold, with varying degrees of conscious awareness, is what my proposal for teaching philosophy to undergraduates is meant to assist. One thing we can be sure a student brings to class is his or her biography. The task is to help, maieutically, its expression in terms of held beliefs.

The Psychology of Present Constructs

In the view of Professor J. P. Corbett:[4]

> the work of philosophical education must begin by raising radical doubts. The teacher must apply his energy and skill to throwing the convictions of his student into disarray. He must personify the malignant demon of Descartes and stir up every doubt he can. This is the only way in which accepted principles of validity can be dredged up to the surface of the mind

for examination. But principles of validity do not rest inside a personality, detached from the emotions and the will, they are an integral part of the personality; they are, in a very real sense, what a man is and how he lives.

This dredging up of one's "principles of validity" is very like what George Kelly suggests in his psychology of personal constructs when he says we can explore the subjective maps that people chart to deal with the psychological terrain of their lives. Or, in a slightly different way, we can understand that "man looks at his world through transparent patterns or templets which he creates, and then attempts to fit over the realities of which the world is composed."[5]

I anticipate an objection at this point over the fact that Kelly is a psychotherapist and that teaching philosophy is not, whatever else it may be, psychotherapy. Besides, a philosopher or a philosophy teacher is not trained for theraputics and therefore should not act therapeutically, or deal directly with the "personality." For the sake of getting on with a discussion of the Belief Profile, I will not dispute this objection by arguing over the relations between teaching and therapy, between learning, healing, and health. I will instead sustain the objection on the grounds that one can deal with another's beliefs, some of which can be likened to "principles of validity," some to "subject maps," some to "templets," which are created constructs meant to help interpret the world, without assuming a therapeutic role or frame of mind, but solely through the use of a diagnostic instrument designed to yield a profile of existing, held beliefs. Before discussing the Profile itself, however, I would like to elaborate just briefly Kelly's theory of personal constructs because the theory has been of significant influence in the development of the Profile.

Kelly's psychology of personal constructs is of a category in the field of personality studies called "phenomenological theory," a category which embraces the theories of Kurt Lewin, Carl Rogers, Gordon Allport, Frederick Peris, and perhaps R. D. Laing, as well as Kelly. The theories of this category are normally contrasted with Type and Trait theories (Sheldon, Cattell, Guilford, Eysenk, and sometimes Jung), with Psychodynamic theories (Freud, Jung, Fromm, Erikson, Adler, Sullivan, Horney, Dollard and Miller), and with the Social Behavior theories (Watson, Skinner, Bandura, and perhaps Glasser).

In contrast to Psychodynamic theory wherein *motive* and *unconscious conflict* are, respectively, the prime units and process, Kelly emphasizes a person's own constructs, or categories or templets, which one uses to sort out the important from the matter-of-fact, as Whitehead would put it, in order to exercise some degree of control over those events which affect one's life. The critical elements of the theory are these:

1. People perceive and construe behavior, and they generate abstractions about themselves and others.
2. These perceptions-turned-abstractions are called constructs, which act as patterns or templets for interpreting experience.

3. All people are like scientists in that they generate hypotheses and constructs which help them anticipate, predict, and control events in the world with which they are involved.
4. One way a person tries to improve his constructs, to give them a better "fit," is to subsume them with superordinate constructs or systems, which are, for the most part, systems of belief.
5. A major presupposition of the theory is that "all of our present interpretations of the universe are subject to revision or replacement." (Although we all do have, inevitably, a biography, we are not inevitably *victims* of that biography.)
6. Sometimes we hesitate to experiment with our construct systems because we fear the ambiguity that may result if we lose the ability to predict and control.
7. A person is not necessarily articulate about the constructs and construct (or belief) systems he places on the world.
8. A superordinate construct has a deterministic control over its element, but the elements do not determine the constructs which are used to subsume them. A person, then, to the extent that he can construe his circumstances, can free himself from their dominion. A man can enslave himself, but he can free himself also by reconstruing his life, or part of it.
9. The concern of the psychologist or psychotherapist is the utility of the constructs in question, not their truth: the object of therapy is to provide conditions for the person to elaborate and test for implications his own operating set of constructs, or beliefs, which is to say, controls. In light of new experience they may be modified.

Belief Constructs and Belief Profiles

What Kelly calls a superordinate construct or system is very like Boulding's notion of "social image"[6] through which we filter messages that we call knowledge. Another conceptual similarity worth noting here is the one between Corbett's "principles of validity," which are "what a man is and how he lives," and Quine's view of believing as a "disposition to respond in certain ways when the appropriate issue arises."[7]

Now, insofar as holding a philosophical view can be likened to holding (consciously or not, articulate or not) a superordinate construct or system, or a social image of knowledge, or a set of validity principles, or that the disposition called believing, and insofar as these aspects of human living are *inevitable* constituents of one's own biography, then holding a philosophical view is *inevitable*, whether one has been instructed in philosophy and its refinements or not. Insofar as one has construed one's own experience, abstracted some of these constructs, appealed to principles of validity in the course of one's daily living, and been disposed toward believing, one has been "speaking philosophy" just as surely as M. Jourdain had been "speaking prose" those forty years before he knew what to call it.

Assuming that we all do have, in the lines of our own biographies, beliefs on philosophical issues, we still have the question of what a paper and pencil Profile has to do with them. It has been my experience that instruments, devices, machines and the like devised to increase the economy of some aspect of human affairs (in this case introducing students to philosophy) have in them inherent invitations to superficial thinking. Jacob Burckhardt predicted from his century that our century would be one of "great simplifiers," tempting us away from complexity and toward the essence of tyranny. I do not wish the Belief Profile to be understood or used as a great simplifier.

John Dewey[8] held that the most pervasive fallacy of philosophic thinking is the neglect of context: such neglect takes two forms; the *analytic fallacy*, wherein distinctions and elements that are discriminated are treated as if they were final and self-sufficient (leading to various forms of atomistic particularism), and the *fallacy of unlimited extension or universalization*, wherein distinctions and elements discriminated are lost altogether when the contextual limitations under which such discrimination take place are ignored in the metaphysically anxious rush for Coherency and Unity. Any instrument designed to represent the views or beliefs of persons is subject to both of these fallacies which are two of philosophy's great simplifiers. I hope to avoid charges of yielding to these wily invitations to fallacy by stipulating some limits of use for the Belief Profile.

1. It is meant only to be used as an aid in deciding how specifically to introduce beginning students to philosophy.
2. It is not to be thought of as a summary of any one philosopher's views, nor of a student's beliefs in a given area, nor of the area itself. It is merely an indicator of likely connections between a student's held beliefs on a given issue and a recognized philosopher's held beliefs on the same issue.
3. It is not to be used as an evaluative examination.
4. It is not to be used as a text or syllabus substitute.
5. It is not to be used as a substitute for teacher-student conferences and dialogue; it is to be used to promote and prepare for conferences and dialogue, and perhaps class debate.

The application of the Belief Profile would go something like this: (*a*) at the start of a class or a unit of a class, the student would mark, for example, the ethics section of the Profile according to instructions, (*b*) the teacher checks each Profile for clusters of "Strongly Agree" and "Strongly Disagree" items, (*c*) the teacher compares these belief clusters with a reference list (not completed as of this writing) coded to match the numbered items of the Profile, (*d*) on the basis of this comparison the teacher recommends a selected bit of reading calculated either to give the student an experience of seeing his own beliefs stated in the words of a *bona fide* philosopher or to confront the student with a succinct statement supporting the opposite or at least conflicting point of view, (*e*) the student does the suggested reading and reports his reaction to the teacher, which in turn provides the teacher with some immediate feedback as to how well he is "reading" the student's beliefs, how well he is matching those beliefs, and as to what the next step in this process might be.[9]

Two assumptions lurk beneath this application description. First, I am assuming that a student will be at least surprised if not pleased or even flattered to find that he thinks somewhat like a philosopher, or that he has thought about philosophical issues and questions already. Second, I am assuming that such a reaction will breed a certain motivation, by virtue of association with a model, a philosopher, that would otherwise not have shown itself—at least not so soon. If these two assumptions hold, the question "What does philosophy have to do with me, or with real life?" will have been answered by an actual demonstration of such a connection.

Notes

Presented at the American Philosophical Association (Western Division) Annual Meeting in Chicago, April 26, 1973. Published in *Metaphilosophy* 5 (1974).

1. Michael Scriven, *Primary Philosophy* (New York: McGraw-Hill, 1966).

2. Friedrich Nietzsche, *Beyond Good and Evil* (1.6): the Kaufman translation (New York: Random House, 1966) has "memoir" where the Zimmern translation (New York: Modern Library, 1954) has "biography."

3. G. J. Warnock, *English Philosophy Since 1900* (London and New York: Oxford University Press, 1969, 2nd ed.).

4. J. P. Corbett, "Teaching Philosophy Now," in *Philosophical Analysis and Education*, ed. R. D. Archambault (London: Routledge and Kegan Paul, 1965).

5. George A. Kelly, *The Psychology of Personal Constructs*, vol. 1 (New York: Norton, 1955).

6. Kenneth Boulding, *The Image* (Ann Arbor: University of Michigan Press, 1956).

7. W. V. Quine and J. S. Ullian, *The Web of Belief* (New York: Random House, 1970).

8. John Dewey, *On Experience, Nature, and Freedom*, ed. R. J. Bernstein (New York: The Liberal Arts Press, 1960), chap. 4, "Context and Thought."

9. "The next step in this process" is not strictly implied by the Belief Profile. It should properly be the function of the interaction, or transaction, between the teacher, the Profile, and the student. An example of a possible, and feasible, "next step" would be to assign 3–5 students who show similar belief clusters to meet together in order to discuss the first assigned readings, and to reinforce each other's beliefs. Then pit one of these groups against another, which represents a conflicting cluster of held beliefs on

generally the same issue. In this way, the teacher could assess the degree to which the students understood the assigned reading and, by implication, their own beliefs, and he could point out, using the debate as an example, how difficult and emotion-laden discussion of philosophical issues can become, especially when dealt with on the level of beliefs.

Appendix 1
DANYBERG Belief Profile: Ethics

Please indicate your response to each item
by checking that part of the scale which corresponds to your present belief.

| strongly agree | somewhat agree | slightly agree | neutral | slightly disagree | somewhat disagree | strongly disagree |

1. There is essentially no difference between "factual" statements and "value" statements.

2. Anything that is "good" is also "right."

3. Anything that is "right" is also "good."

4. A "value" judgment is also a "moral" judgment.

5. It is possible to find a criterion for determining the "validity" of ethical judgments.

6. Value statements such as "Democracy is good and communism is bad" are really commands that mean "you should choose democracy over communism."

7. One cannot deduce an "ought" statement from a series of "is" statements (e.g., man is a rational animal, so man ought to act rationally.).

8. There is such a thing, or quality, as "intrinsic" good.

9. It is possible to make moral judgments that apply to all people.

10. It is possible to make moral judgments that apply to one person at all times.

11. If one "senses" an obligation, one "has" an obligation.

12. Intuition is the best source for moral judgments.

13. Revelation is the best source for moral judgments.

14. Rational thinking is the best source for moral judgments.

15. Empirical, or scientific data are the best source for moral judgments.

strongly agree	somewhat agree	slightly agree	neutral	slightly disagree	somewhat disagree	strongly disagree

16. "Science" is no more related to "morality" than blacksmithing.

17. Everything in the world has ethical aspects and implications.

18. "Morality" is a function of convention, not nature.

19. "Good triumphs over evil;" therefore, what survives, what is strongest, is "good."

20. It is not possible that one who really understands what is "good" could then choose to do bad or evil.

21. It is not possible that pain can ever be thought of as a "good."

22. If I can decide the question "What should I do?," I can also then decide the question "What should you do?"

23. An act can be "wrong" and "good."

24. There is essentially no difference between deciding what is hot, hotter, hottest and deciding what is good, better, best.

25. It is impossible to understand the term "guilt" without first understanding the term "ought."

26. There exists a "level of being" higher than human life which is the "real" source of morality.

27. What we call "morality" is at bottom no more than a desire, or choice to believe this rather than that: one can change one's "morality" merely by changing his mind.

28. There can be no "morality" that is not "just."

29. Man invented the concept of "justice"; there is no example of "justice" to be found in "nature."

30. "Evil" means the same as "bad."

PART III:

NEW CLASSROOM ACTIVITIES

Teaching and Learning Philosophy in a Classroom

MARK LEVENSKY

If there's one thing most philosophers have in common, it's that they're teachers. That's how they earn their living. But strangely enough, most philosophers never admit they're teachers. Not in print, anyway.

I

When I was a teaching fellow at the University of Michigan, I used to teach recitation sections of a large introductory course in philosophy. At the end of each term everyone teaching in the course would get together in one room to read final examinations. Soon after we started reading these examinations, someone would suddenly groan. And once we were well underway, someone would read out some crazy passage from some exam he was reading and we would all laugh and begin to look for more crazy passages to read aloud. Some of the passages we picked out sounded like this:

> Descartes said that there were these two substances. Mind and people's bodies. Berkeley said that there was only this one substance. God's Mind. They differed about wax. Descartes said that wax exists. And that it will melt. He said that wax won't melt because wax is in God's mind and God's mind won't melt. Descartes said that God exists because existence is a predicate. G. E. Moore said that existence isn't a predicate. Berkeley didn't think of predicates.

From time to time someone would say something about how terrible most of the exams were and we would all agree and sigh and read on. Eventually, when all of the examinations had been more or less read and graded and the grades recorded and the exam books sorted and tied into bundles and stacked, we all got up and went home. It was an incredibly depressing experience.[1]

In thinking about this experience since, I have been struck by a number of things that I think may be of some general interest. For one thing, I think that we were probably right in thinking that most of the examination papers were just awful. As I remember them they were, for the most part, barely legible, filled with inconsistent accounts of misunderstood views, vague recollections of distant blackboards and far off lectures, and, worst of all, they contained almost no direct evidence as to what the students thought or felt about anything. Secondly, I think that we were probably wrong about why the examinations were so bad. I think that most of us probably thought that they were bad because the students were bad—they really were pretty dumb, or, at least, they couldn't argue philosophically, or that they didn't bother to read the texts or come to class, or, more simply, that most of them didn't do any work. But none of these explanations will do. Generally, our students were smart. They were at Michigan. And they *could* argue philosophically. They argued philosophically with their friends. And they did read the texts. They underlined them in yellow and made notes in the margins. And they did come to class. The seats were always filled. And they did all the written work that we asked them to do. We kept records. Sometimes when the uncomfortable subject of our student's failure to learn what we wanted to teach them came up during the term, we would blame the course or the books: "If only the courses were different . . . if only we could teach Austin and Quine." But then we all got to teach different courses, and then we all got to teach Austin and Quine. I now think that the reason that the final examinations were so bad is that in spite of our knowledge, ability, and good intentions, *we* failed as *teachers*. Not only did *we* fail to teach most of these students anything that *we* wanted to teach them, or, more importantly, anything *they* wanted to know, but we probably taught some students to *hate* philosophy as much as they hated anything. (We never considered the possibility that some of our students had *intentionally* written crazy dumb answers to our examination questions.) And I think that one of the main reasons that we failed as teachers is that we all tried to teach philosophy pretty much the same way, and generally that way doesn't work.[2]

II

How, exactly, did we try to teach philosophy in our classrooms? What, exactly, did we do? Let me speak for myself. The first day of my recitation class went something like this. Twenty or twenty-five students appeared in my classroom. They came for a variety of reasons. Some because it was a required course. Some because they wanted to fill an hour. Some because they had some real interest in philosophy. And they came with a variety of questions that they wanted answered—what is philosophy and who is Wittgenstein and what about the meaning of life and can all proofs for the existence of God be refuted and what is Zen—and with a variety of their own views that they wanted to discuss, views about the relativity of all moral values and views about the uncertainty of all our knowledge of the external world. Then I appeared. I appeared because it was my job. But it wasn't just a job. I wanted to teach. I formally introduced myself to my students by writing my name on the blackboard and pronouncing my name aloud. I introduced my students to myself and to each other by reading their names aloud and watching their hands go up. Then I introduced the structure and content of our course by telling my students what we would, and hence, wouldn't cover during the term, what texts they should buy and read, and what papers and examinations they would write and when. Sometimes I even handed out a course assignment sheet with each day's work spelled out in detail. Then I stopped, paused, and asked for questions. When the questions stopped, I stopped, made an assignment for next time, and left. After I left, my students got up and left too. I think it would be fair to say that at that point, for all practical purposes, the course was over.

The normal day to day, hour to hour life in my recitation section was probably like the normal everyday life in most classrooms. I lectured a lot. Sometimes I prepared my lectures rather carefully. Sometimes I just talked off the top of my head. I got better at talking off the top of my head as the term wore on. It was easy and fun. I soon discovered that I could talk about anything—philosophy, sports, politics, myself, the world—and the students would apparently listen. Just so I didn't run over the hour. Whether I prepared my lectures or not, I thought my lectures were better than the lectures of the lecturer in the course. I corrected his mistakes in my classroom.

I also tried to get discussions going in my classroom and sometimes I thought that I had succeeded. These discussions usually consisted of my asking my students a question about an assigned text and receiving, in return, no answers, or wrong answers, or non-answers. I almost never asked a question that I didn't know the answer to. My students almost never talked to anyone in class but me, even when they were replying to something that a fellow student had just said. One reason for this was that while all the students in the classroom could see my face, most of them could only see the backs or sides of each other.

In addition to giving lectures and leading discussions, I used our classroom time to assign paper topics, hand back papers that I had read and graded, arrange for conferences with individual students who wanted mostly to talk to me about some grade I had given them, and sometimes, I used this classroom time to give a pop quiz:

What is the dream argument in "First Meditation" and is it any good? Why or why not?

In doing all of this I thought that I was teaching well. The philosophy department also thought that I was teaching well. They helped me get a good teaching job.

III

Why did I teach this way—on the first day and throughout the term? What made me so sure that teaching philosophy in a classroom consisted of giving lectures, making assignments, and grading papers? And why did I continue to teach this way after it was obvious to me and to everybody else that teaching philosophy this way generally doesn't work? One reason that I taught this way was that for the most part, this was the way that I had been taught (or not taught) everything in school. From the first grade through my graduate work. Of course, I had been in plenty of recitation sections, discussion classes, and graduate seminars. I had even spent one year in law school where otherwise gentle men practice their own peculiar version of the Socratic Method. But these courses all turned out to be lecture courses too. If the teacher didn't lecture someone else did.

I must say that I often hated these lectures. By the time I was a graduate student this lecture series had lasted fifteen years and I was tired of it. It was always the same story whenever I walked into a classroom. Some person standing up there talking all of us to death. So why, in a classroom, did I do the same thing? Well, as I've mentioned, I discovered that lecturing, as opposed to listening to lectures, wasn't awful and boring, but fun. And I thought that *my* lectures, unlike all the lectures that I had to listen to all my life, were *interesting* and *good*. They could teach people something, if only the people would listen.

Another reason that I taught this way was fear. Teaching is a scary business. I was afraid of standing up and talking to strangers, afraid of revealing that I didn't know as much philosophy as my students probably thought I knew, afraid that if I didn't talk no one would, afraid that at any moment the class would get out of hand and fall apart, afraid that if I didn't give assignments, examinations, and pop quizzes, then no one would do any work. As a consequence of these fears and others, I kept my students strangers and distant, I saw to it that we only considered questions that I knew a lot about, I kept as much control as I could of what publicly went on in my classroom, I made a lot of assignments, and I gave a number of pop quizzes.

A fourth reason that I taught this way, and that my students allowed me to teach this way, has to do with something that we all believed at that time. My students and I believed that while I obviously had something of real value to contribute to our class, none of the students had anything of value to contribute. I was a philosopher and a teacher. They were simply students. And beginning students at that. Hence, with the students' implicit approval, or, at least, without any student's explicit objection, I ran all of our classes, I did most of the talking, all of their comments in class were directed at me, discussions never got going, I made all of the assignments, I graded all the exams and papers, and students never said, or seemed to say, what they thought or felt about anything. And surely we weren't alone in thinking that while I, as teacher, had something important to offer the class, the students, as students, had nothing to contribute. I think that this general view was shared and is shared by teachers and students throughout the land—beginning students and graduate students, teaching fellows and full professors. And not just by philosophy teachers and college students, but by teachers and students in classrooms everywhere. One everyday symptom of this disease is that when a teacher doesn't show up for his class, the students pick up and leave. Or if the teacher has to leave his class early, the students leave too.

Each of these things, then, my lifetime of being lectured in school, the fun I had lecturing and my thought that I was lecturing well, my natural fears of teaching strangers in a classroom, and our belief about what I had to offer my students and what my students had to offer me, led me to teach and fail to teach in the way that I did. And perhaps some of these reasons also explain why I continued to teach this way after it was obvious to me that my teaching wasn't any good. At the time there seemed to be no alternative. For better or worse, there was nothing else that I could do.

IV

How can a philosopher teach philosophy well in a classroom? In particular, how can a philosopher teach philosophy well in a classroom filled with twenty or thirty people who have come to the classroom with a variety of desires and expectations, who have a limited amount of time and energy to give to the class, and who have already been thoroughly educated about teaching and learning in school during their own lifetimes of sitting in classrooms? Given our times, a more pressing question is probably how to teach philosophy well outside of classrooms, or in classrooms filled with hundreds of people rather than classrooms filled with thirty. However, most of my experience trying to teach philosophy has been in classrooms and with groups of twenty to thirty people. So that is what I want to talk about here. But I think that part of what I say here might be helpful to philosophers trying to teach hundreds or, someday, even thousands of people at a time. For example, if what I have already said is true, then a good solution to the problem of teaching philosophy to huge groups of people is not, or is not just, finding some way to break the huge group up into smaller groups and giving each smaller group its own philosopher.

One suggestion for how to teach philosophy well in a classroom is this. Do just what I did—lecture, ask questions, answer questions, make assignments, grade papers, give examinations—only do it *better* than I did. Give better lectures, ask better questions, give better answers, make better assignments, write better comments on papers, and give better examinations. This suggestion is an instance of an attractive solution to many human problems: "Do just what you're doing now, just do it better. Then everything will be lovely." And the present instance of this general solution might seem to have some fairly strong support. For example, someone might argue as follows: It is surely no accident that this method of teaching is far and away the most widely used method of teaching in classrooms. Most philosophy teachers want to teach something. Most students want to learn. If there was a better way to do both in a classroom then surely over the last thousand years it would have been discovered, and its use would be widespread. Of course, there may be technological reasons why a better way of teaching and learning philosophy in a classroom wasn't discovered, or isn't now widespread. Still, the lecture-question-assignment-paper-examination-grade method of teaching has evolved over a long period of time and has survived a good deal of criticism, experimentation and despair. And that must be in its favor. Secondly, we know on the basis of our own teaching and learning experience that when this method of teaching is used well, it does work. Students do learn some philosophy. Not all students do. Perhaps not even most students, except when this method is used brilliantly and with highly motivated and prepared students. But a few will learn something—something that their teachers wanted to teach them and something that they wanted to know. Of course it's not always easy to say how much philosophy a particular student learned, or what philosophy he learned. The student often doesn't know. Philosophy is such that the results of successfully teaching philosophy are often invisible or small—a person becomes a tiny bit better at justifying his beliefs, a person comes to understand something about an issue or a form of argument that he didn't understand at all before. And as for the students who don't learn any philosophy, many will be excited enough by what happened in the classroom to take another philosophy course where they do learn something, or go on to learn some philosophy on their own. This is the most that we can hope for. And it's a lot.

    I have mixed feelings about the suggestion that the way to teach philosophy well in a classroom is to do what I did only do it better than I did. Sometimes I think that this might be right. But most of the time I think that this is probably wrong. One reason that I think that this is probably wrong is that the reasons that seem to support it don't support it very well. Consider the argument that this teaching method was developed over a long period of time by sincere, interested, and concerned people, and that it is now being used by philosophy teachers everywhere; hence, it must be a good method, or at least, it is the best available. The force of this argument is weakened for me by the fact that I have rarely seen the negative consequences or non-consequences of teaching this way affect this method of teaching. When things don't go well and learning doesn't happen students are blamed, the material is blamed, sometimes the teachers using the method are blamed by other teachers, classrooms are blamed, society is blamed. But the method is seldom blamed. And if the negative consequences or non-consequences of teaching this way are seldom allowed to affect the method, then the fact that this method has been around so long, and is used so widely, doesn't mean so much to me.

    The second argument isn't much of an argument at all. I am willing to admit that on the basis of my own teaching and learning experience I know that when this method of teaching is used well, it works. Some of my students have learned something. I have. Friends have. And people are sometimes inspired to go on to learn philosophy in other classrooms and on their own once they have been in classrooms where philosophy is taught in this way. But I don't think that this is the most we can hope for. I think that I have discovered a way of teaching philosophy that is even better than the one I have been discussing, a way that makes even more learning possible. And what I would like to do now is to describe to you how I came to think of this method, or series of methods, and tell you what some of these methods are.

V

I began my search for a more successful way of teaching philosophy in a classroom by considering what seemed to me to be obvious instances of one person successfully teaching a group of people something in a classroom. The instances that I considered were one person teaching a group of people a craft like potting, trade like carpentry, a game like chess, a language like French. Then I tried to discover some general features of this teaching and learning. Some of the things that I came up with are: (1) The teacher talks a lot, but he doesn't try to teach anyone anything just by talking or writing things on the board or reading from books. One thing that he does in addition is to demonstrate *physically* the meaning of his words. For example, after talking about centering the clay on the wheel, he does it. Over and over again. (2) The students come to understand the meaning of the teacher's words and the meaning of his physical demonstrations by talking and by physical demonstrations of their own. For example, a student understands what the teacher meant when he held the saw a certain way, when the student asks some questions, has the saw in his hand, and is sawing. (3) The teacher and student correctly assume that even if the students are beginners, they are not starting from scratch. For example, in learning how to play chess the teacher and students correctly assume that the students know what a game is, the connection between games and rules, and the difference between winning and losing. (4) The teacher fully structures the learning environment of the classroom, and structures it in such a way that (*a*) the students are constantly presented with a variety of tasks to perform in the classroom, and (*b*) at the same time the students have the freedom to move around the room, ask questions and say things, look at what others are doing, talk informally, start working, and stop working. (5) The students memorize and practice basic techniques, they put these techniques to original-for-them use, they receive encouragement and criticism from their teacher, fellow students, and themselves, and they want to improve the quality of their work.

Now it seemed plausible to me at the time, and it still does, that these general features of these teaching and learning situations might be part of the reason that *successful* teaching and learning took place. It also struck me that it was just these features that were not present when I taught philosophy as a graduate student, or when most people teach philosophy in any classroom anywhere. As I have said, when I taught philosophy as a graduate student, and for some time after, I thought that I could teach philosophy just by talking; I thought that students in my classroom could learn just by listening to me; most of my students and I thought that while I had something of value to say in the classroom, no one else did; while I fully structured the learning environment of the classroom I structured it in such a way that (*a*) the students were constantly presented with only two tasks to perform in the classroom—listening to me and answering my questions, and (*b*) at the same time the students did not have the freedom to move around the room, say things, look at what others were doing, or talk informally; and while my students presumably wanted to improve the quality of their work, they were not given much opportunity to learn or practice the basic techniques that I was trying to teach them, or put these techniques to original-for-them use, or receive criticism from anyone but me. A third thought that I had at this time was that it might have been partly because these general features were not present when I and others taught philosophy that we succeeded in teaching so little.

As a consequence of these ideas, I decided to try to make these general features of teaching crafts, trades, games and languages part of my own way of teaching philosophy in a classroom. Now some of you might think that this was a very unpromising thing to do. And one reason that you might have for thinking so is the following: Let's assume that the instances of teaching that I mentioned are instances of successful teaching and learning in a classroom. And let's assume that I have picked out some general features of these instances and that these general features do partly explain why these instances of teaching and learning in a classroom are successful. Now even if all these assumptions are true, this probably wouldn't help me at all in figuring out how to teach *philosophy* well in a classroom. For there is a difference between *what* one is trying to teach in teaching crafts, trades, games and languages and *what* one is trying to teach in teaching philosophy. In teaching the former, the teacher is trying to teach students *how to* do something, or *to do* something—throw a cylinder, plane an edge, move the rook, use the subjunctive. But in teaching philosophy, presumably, the teacher is trying to teach students *that* something is so—that Plato held a particular view about universals, that there is a difference between knowledge and true belief, that statements of value are never entailed by statements of fact. And this difference probably makes the ways of successfully teaching crafts, games and languages in a classroom quite inapplicable to teaching philosophy anywhere.

I have two responses to this suggestion. First, I think that this suggestion contains a correct characterization of what teachers of crafts, trades, games and languages are trying to teach their students. But I think that it contains a mistaken account of what philosophers are trying to do. Pottery teachers are primarily trying to teach their students *how to do*, or *to do* certain things. But *so* are philosophers. In teaching philosophy, my primary aim, and I think the primary aim of many philosophers, is to teach a discipline. In particular, I want to teach students effective methods, strategies, rules and procedures for coming to understand traditional philosophical problems and texts, for evaluating the views of others and justifying their own views more rationally, and for making the philosophical discoveries that they want to make their own. In short, I want to teach students *how to do* and *to do* a number of very difficult things. It may be that in order to teach students these things, I have to teach them that a hundred particular things are so. But what I am primarily trying to teach my students in teaching them philosophy is *how to do* and *to do* some things, and not that any particular somethings are so. Hence, there isn't this essential difference between *what* I am trying to teach in teaching crafts, trades, games and languages, and *what* I am trying to teach in teaching philosophy.

My second response to this suggestion is that my subsequent experience does not support it. For when I did try to make these general principles part of my own way of teaching philosophy in a classroom, I achieved some success. More success, in fact, than I think I have ever achieved in teaching philosophy in a classroom before. I now want to describe briefly what I did. In particular, I want to describe to you some of the things that I did in teaching philosophy of art.

VI

There were twenty students in my philosophy of art class. We met once a week for three hours. We met in a medium sized living room type classroom. There were moveable couches, wooden chairs, and there was a rug on the floor. I limited the enrollment to twenty volunteers, divided up the class-time into three parts with two breaks, and dictated the kind of activity that took place during each of these periods. I also allowed and encouraged each of the students to *use* this time, these activities, each other, and me to learn anything that they wanted to learn about philosophy of art.

The first part of the class period lasted an hour. It was spent in discussion. Sometimes we sat as one large group and I would begin the discussion by saying, "What's on your mind?" or by silence. Sometimes I would divide our large group into groups of two or three or five people and we would talk to each other about what we had been reading or writing or thinking. During these large and small group meetings I pushed, pulled and searched for what I wanted to know and encourage others to do so as well. Sometimes during this period I would give a fifteen minute lecture to the whole group. I would try to summarize what we had discovered over the past few weeks, or suggest some new generalization to fit our combined experience, or make some wild or considered guess as to what we might discover next, or explain as best I could some traditional or contemporary view in philosophy of art, or set out some view of my own, or answer questions. Once in a while someone else in the class would lecture.

The second part of our class period lasted about an hour and a half. It was spent in a group exploration of a particular work of art—a piece of music, a parable, or a color slide—and in sharing our individual experiences of the work with each other. I selected the works for exploration, introduced easy exercises to help students explore the work of art and share their experiences with each other, and I more or less guided this exploration and sharing. I encouraged the students by what I said and by what I did to carry out this exploration and sharing as seriously and as fully as possible. I said, again and again, that this was another opportunity for them to find out what they wanted to know about philosophy of art. The more we did the exercises, explored the objects, and shared our experiences with each other, the better we got at it and the more we learned.

The last part of the period lasted about half an hour. It was spent in discussion. We usually met as one group to consider what had happened so far during the class period, how this connected with what we had read or experienced or learned or hoped for or guessed at or feared before, and what now, finally, could be *said*. I led these discussions, asked for energy and insight, and usually at some point had my say. Many others had their say too. At the very end of the period I made a reading assignment for the next meeting and suggested topics for further discussions and explorations. Students often made suggestions of their own. Three times during the term I also assigned a short paper and a written course evaluation. Each person's paper and evaluation was read and responded to in writing by another member of the class. I also wrote papers, evaluations, and responded in writing to someone else's paper. Some of these papers and course evaluations were discussed formally or informally in class.

Another way of describing what happened in the classroom is this. During the three class hours I talked a lot, but I didn't try to teach anyone anything just by talking or writing things on the board or reading from books. When students discovered the meaning of something that I said or did, or what a book said, or what someone else said or did, or when students learned anything else in that classroom, they seemed to do so mainly by talking with other students, by doing exercises, by exploring works of art and sharing their experiences of these works of art with others in the class, or by writing things down. At the start of the term I said that each of us already knew some things of philosophical importance about art, about what art is and what gives it meaning and what gives it value. As the term went on many of us discovered that this was true. I structured the learning environment in such a way that (*a*) students were presented with at least four distinct tasks to perform during each period—(1) discussion, (2) exploring, (3) sharing, and (4) theorizing, generalizing, or explaining, and (*b*) at the same time the students were free to use or not to use these opportunities as they pleased, and they were free to move around the room during some of the activities, ask questions and say things to me and each other, look at what others were doing, talk informally with me and others during breaks and during and in between activities, start working, and stop working. And during each class period many of the students learned and practiced some basic techniques for discussing hard stuff without wasting time, for exploring works of art and sharing what you have experienced, and for theorizing, generalizing, or explaining. Students also received encouragements and criticism from me, from fellow students, and from themselves along the way.

In briefly describing this class to you I hope that I haven't given you two false impressions. First of all, I hope that I haven't given you the impression that once I decided I wanted my classroom to be like the classroom of a potter, I simply broke up the class time in rather arbitrary ways and insisted on lots of different kinds of activity on the part of the students, any kind of activity, just so long as it wasn't just sitting there listening to me or answering my questions or staring off into space. This isn't what happened at all. I planned each activity with a view to the pottery teacher *and* with a view to my primary aim in teaching philosophy. For example, during the second part of the period I taught and encouraged students to explore individual works of art in particular ways. One reason I did this was because I think that this kind of exploration is one way to discover the meaning and truth of some important philosophical views of art. For example, I think that this is one way to discover the meaning and truth of the view that John Dewey expressed in *Art as Experience* when he said:

> In common conception, the work of art is often identified with the building, book, painting, or statue in its existence apart from human experience. *Since the actual work of art is what the product does with and in experience*, the result is not favorable to understanding.[3]

A second impression that I hope I haven't given you about this class is that it was a huge success. It wasn't. Some students hated the class and probably learned nothing. Others probably didn't learn much. But I do think that in teaching philosophy of art this way I came the closest that I have ever come to my primary aim in teaching philosophy. I think that I was able to teach many of the students how to come to understand some traditional problems and texts in philosophy, how to evaluate the views of others and justify their own views more rationally, and how to make some philosophical discoveries about philosophy on their own. Of course, it *isn't* so easy to tell for sure. I certainly have no *proof* that I taught these things or anything else. But my clear sense of what happened in that classroom during that term, based on what I saw and heard and felt and read, is that some really successful teaching and learning did take place there. I learned and I think that many of my students did too. And I continue to think that part of the reasons that successful teaching and learning did take place there is the model of teaching and learning that I brought into the classroom with me. For the first time, I wasn't a public lecturer hoping for the best, but a teacher of some useful skills doing what I could.

VII

Philosophers sometimes say that while you can teach some things differently and better than people usually teach them in a classroom, you can't teach philosophy differently and better than it is usually taught in a classroom, or, at least they can't. Not in a classroom, anyway. These are very comfortable ideas. They allow everything to stay so still. But I also think that they are false ideas. I think that philosophy can be taught in a classroom and taught differently and better than it is usually taught in a classroom. I hope that I have been able to give some suggestions for how this might be done. Not every philosopher will be able to use these ideas or others that he or someone else might think of. Some philosophers, for better or worse, can only teach the way that they do teach. Their personalities, or the size of their classes, or the administration of their schools makes change, for them, practically impossible. I once suggested to a philosopher that he begin his first class of the term by asking all of his students to stand up, clear away all the chairs from the middle of the room, and then spend the next twenty or thirty minutes informally introducing themselves to each other. He said that he couldn't. He said that the chairs in his classroom were bolted to the floor. But for most of us, change is possible. Our personalities will bend without breaking, our classes and classrooms can be reorganized at a moment's notice, the administration can be avoided by silence. It is only a matter of our believing that change in the way that we teach or try to teach philosophy in a classroom is not only possible, but is of the first importance to the philosophical lives of our students and ourselves.

Notes

A draft of this paper was read to the Foundations of Education Department at the State University of New York at Albany. It was later published in *Metaphilosophy* 2 (1971).

1. It might be worth mentioning here that most of these examinations were never read again by anyone. It was a *departmental policy* that these examinations could not be returned to the students who wrote them, although a student could, if he insisted and if the examination was to be found, look over his examination with his instructor. What was this departmental policy? We never asked and we were never told. Whatever the reason, I think that we were all quite relieved that this was a departmental policy.

2. It is probably a general fact about teachers that no matter where or what or who or how they teach, when things go badly in their classrooms they never say it is their fault, or the fault of the way that they teach. I once heard a grown up man say that it was impossible for anyone to teach philosophy well at this University because out of an enrollment of five thousand students there were only thirty or so who were interested in philosophy, and out of the thirty there were only five or six who were capable of doing philosophy. Recently another teacher of philosophy said that one reason that she had trouble teaching philosophy at any Ivy League college is that her students couldn't think.

3. John Dewey, *Art as Experience* (New York: Minton, Balch and Company 1934), 3. Italics mine.

Is There an Innovative Pedagogy for the Teaching of Philosophy?

Karl F. Hein

Before tackling the question raised above, it will become necessary to set out this author's conception of the purposes for teaching philosophy. For depending on one's aim in teaching philosophy, it may appear that the question raised in the title is irrelevant, frivolous, or unaware of what teachers are already doing in the classroom. I take the position that the chief goal of teaching philosophy is to teach students to philosophize themselves, i.e., to develop the philosophic skills and abilities necessary for one to properly *do* philosophy. I think this goal is what is spoken of when philosophy teachers speak of teaching critical inquiry, analysis, logical thinking, etc. Yet, I wish to stress the active, behavioral aspect of this matter rather than phrase it in terms of subject matter areas to be learned. Beyond this primary goal are other goals which stress the application of these philosophic skills to analyze and inquire into the varying conceptual frameworks different people and cultures have. And beyond the analytic view of these "world-views" (philosophies, ideologies, religions, systems of thought, etc.) a further goal would be for the student to exercise his philosophic skills to describe and synthesize his own "world-view" from the varying models he has around him. Hopefully, in relating the methodological aspects of philosophy to various conceptual frameworks, the student will be able to derive concrete and useful benefits from being able to recognize, analyze, and resolve (or at least grapple with) personal questions and issues that confront him in his daily life, questions which also are rooted in the traditional philosophic literature: "Should I go to war?"; "Should I believe in God?"; "Should I obey my conscience?"; "Should I engage in violent revolution?"; "Should I take drugs?"; "Should I alter my values?"; "Should I conform?"; "What should I do with my life?"

These goals are not radically different from what most philosophy teachers would cite; however one must now ask what means have been traditionally employed to carry them out. I believe that the following list includes most (if not all) of the typical ways philosophy gets taught:

1. A teacher lectures using either his own notes, a textbook, or both.

2. A teacher lectures and then allows for discussion between himself and members of the class.
3. The teacher employs what is affectionately called the "Socratic technique," presenting questions which the students are pressed into answering.
4. The teacher sets criteria for grading and does the grading.
5. The teacher "manages" the behavior of the class by establishing certain (perhaps tacit) rules in regard to noise, tardiness, seating, etc.
6. The teacher sets the curriculum for the course, the books to be read, any audio-visual materials, outside speakers, etc., on the basis of what he feels is good philosophy and what is needed by and relevant to the students.
7. The teacher speaks authoritatively from his academic background and the particular area of his expertise.
8. The teacher is responsible to see that students follow the plan for the course, for he is accountable to others to produce certain results in the time allotted to him.

I would now like to turn to some of the results of this manner of teaching philosophy which seem to stem from the pedagogy employed rather than from the nature of philosophy itself.

Among the conspicuous features of the above sketch are:

a. There is a stress on the teacher as a lecturer, the arbiter of class discussion, and the initiator of discussions and questions.
b. There is a marked emphasis on having a structure there for students to accommodate themselves to; this shows up in regard to course content, the manner of class discussion, the physical situation in the room, etc.
c. The teacher is seen as an authority of a sort. This seems to imply that the primary function of the student is to apply what the authority releases (from his background) to the group.
d. Criteria for grading and the process itself are seen to be the task of the teacher, rather than the students.
e. There is little, if any, opportunity for students to engage in dialogue with each other.
f. Physically speaking, the teacher stands before a group of students who sit, all facing the teacher instead of each other.
g. There is a rigidity of posture, attitude and emotion in this class situation. Movement would seem to be inappropriate, laughter or noise would seem unacademic, and the teacher taking a seat or leaving the room would seem to indicate impending chaos.

Of course, no one who reads this will recognize himself in the above sketch, but try, for the moment, to remember your own student days in college, high school, or whatever. I submit that your own experience, like mine, conforms fairly well to what has been said so far. (The problem is we tend to take it all for granted.) But all we have done is described what is there in many classrooms where philosophy is taught; what possible criticisms are there for the way philosophy is taught when this account represents how even the best of classes is conducted? For one possible objection to this essay is that it does not apply to the teachers who can generate excitement in their lectures, whose students would hate it if the teacher did not conduct the class in the manner outlined above, and who agree that this is how philosophy ought to be taught.

My reply is to say that I realize there are dedicated, exciting lecturer gadflies. But what I object to is a pedagogy which appears diametrically opposed to the stated goals one wishes to achieve in teaching philosophy; one's teaching methods must be in harmony with and must directly further the stated goals of the course one is teaching, otherwise there may be a negative force moving against accomplishing these goals which may even result in students finding it close to impossible to achieve them. What we need to ask ourselves at this point is, "Which means best serve the goals we have already set out?" And to answer this question accurately we must also inquire how pedagogy reflects the matter one is working with.

If our aim, as we have stated earlier, is to create philosophers of our students in the sense that they will learn to develop certain philosophic skills and abilities, then is the model of teaching outlined above the most efficient way to realize this end? If not, then what would work better and why?

What seems apparent is that the model of the classroom sketched above relies upon the concept of teacher as authority, arbiter, and leader. Material is presented to students, questions are asked on what the teacher has lectured, decisions finally come down to be the teacher's responsibility. In the making of rules, the designing of a course curriculum, the managing of the daily life of the class in the classroom, and initiating new policies, the teacher is the stimulus to which students respond in basically pre-structured ways. The model of learning is basically "deductive"; students are only able to apply something after it has been given them by the teacher; the actual starting point is determined by the teacher—it is his feeling of where the students "are at" that sets the tone for the rest of the course. The form of classroom behavior is largely one-sided: the teacher does most of the talking; when students do talk they are talking to the teacher in response to something he has said or asked for; students sit facing the teacher and conform to the model of behavior he establishes as the classroom norm. In short, the model of "inter-personal" activities briefly described here does not seem to me to be a surefire model for accomplishing the goals of developing the abilities to think independently, critically, to argue with one's peers, to detect faulty reasoning, to argue for a position rationally and effectively, to analyze complex personal questions that are directly relevant to one's own life, to explore a multiplicity of points of view, and to share in a budding philosophic dialogue with one's fellowmen.

I submit that the typical class in philosophy does more than merely not carry out the goals stated above, it actually stifles their achievement and directly prevents them from being realized. In short, the pedagogical "medium" is not suited for the "message" it intends to carry; in fact, it may just be that the medium, i.e., the pedagogical manner a teacher employs in philosophy, is at the heart, and to some degree, constitutes the very content that is being attempted to be taught. The form and behavior of the class must serve the ends of the class; in philosophy this means that the actual classroom structure, the way the teacher talks, allows the students to participate, structures activities that will allow for dialogue between students to be achieved as well as between teacher and students, all these things must be important considerations for the philosophy teacher and some decision on each of them must be reached, either by consciously reflecting on their pedagogical purpose in furthering the aims of the course or else unconsciously slipping into the typical teaching style which bored all of us in our youth and bores our students yet.

What then can be done to match one's pedagogy with one's stated aims in teaching philosophy? I believe that a completely different model should emphasize dialogue among the members of the class, rather than just between the teacher and selected individual students. The new model should attempt to structure the class so that the very processes of evidence-gathering, analysis of criteria, and the responsibility for making decisions rests with the student and teacher rather than only with the teacher. In this manner, the day-to-day life of the class will more accurately mirror the intellectual processes and methods of inquiry, decision-making, and supporting one's own choices that occur outside the class which students engage in very day to some degree. The model we are pushing here places much stress on starting with the real needs and desires of the students themselves, rather than someone else's interpretation of what their needs are. For this to occur, the teacher must be willing in inquire himself of the students' needs, desires, and questions. In addition, the teacher must be willing to listen as much as talk; he must be patient enough to allow time for intellectual struggles and the confusions and frustrations these struggles often entail. The teacher must structure a pedagogical model such that there is built within its limits the means to facilitate the open exchange of differing viewpoints and the examinations of these views in a critical manner. To accomplish this, it would seem more natural to allow students to discuss questions among themselves in groups smaller than the whole class. It would also seem to follow that students must be able to practice a fairly large degree of freedom and also bear the consequences of such freedom in terms of behavior, tardiness, tests, make-up work, etc. It is obvious that the teacher can do all these things, do them efficiently and save much time and avoid many hassles. Yet, if one's aim is to foster the development of critical thinking and solving complex problems with one's peers, what better place to begin than in the decision-making process which will determine how the members of the class are to conduct themselves with one another and with the teacher?

Another concern for the teacher who wishes to adopt a new model of teaching philosophy is to structure the model in such a way that it avoids the grave danger that the class will amount to little more than an aimless "bull session" with the more talkative students dominating the rest and the teacher relegated to a sideline spectator reluctant or afraid to enter into the discussion to give it form and direction.

Every classroom situation will have a structure of some sort, even if it is one in which everyone tries to talk at once and people leave when they have had their say or when they can't take the rest of their fellow students anymore! The point, however, is what type of structure(s) are most conductive in developing philosophic abilities and attitudes. Other curriculum areas are also faced with this task: how can one teach the natural and social sciences in such a way that the students not only learn what is important content material in their fields, but also learn to employ the scientific method as they deal with such content; how can English and Humanities be taught such that the creative process be explored actively rather than merely be read about in books about artists?; how can mathematics be taught in a way that allows students to exercise their skills in math rather than restrict them to memorizing more and more abstract formulas, etc?

In philosophy, the question of the most efficacious pedagogy is of the utmost importance. For how can students ever develop their own powers of analysis and reflection if they are forced into either an authoritarian or aimless situation? If philosophy is understood as an activity rather than merely a body of data to be learned, then the class would seem to function best when structured in such a way that students engaged themselves in activities designed to foster the development of philosophic skills.

The main features of the model that has been suggested as more innovative than the traditional model are:

1. The teacher is a participant in the class activities rather than the sole authority.
2. Students are encouraged to engage in dialogue amongst themselves rather than limit their talk to responses to the teacher.
3. The starting points are real questions which students have and are concerned with rather than issues the teacher feels they should have knowledge of.
4. Students share in the decision-making processes which affect their behavior in class, the work they are expected to do, and the manner of grading which they will be subjected to.

5. The classroom is utilized in ways that will foster dialogue among students including breaking the class up into smaller groups, meeting in other places and at other times than the regularly scheduled class, and allowing for students to move about, express their dissatisfactions with what is going on, and suggest future activities.

6. While the teacher has responsibility to the class, he also must allow for genuine intellectual development by avoiding the easy response of saving the students time by giving answers when their inquiries become difficult and time-consuming. To do this for someone else is to short-circuit the whole process of developing abilities to think critically for oneself.

7. Built into the structure of the class activities are ways to engage the interest and participation of the maximum number of students in speaking, writing, and taking a leadership role in helping to organize group activities and helping to plan the future activities for the class.

8. In order to make philosophy both "intellectually respectable" and "relevant" to students' interests, the teacher must plan ways of linking the course to the students' other courses and to the extra-academic world.

9. The teacher must inquire into the abilities, desires, and frustrations of the persons in his class, and must take as part of his or her responsibility the gauging of the course in relation to the varying degrees of ability and interest the students bring into the class. Conferences with each student as well a with the students' other teachers and their advisors or counselors are essential to this end.

10. The teacher is seen as a resource for the students' use in a similar way that the library, audio-visual aids, books, outside speakers, etc. are seen as aids and guides for personal development. While the teacher knows a lot, and surely knows more philosophy than the students, the teacher and the students together are actively involved in an inquiry, a genuine search for methods to find the truth and the resolution of perplexing problems. The teacher is a helper and fellow participant, not the resident guru with all the answers.

11. The teacher and students work together to devise activities and select content materials which will be of use in accomplishing the goals of the course. This entails that revisions will probably have to be made as the course progresses and that there will be an opportunity of choice available to students in regard to what books they will read, speakers they will hear, movies they will attend, etc.

The model entails taking many risks, both on the part of the teacher and also by the students. To many it may seem both too idealistic and too impractical to work in anyone's particular teaching situation. But if one agrees with the presuppositions which lie behind it, then it at least deserves the benefit of a test. Presupposed in all that has been said are several fundamental beliefs: (a) philosophy is chiefly an active process; (b) students should be regarded as having the freedom and responsibility to help shape their academic lives; (c) the philosophic enterprise should serve pragmatic ends—helping to clarify and resolve real questions; (d) the classroom should be itself a model for the philosophic activity of dialogue, analysis, inquiry, and decision-making; (e) the concept of the teacher as the giver of answers subverts the philosophic enterprise; and finally, (f) traditional pedagogy fails to fully realize these values—innovation is truly necessary.

But more precisely, what specific teaching "activities" fit the model herein suggested for use? How does one actually organize a class and set up conditions so that it can function according to the goals set forward here? What follows are but a few of the techniques one can employ to structure the philosophy class to facilitate the "doing" of philosophy:

1. Mock trial concept:
    a. division into groups both pro and con
    b. evidence gathering and analysis
    c. presentation of an argument
    d. cross-examination of evidence and rebuttal
    e. utilization of logical skills
    f. aids in the development of writing and speaking
    g. can be applied to many contemporary problems which actually have bearing in the judicial process, e.g., censorship trials; trials of political prisoners, etc.
    h. part of the class, as jury, has to render a decision based on the arguments heard
    i. can also lead into a discussion of the whole notion of justice and process of the courts

2. Town-meeting concept:
    a. necessitates full student participation
    b. each "citizen" formulates a "position paper" or bill to be voted on.
    c. the citizens have to elect officials and set up the rules for the community and how the meetings are to be run
    d. the technique lends itself to many social issues; who shall vote? who shall pay for what services from the town? where shall the town's monies and resources be placed? what motivations guide the decisions of individuals? of interest groups? is "democracy" the best system for this town? the most efficient?

3. Expositant/Critic concept:
    a. each student to write a paper and defend it

b. in turn, other students to act as critics and write papers arguing against the first position or pointing out its weaknesses
   c. expositant has opportunity to rebut his critic
   d. class as a whole adds criticism of both expositant and critic
4. Collective bargaining concept:
   a. role-playing of workers and levels of management
   b. utilizes issues in social-political philosophy such as "exploitation," "alienation," profit as basis for capitalism, rights of workers, etc.
   c. requires the arguing of positions and finding weaknesses of same
   d. discussion on the actual social process and whether the class activity manifests similar features
   e. can be used before reading works of social philosophy, e.g., Marx's "Alienation of Labor"
5. Editorial writing concepts:
   a. analysis of local newspapers' editorials and/or letters to the editor
   b. use of epistemological skills to detect fallacies
   c. writing exercises designed to lead to editorials or letters to be submitted for publication in school paper or local papers; can be done by individuals or small groups working together
   d. in-class analysis of editorials written by students
6. Class organization concepts:
   a. useful in initiating discussion on the aims and rules for class participation, grades, projects, etc.
   b. argumentation for certain positions and counter-argumentation
   c. relevant to issues in the purposes for education and ethics (should the class have the right to decide what it will be responsible for?)
   d. can extend to a critique of the contemporary educational system(s)
   e. can extend to the class voting on the ways it will spend its time and how grades should be determined (e.g., should contract grading be employed?)

These are but a few suggestions of techniques which could be employed to make a class in philosophy a full participating body involved in the active processes of evidence-gathering, analysis, argumentation and counter-argumentation, decision-making, and reflection upon the actual processes in society which these activities, to some degree, mirror. They are not intended totally to supplant the reading of philosophic texts or the lecture/discussion method; they are intended mainly to support the learning of philosophy by engaging the student in active dialogue with his peers and with the teacher and in so doing clarify the issues philosophers raise which have relevance to the crucial decisions people must make today.

Perhaps the specifics mentioned above do not go far enough to satisfactorily answer the question raised in the title to this essay—hopefully, this essay has provided at least one possible direction innovation in the teaching of philosophy could take. My own experience using these techniques indicates they may not only facilitate learning the "doing" of philosophy by having students actively participate in philosophic dialogue, but they also generate more interest and enthusiasm than the traditional methods I have employed. Before philosophy teachers dismiss them as "games," "gimmicks," "tricks," or "childishness," it might be practical to give them a test: if they engage students' participation and interest and at the same time foster genuine learning of philosophic skills, concepts, and content material, what reasons can be given for clinging to the traditional pedagogy?

Note

Originally published in *New Directions in Teaching* 4 (1973).

A Hierarchy of Values:
An Approach to the Teaching of Philosophy

RONALD H. EPP

One of the few characteristics many academics share, and too few of us ever mention in print, is the inadequacy of our preparation for the teaching of philosophy. Our graduate student days provide the opportunity for colleges and universities to draw upon this cheap labor force for the teaching of elementary courses. By their own example our mentors illustrate methods that we find successful in our learning experience, yet there is little—if any—direction or supervision of our initial attempts to teach. Unfortunately, those first few courses that we teach do more in the way of educating the novice teacher than the new student. In a nutshell, we learn what is effective by the slow, laborious, and solitary process of trial and failure.

The unique series on the Teaching of Philosophy which was recently inaugurated in this journal partially remedies this deficiency in graduate education. What I would like to share with you is a methodological approach which I have found enormously successful in my repeated attempts to be an effective teacher of philosophy. In structure this approach may be workable in a variety of courses, yet I have found it more effective in a problematic approach to Introduction to Philosophy and Problems in Ethics.

My Introductory course was structured in terms of key philosophical problems, divided into the traditional areas of epistemology, metaphysics, philosophy of religion, political philosophy, and ethics. With varying approaches I had achieved success in all areas, save ethics. In traditional fashion I covered various types of ethical theories and their foremost representatives. However, not only examinations but the temper of the class made it abundantly clear that my students were not reflecting on their *own* value commitments. Ethics remained for them an inquiry into conflicting and irresolvable ethical commitments of *other* men.

In April of 1970, the popular periodical *Psychology Today* published Milton Rokeach's "Faith, Hope and Bigotry."[1] As a social psychologist, Rokeach was deeply interested in the origin and nature of value preferences, especially as they are revealed by representative opinion sampling. In this article he was concerned with the relationship of religious belief and bigotry, and his methodology seemed applicable to my struggles in teaching ethics.

Paraphrasing Rokeach I developed a questionnaire which was given to each student prior to any discussion of ethical commitments. The instructions of this questionnaire were as follows:

> This questionnaire is directed toward the revealing of what *you* believe to be of worth, of value to you as an individual. The questionnaire is composed of parts A and B. Part A lists eighteen End Values, and terminal values or goals that most of us strive for. Part B consists of eighteen Mean Values, the tools or instrumental values that we employ to attain End Values. Working with these value terms and what they mean to you, arrange the values of each list hierarchically to their importance to you as guiding principles in your life. Keep each list separate and work only with the value options that I have given you.

The End Values[2] were randomly listed on page one which was blocked into sections to facilitate the cutting of the sheet into eighteen separate pieces of paper, each labeled with a value. Page two repeated this schemata with the Mean Values.[3] The student was instructed to spread these values on a table and proceed to arrange them in order of their importance, and I cautioned them that there would be frequent shuffling of paper slips until they arrived at a satisfactory ranking. The student was verbally instructed to bear in mind the consequence of ranking. Namely, would he be willing to sacrifice End Value number three in order to preserve End Value number two, and risk number two in order to preserve End value number one? The students were asked to complete this questionnaire at their leisure before the next class meeting, listing on a separate sheet the results of their value card shuffling. Lastly, the student was assured that there would be no public disclosure of their personal value hierarchy. The list would not be seen by either the instructor or their fellow students, for I hoped that this insistence on the privacy of the questionnaire would insure a more authentic response.

The next class meeting was marvelous! The students were "sitting on the edge of their seats" in anticipation, and before I could initiate my presentation they queried me as to the origin, function, and ends of the questionnaire. I informed them that their personal value scale would now be contrasted with a representative sample of the American public (the results of the Rokeach Survey). However, rather than listing on a handout or the blackboard the Rokeach results, I employed the following pedagogical tool.

I began by asking the class to offer verbal suggestions of what they believed the public might hold to be the highest ranked End Value. Past experience indicated that several values would be suggested before the correct answer (i.e., number one on the Rokeach survey) would be identified. As each suggestion was offered it was listed beside the appropriate number on the blackboard until the End Value scale was completed. This process of soliciting their suggestions had a threefold effect: (1) it brought even the least vocal students into the search; (2) it encouraged the students to question and weight the various values in light of their appraisal of social norms; and (3) the impact of the survey was more dramatic due to the frequency of their errors. However, the meaningfulness of this approach to the survey is best attested by the gasps, moans, and opinions that soon reverberated in the classroom. Most members of the class were surprised and annoyed at their failure to correctly identify public value preferences in the Mean Value Survey.

The results of the Rokeach Value Survey show that honesty was valued more highly than any of the eighteen Mean Values. However, more than a dozen other values were suggested before I listed honesty beside number one. The class reaction was spontaneous outrage. As I proceeded to complete the Mean Value list the class queried me with the following questions: How can the public rank honesty first when they repeatedly sacrifice it for the sake of ambition (number two on the Mean Value Scale)? Do people correctly understand what honesty involves? How can the public respond so hypocritically?

Before I continue with an account of the next stage in administering this questionnaire, I would like to share several observations that should be anticipated by the teacher who employs this survey. First, the media repeatedly report that today's college student is apathetic and indifferent. Consequently, to discover the shock that is written on their faces proves instructive to both teacher and students. Furthermore, anticipate striking differences between student value preferences and the Rokeach profile. Yet it is not the differences that are unanticipated; rather, it is the class reaction to these differences. With all the proud affirmation that today's counter-culture—the strong individualism in dress styles, sexual habits, occupational preferences and the like—it is curious to discover that students actually dislike their alienation from commonly accepted values. Lastly, anticipate probing questions concerning the motives which prompted the responses of those who participated in the Rokeach survey. Students become intensely curious as to the reasons for value commitments, besieging me with questions such as: what are the sources of one's ethical commitments, how strongly is the public committed to these preferences, and what grounds do they have for their convictions? It does not take much ability to turn these same questions back on the very beliefs of students themselves.

Another line of inquiry that I pursue concerns the nature of the questionnaire. I suggest that they examine the following hypothesis—that the character of the questionnaire is responsible for the oddness of both the Rokeach profile and their own personal value scale. The student critique of the questionnaire not only encourages them to be more critical of statistical analyses, but also leads them to observations which open more comprehensive axiological problems. Student criticism comes in the form of questions: How was the test administered? Orally or in written form? Was the party questioned confident that his responses were not open to public airing? Was there a time limit imposed on completion of the questionnaire? Yet if the method of testing was under review, so were the motives of those examined: were those tested stating what they did value or what they would ideally prefer to value? Did they regard the questionnaire as a cute game or an opportunity for serious introspection? However, the most pointed criticism aligned them with Socrates' renowned concern. That is, how can one know what is to be valued if one has not examined the adequacy of ethical grammar? In brief, the Rokeach survey is premised on a standardized grammar. Yet, common usage is notoriously confusing and one man's freedom is another man's slavery. The able dialectician has enabled his students to discover the need for clarity in ethical terminology, and without some accompanying glossary for selecting one's value preferences, the questionnaire is rendered useless by the ambiguity of moral grammar.

At this point the class usually ends with the resounding shrill of the bell. Students are often annoyed that we cannot continue and here and now resolve these perplexing problems. In subsequent class periods the interest generated in this initial meeting usually sustains us as we cover some of the traditional ethical theorists. Kant, Bentham and Sartre are no longer viewed as historical curiosities pontificating on problems of small consequence. To the contrary, not only are the students sympathetic with the struggles of these theorists, but they are intensely demanding in their desire to discover solutions that are personally meaningful.

Readers of this journal should be conscious of the repeated pedagogical message that has been stated, argued, and echoed throughout these essays on The Philosopher as Teacher. Namely, what is preferable to traditional lecturing is the application of the Socratic technique of midwifery which enables the "teacher" to elicit ideas born in the mind of the student and delivered through the ministration of the "teacher." It has been my contention that the Rokeach profile coupled with a dialectical approach enables both student and teacher to experience many of the features that are the substance of a liberal education:

1. *Discussion.* The contrast of personal values (often newly discovered) with the Rokeach profile encourages a heightened degree of interaction and personal involvement among all participants.

2. *Exploration.* The instructor who implements this questionnaire does not begin with the proverbial blank slate, but with the convictions and assumptions of those surveyed. The students are not exploring uncharted territory, but rather are critically assessing commitments that were previously unknown or unexamined. This survey not only opened the student to consciousness of his basic commitments, but may have encouraged a partial *liberation* from the unsatisfactory edifice that supported his value preferences.

3. *Sharing.* Unlike Descartes who searched in solitary fashion for some indubitable truth, the use of this approach precipitates the involvement of many minds in a common quest. Whereas at the outset of the survey I noted that each students value scale would remain solely in his possession,

the reaction of the students was such that they volunteered their personal ranking preferences and encouraged others to do the same.

4. *Theorizing*. Not only were students critical of both public and personal value preferences, but they were able to sense the need to stand apart from the values of their culture and consider whether any abstract ethical principles would hold universally.

5. *Relevance*. What may have appeared at the outset to be a trite exercise, became in time an issue of crucial importance. In fact, many students requested additional copies of the questionnaire. Later I discovered that these budding dialecticians broadened their knowledge by encouraging their acquaintances, friends and relatives to take part in the survey.

I am still refining the above technique and recognize that it should be altered and amended as befits the temper of the class and its teacher. I have offered this account not only to encourage its use elsewhere, but to stimulate the publication of other methodologies that might be helpful to teachers in their quest for relevant and stimulating aids in the teaching of philosophy.

Notes

Originally published in *Metaphilosophy* 5 (1974).

1. *Psychology Today* 3(10) (1970): 33ff. This article is an outgrowth of findings published in "Value Systems in Religion," *Review of Religious Research* 11 (1969): 3–23.

2. The alternative End Values were: an exciting life, family security, inner harmony, a sense of accomplishment, self-respect, a world at peace, wisdom, a comfortable life, mature love, pleasure, freedom, equality, salvation, a world of beauty, social recognition, true friendship, national security, and happiness.

3. Alternative Mean Values were: self controlled, independent, helpful, imaginative, obedient, polite, capable, courageous, ambitious, forgiving, clean, cheerful, logical, intellectual, loving, honest, responsible, and broadminded.

A New Medium for Teaching Philosophy

DAVID WEST

The phrase "teaching philosophy" often appears to have an air of oddness about it, for teaching is frequently taken to mean something like "imparting truth." The idea of imparting truth seems to require that there be both a clearly defined set of problems and a clearly defined set of answers, requirements that are not satisfied in the activity of teaching philosophy.

I do not wish to speculate upon the similarities or differences that philosophy shows in relation to other activities or disciplines except to say that in some areas of university teaching the notion of imparting truth does have some validity. However, philosophy is essentially an activity in itself and not a body of knowledge which may be applied to an activity. It is primarily "doing" and not "knowing." There *are* good philosophers but such men are not necessarily those who know more "about" philosophy.

In saying this, I imply that there *are* things to know about in philosophy but that this is generally less important than doing philosophy. A good philosopher is not necessarily one who knows all about the arguments and theories of other philosophers. Wittgenstein, who was certainly a good philosopher, does not demonstrate in his writings a massive knowledge of the ideas and systems of other philosophers, and is said to have maintained that reading *Mind* was inferior to reading detective magazines. Indeed it may be claimed that there can be such a thing as too great an immersion in the theories of philosophers since philosophy as an activity is as much concerned with *questions* as with *answers*. Our way of arguing with Descartes or Locke, for example, is frequently to show that they were asking the wrong questions. This claim may be dubious in that what are wrong questions for us may not have been for the seventeenth century, but the point may be made that if philosophy can be characterized as the attempt to make sense of man's position in his world, the problems may, and will, change as the way the world appears to us changes.

Given this, the notion of "imparting truth" does appear to be rather odd as the function of teaching philosophy in the university. The aim of philosophy is wisdom and knowledge and it may be wiser to say that there are no eternal truths in philosophy—at least in the way that science claims eternal truth for some of the natural laws that it claims to have discovered.

I will not deny (indeed it would be foolish to do so) that the study of Plato, of Descartes, of Kant, and of Russell is a valuable activity, and it may appear that there are certain facts which can be learned in this regard. There is "what Plato said," "what Descartes meant," "the implications of what Kant thought," and so on. Teaching these may be imparting truth but if doing philosophy is also generating questions, it may be both that what is to be gained by the historical greats may not remain constant and that some of the questions that they ask may be hindrances to attaining wisdom.

Wittgenstein often thought of philosophy as therapeutic—it sometimes appears that in teaching the history of philosophy we are making people sick in order to cure them. Whatever is the truth of this, it seems that one of the aims of teaching philosophy is to enable students to look critically, not only at answers, but also at questions. Even in teaching the history of philosophy, we are, or should be, *doing* philosophy, and this is what students should gain from our classes, the ability to *do* philosophy. Philosophy is an activity, philosophy is *doing*.

Thus, teaching philosophy has something in common perhaps with teaching people how to swim. In teaching swimming, the instructor does not *tell* people how to do it but *gets them to* do it. Of course, from such instruction, the pupil learns how to swim in a certain way, be it breast-stroke or crawl. The difference between teaching swimming and teaching philosophy is that in the former there are certain principles which can be established. In philosophy, it seems that each philosopher has his own principles. Often a revelation in philosophy comes about when one sees a new method, but the method itself is the subject of philosophical scrutiny.

It seems therefore that the notion of "imparting truth" must play a fairly subordinate role in teaching philosophy and that these implications of the word "teaching" should be resisted. If this is so, then surely the methods of teaching philosophy in the University should reflect the aims of such teaching, i.e., to bring it about that students can *do* philosophy. However, it seems largely that methods in use do not properly do this.

The main emphasis of teaching in the universities appears to be on the lecture method, which despite its merits in achieving certain aims does not appear, from the research carried out, to be very effective in enabling people to *do* things.

J. D. Barnard,[1] although talking in terms of science education, finds that the discussion method of teaching is superior to the lecture-demonstration method on measures of problem-solving, though inferior on a test of specific information. Dawson[2] found the same superiority in problem-solving but also found that the discussion method was equal on tests of recall. On the gamut of research on teaching methods W. J. McKeachie sums up:

> Despite the many findings of no significant differences in effectiveness between lecture and discussion, those studies which have found differences make surprisingly good sense. In only two studies was one method

superior to the other on a measure of knowledge of subject-matter; both studies favored the lecture method. In all six experiments finding significant differences favoring discussion over lecture, *the measures were other than final examination testing knowledge.* When one is asked whether lecture is better than discussion, the appropriate counter would seem to be, "For what goals?"[3]

The effectiveness of lectures per se is much under dispute, even when considered in terms of goals opposite to it. McKeachie reports that Greene[4] shows that college students may learn as much from reading a passage in a book as from hearing the same material in a lecture.

Jones[5] reports the following percentages of retention of material in a lecture on the part of students:

Immediate	*3 days*	*7 days*	*14 days*	*8 weeks*
62	50	37	30	23

McLeish is even more pessimistic concerning lectures. He claims that retention is likely to be about 40 percent immediately after a lecture and 20 percent after only 1 week.[6]

If the aim of a lecture is the transmission of information then it would appear not to be very efficient. However, in another place,[7] McLeish concedes that the lecture method is useful for inspirational purposes, didactic purposes, to give the latest findings and for passing examinations! However, more importantly, he holds that it cannot be dispensed with *for reasons of economy.*

This last argument, the economic, is often presented in defense of lectures, but how valid is it? In general, it seems specious and in reference to philosophy, vacuous. If one's aim is A, and one uses a method suitable to achieve B, then to defend the method as being cheaper is ridiculous. It as if seeking an implement to dig my garden, a shop assistant were to tell me that while a screwdriver will not do it, it is cheaper than a spade. Of course one *could* dig a garden with a screwdriver but saying that one has to do so for reasons of economy is a pretty sorry picture of university education.

The alternative to lectures has traditionally been the seminar or tutorial method and it is true that these methods are expensive. Research tends to hold that the optimum size for discussion classes is between seven and nine,[8] and this demands, of course, a high staff-student ratio. Instructors with introductory courses face classes of thirty and upwards. At Acadia, in a small philosophy department, we have about 150 students at an introductory level, which we divide into three classes, an instructor to each. Thus, it often appears that the only way to handle such classes is to lecture. However, it is at this level that most students gain their awareness of philosophy, and if the lecture method is the sole medium in use, they may gain a pretty poor picture.

In an introductory course that I ran in 1970–1971, I made attempts to achieve some form of participation. A questionnaire study carried out at the end of the course indicated that those students who had not participated felt that the benefit of the course had been in (*a*) finding out what philosophy was, and in (*b*) making them question more. It was these students who did not wish to continue philosophy and, although the study was relatively informal, I suspect that they felt philosophy to be simply the asking of questions without answers—a negative attitude. It is my view that it is this attitude which is largely responsible for the bad name that philosophy has in many circles.

It seems imperative, if philosophy is to be a success in the university environment, and the "numbers racket" is unfortunately the financial criteria for success, that students are enabled to see the positive side to philosophy. This is achieved only by bringing about their *involvement* in courses. Lectures, or at least lectures alone, will not achieve this.

Apart from economic considerations, there are other drawbacks to the seminar method. Too much intervention by the instructor produces question-answer instructor-led sessions that are discussion classes only in name. however, too little intervention may have equally undesirable results. As McKeachie says:

> in creating 'groupy' classes an instructor may sometimes help his students develop strength to set low standards of achievement and maintain them against instructor pressures, or at least develop goals different from their normal academic goals.[9]

It is often said that teaching by means of seminar methods is far more demanding and difficult than teaching by lecture methods. The need for control and the difficulty of maintaining it while setting up an informal atmosphere demands great sensitivity and quick-wittedness. Many seminar courses fail, I think, because instructors do not realize the difficulties of running them.

Insofar as philosophy is an activity and as teaching philosophy is communicating abilities and insights, discussion methods appear to be best. It is true that lectures may be valuable on occasions for they may be used as ways to make quickly available certain theories beneficial to the discussion. They also have the benefit over books in enabling the instructor to shape input in terms of the needs of a class at a particular time but they cannot be the basic medium for philosophy teaching. This is more true of some courses than others but in general it holds good.

Given this, a medium is required which will

(a) Create conditions suitable for creative participation on the part of the student.

(b) Enable the instructor to control procedure and aims.

(c) Be economical in terms of staff-student ratio.

One should further add that such a medium should

(d) Foster good instructor-student relations.

(e) Be *practical* and *useful* in the present university environment.

(I add the last requirement because I am always annoyed and exasperated by teaching theories which require massive social change for their adoption. We need new methods *now*, not in some distant Utopia.)

I believe that I have found a medium which will satisfy these criteria, and one which has already been seen to work. I shall call this medium "instrumented design." It has been used for some time in managerial training in the business world where a great deal of research on teaching and training methods has long been carried out. The medium, as I use it, is a development of that used and refined by W. J. Reddin of the University of New Brunswick. I make no claim, therefore, to originality but have simply adapted this medium to the teaching of philosophy.[10] In this connection I owe a debt of gratitude to my colleague, Robin Stuart-Kotze, and the School of Business Administration at Acadia University.[11]

The medium is based upon the following scheme. In a class the method is as follows:

(1) The instructor sets each individual in the class a task to perform privately. The task is set out on what we will call the "instrument."

(2) The instructor divides the class into teams and asks each team to REACH CONSENSUS on a team answer to the task.

(3) Each team DISPLAYS its CONSENSUS on a large sheet of paper which is posted in front of the class.

(4) Depending upon the objectives, the instructor brings about DISCUSSION of the teams' CONSENSUS, or comments upon it.

Ideally, the steps (2)–(4) are completed within the bounds of one class meeting, the first step being carried out by each student as pre-work. The best system is to run one three-hour class per week. The medium is particularly suited, also, to summer school sessions. I do use the medium in a class which meets three times a week for one hour each time but this is not highly recommended.

Let me now explain the use of this medium in detail. In doing this I shall show how lectures, essays and evaluation methods can be built in.

The Tasks

The name, "instrumented design," is derived from the fact that a course, using this medium, involves the design of a connected series of instruments, each of which sets the class a task to perform.

The objectives in setting such tasks are to (*a*) get the student to consider privately a problem set by the instructor and to reach some conclusions on it; (*b*) get the student to argue over the matter of the task with his peers.

Thus, when the student completes the task privately, he is asked to make a series of decisions and commits himself, to a greater or lesser degree, to his answers. When faced with the answers of his fellow team members, many of whom are likely to disagree with him, he is led to defend or reject his own answers in the face of the arguments of his peers. Thus, the student discusses, sometimes in great emotional heat and in great detail, the task set by the instructor. In other words, participation and argumentation is achieved.

The tasks themselves may be set out in a variety of instruments. The most simple is an "agree-disagree" questionnaire. In this task (see Figure 1), the student is faced with a series of statements and asked to decide, and mark on the instrument, whether he agrees or disagrees with each. Teams are asked to reach agreement on the task and in doing so are led to discuss statements which the instructor wishes them to.

Name ....

Class ....

    Mark each of these statements true or false, by circling T or F respectively. Thus, if you think statement (1) is true, circle the T.

1. The universe will come to an end .... T   F
2. The history of creation is a history of advancement .... T   F
3. Values are objective .... T   F
4. Man is simply an animal .... T   F
5. What we see is not what is really there .... T   F
6. The soul is immortal. .... T   F
7. The universe is finite. .... T   F
8. Mind is merely matter .... T   F
9. Time is an infinite series .... T   F
10. There is a scale of being with man at the top .... T   F
11. All change is illusory .... T   F
12. Morality is a matter of feeling .... T   F
13. Man can perform miracles .... T   F
14. All is one .... T   F
15. Death is the end. .... T   F

Figure 1

    This instrument and task is designed *with a point in mind*, as are all such tasks. In the example instrument shown the objective was threefold.

(a) To break the ice and get the students talking.

(b) To get students to realize the vagueness and ambiguity of many "high-sounding" phrases and statements.

(c) To demonstrate the difference between holding an opinion upon certain grounds and holding it as a matter of faith.

All three objectives were achieved when the instrument was used in my introductory course.

Another form of task, which looks like a personality inventory test, is more fun though more difficult to devise. Two or more theories are taken and a set of statements deducible from each are opposed to each other in pairs. The students are then asked to divide three points between each pair, 3-0, 2-1, 1-2, or 0-3. They are asked to answer every question and not to use half-points. A key is later given which "tells" the students to which theory they adhere.

Thus, an instrument that I designed set up two "theories," free will and determinism. The key "told" the students whether they were determinists or not and to what "degree." Such an activity, especially when combined with a team discussion and consensus, can lead to attacks upon the key and thus to detailed discussions of the implications of the "theories" of free will and determinism.

In later stages, the instrument may be set out in form like an essay topic. Thus, one may ask each student to evaluate, say, the causal argument for the existence of God, and then, in teams, to reach consensus on the three (or some other number) most important points they wish to make about the argument. (Figure 2 is an example of such a form. The page references are to Baldwin and McPeek, *An Introduction to Philosophy Through Literature*.[12])

A View of Man and a View of Beauty

Problem: Can a sense of beauty be taught or learned?

Objective of task:

(1) To use the groundwork laid by our discussions of man and free will to investigate man's relation to his environment from another angle.

(2) To grasp the structure of a philosophical argument.

Pre-work:

(1) *Reading.* Whitman (43)   Santayana (53)
Millay (43)   Schiller (58)
Emerson (44)   Plato (63)
Santayana (45) Wilde (67)
Nietzsche (48) and any other
Joyce (49)   selections that interest you

(2) *Thinking.* Reflect upon these writings and ask yourself about the form or nature of statements that something is beautiful. Then ask how a realization that x is beautiful comes about.

(3) *Writing.* Note down some thoughts on whether a sense of beauty is something that can be taught or learned.

(4) *Teams.* Reach consensus upon (3)—in particular upon a yes/no answer to the main question. Give reasons.

(5) *Class.* Examine the results of team consensus in order to ensure that all points are covered.

(6) *Class.* (ongoing)—decide upon the next steps in an investigation of man's relationship to art and nature.

Figure 2

The essence is that the students are brought to discuss, in varying detail, problems set by the instructor. It is, of course, essential also that these tasks form an integrated series, developing one from another. This necessity for integration holds for any course taught by whatever method of course but the faults of non-integration will show up more using instrumented design than in any other medium.

In any discussion group, the dynamics of the situation including the personalities of the participants will have a marked effect upon its success. Discussion along the lines suggested will be more free in that it takes place in a peer group but some students may become dominant.

Such dominance may be unconscious or the team may feel loath to take action to prevent it and so some method of identifying and correcting it is necessary. This may be effected by the use of a task which leads the team to investigate its performance.

There are instruments readily available for use in such a task.[13] These instruments ask the individual to decide upon an evaluation of his team along such dimensions as contribution, creativity, leadership and decisions. Teams are then asked to reach consensus on their evaluation and, in doing so, are investigating and discussing their own performance.

This task has a productive "unfreezing" effect and has the additional benefit of making it clear to the students that they themselves are responsible for the productivity of their teams.

Class Meetings

Teams display the results of their consensus during the class meeting. This should take place ideally during the same class period but can be at the next meeting of the class.

The objectives of the class meeting are:

(i) To let the teams show each other their results.

(ii) To compare results.

(iii) To provide the instructor with information on progress.

It is important that the instructor does not turn the class meeting into a lecture but he can, by suitable approving noises, indicate those ideas produced which he thinks most valuable. Still, the instructor should take a back seat (literally) and let the class do the work. Inasmuch as the number of opinions in the class is reduced, in theory, to the number of teams, discussion can be productive. Even if not every student can speak, at least each one feels that he is represented by a speaker.

There is, in this exercise, a constant danger of instructor dominance. If the instructor begins to take over then the value of the discussion is lost. To prevent this occurring and to identify it when it is occurring, it is possible to use similar instruments to those used in investigating the dynamics of the teams. Individuals are asked to evaluate the success of the class meeting and teams asked to reach consensus. During the ensuing class discussion the instructor will receive a great deal of feedback on his handling of the class.

Lectures

Using this medium need not be inconsistent with the giving of some lectures when required. Indeed, a good way to begin using this medium, is to use the team-task exercise as a way of introducing or wrapping-up a topic. The problems of introducing students to the method revolve around their initial feeling that they are not being *told* anything. This of course is true but the "message" of traditional teaching has often and regrettably become that what the student is *told*, is what is necessary to pass the examination. Hence, the use of a medium which devalues "telling" is bound to be strange and not a little forbidding at first. As the medium becomes more familiar, and as the instructor becomes more skilled in its use, so the need for lectures will decrease.

However, a lecture which is used *as an aid* to the discussion, by explaining a theory or by handling a problem which is hindering the teams' advancement, can obviously be of benefit. The main point is that such lectures must *assist* and not *prevent* discussion. They are *aids* and should not be *crutches*.

Perhaps the best way to design a lecture is to take the output from a class meeting as a basis for it.

Essays

It is sometimes said that the insistence upon discussion methods in schools is producing an illiterate society. The importance of being able to express oneself in written form is that complex arguments cannot be followed or given in spoken form. This is particularly true of philosophy. Reading the *Critique of Pure Reason* is tough enough for most of us, but imagine the impossibility of being able only to listen to it spoken aloud.

"Instrumented design" does not interfere with the use of essays. However, essays must be used to enhance the progress of the course in this medium as much as in any other. There are at least two ways to use essays.

Firstly, they can be retrospective over a series of discussions, being used to draw together what has been discovered. Secondly, they may be themselves the output from the teams. This second method can be very powerful in that the teams argue towards what they wish to say and have to consider what research is to be done in dividing responsibilities. The fault with many essays written by students, especially at the introductory level, is that they contain far too many unsupported assertions. Writing essays in teams can go a long way towards correcting this.

Control

It will be appreciated that the amount of control available to the instructor is, in fact, very great. It may be summed up by saying that the instructor controls what is done, while the students control how it is done, which seems to me an ideal balance.

Control is effected by the design of the instruments. Not only is the subject matter chosen by the instructor but he may also design the task such that various steps have to be followed in its completion. "Instrumented design" does not aim at anarchic buzz sessions but at guided discussion.

However, it does free the student to investigate arguments and ideas in his own terms and with his own interests in mind. In a lecture, the student has to follow the steps of the argument at the lecturer's pace and in the lecturer's concepts. Often learning takes place only when ideas are put into terms to which the student can relate and this happens when he puts it into his "own words."

Examination and Evaluation

The problem of discovering meaningful evaluation procedures is not one peculiar to "instrumented design" or to discussion methods in general. Examinations are a powerful motivational factor but unfortunately this power is frequently exerted against the aims of teaching in general.

If philosophy is doing, then a form of examination which stresses memory or which is designed by the instructor without the particular class in mind, will simply act as a hindering force in the progress of the course.

The rules of the game of lectures and examinations involve the assumption that there is a body of information, which if learned and reproduced in the examination will produce a passing grade. This is contrary to the aims of teaching philosophy.

Thus, in the use of "instrumented design" it is important that some form of evaluation be used which produces grades on criteria consistent with the nature of the medium. I offer no detailed solution here except to say that peer-group evaluation, combined with instructor evaluation and the use of "open-book" or some other form of examination may yield more meaningful results. One would like to do away with examinations completely but this is not a desire which can be realized in the near future, and therefore it seems one must live with their difficulties.

Conclusions on the Medium

In this paper, I cannot quote figures to "prove" success but only report my own conclusions based upon observation. It is worth noting, however, that "instrumental design" does appear to satisfy the criteria for successful discussion classes set up by research conclusions. For example, Watt holds that seminar courses depend largely upon four points.

(1) A timetable of reading ahead of seminars should be given.
(2) Some reading should be common to all participants.
(3) All members should be encouraged or required to participate
(4) The course should involve written work.[14]

Points (1) and (2) are covered in the design of the instruments, while (3) is the aim of asking teams to reach consensus. (4) is easily built in to "instrumented design."

Team size can be kept to effective numbers and instructor dominance can be avoided. *Prima facie*, then, "instrumented design" should be successful.

I have found that it can be very effective although there are some difficulties which must be overcome. Primarily one must overcome the students' resistance to the method—a resistance stemming largely from anxiety. The students have to learn the roles in a new instructor-student relationship within an educational context which makes this difficult. McKeachie reports Ross's[15] conclusions regarding relationships between supervisors and workers in industry.

[I]t was discovered that workers were most likely to ask a supervisor for help if the supervisor was not responsible for evaluating his subordinates.[16]

The medium of instrumented design attempts to overcome this by the emphasis upon peer-group discussion, but there is still a great deal of anxiety felt about *how* the students will be evaluated. Most students are educated in a system that stresses *convergent* behavior—i.e., learning "what is so"—while the medium stresses divergent behavior—i.e., creating what is to be said.[17]

Other difficulties revolve around the day to day handling of the class. Tasks must form a coherent sequence but must reflect the students' progress. This requires sensitivity and a good deal of administration. (Perhaps student assistants could be employed in assisting with the administrative load.) There can be also some emotional stress on the instructor particularly in the early stages of a class's introduction to the medium. One feels constrained to give positive help in the discussions and self-control is required. Preventing a university teacher from talking is always difficult!

However, even given such difficulties, the medium is of great value. I have found that it speeds up understanding, unfreezes the class and creates an atmosphere of creativity unlike any other medium that I have ever tried. It has these assets in smaller classes even more than in larger ones and it should not have been seen simply as a way of handling the large introductory classes.

In summary, then, the medium of instrumented design achieves;

(i) 100 per cent participation of members in a class.

(ii) creative participation on the part of the student.

(iii) sufficient control for the instructor.

(iv) good relationship between instructor and student.

(v) the possibility of one instructor effectively handling up to 50 students without constant lecturing.

(vi) the effect of placing responsibility for learning squarely upon the student, where it belongs.

It has, moreover, been widely used and tested in the business world, though the application at Acadia is the first, as far as I am aware, to disciplines other than Business Administration.

Notes

Originally published in *Metaphilosophy* 3 (1972).

1. J. D. Barnard. "The Lecture Demonstration versus the Problem-solving Method of Teaching a College Science Course." *Science Education* 26 (1942).

2. M. D. Dawson. "Lectures versus Problem-solving in Teaching Elementary Soil Sections." *Science Education* 40 (1956).

3. W. J. McKeachie. "Research on Teaching at the College and University Level," in *Handbook of Research on Teaching*, ed. N. L. Gage (American Educational Research Association, 1963), 1127.

4. E. B. Greene. "Relative Effectiveness of Lecture and Individual Reading as Methods of College Teaching," *Genetic Psychology Monographs* (1928) (Reported in McKeachie, *Handbook of Research*).

5. H. E. Jones, "Experimental Studies of College Teaching," *Archives of Psychology* 10(68) (1923).

6. J. McLeish, "Student Retention of Lecture Material," *Cambridge Institute of Education Bulletin* (1966).

7. J. McLeish, *The Lecture Method*, Cambridge Monographs on Teaching Methods, 1968.

8. H. Maddox, "University Teaching Methods: A Review," *Universities Quarterly* (1970).

9. McKeachie, "Research on Teaching," 1135.

10. The medium originates apparently from R. R. Blake and J. S. Mouton as reported in their paper, "The Instrumented Training Laboratory," in *Issues in Human Relations and Training*, ed. J. R. Wechsler and E. H. Schein (National Training Labs., N.T.L. Selected readings, Number 5.)

11. Professor Stuart-Kotze and I have run seminars designed to introduce our colleagues at Acadia to instrumented design. Judging from their comments, it has great possibilities in disciplines other than Philosophy and Business Administration.

12. Robert C. Baldwin and James A. McPeek, *An Introduction to Philosophy Through Literature* (New York: Ronald Press, 1950).

13. From OTL, Box 324, Fredericton, New Brunswick, Canada.

14. Ian Watt, "The Seminar," *Universities Quarterly* 18 (1964).

15. I. C. Ross, *Role Specialization in Supervision*. Unpublished doctoral dissertation, Columbia University, 1956. (Reported in McKeachie, *Handbook of Research*).

16. McKeachie, "Research on Teaching," 1141.

17. These terms are taken from Liam Hudson, in particular from his book *Frames of Mind: Ability, Perception and Self-perception in the Arts and Sciences* (London: Methven, 1968).

Teaching Philosophy by the Guided Design Method

GENE D'AMOUR

Is philosophy being made relevant or is whatever is relevant being made philosophy? This question is inspired by the new breed of introductory philosophy texts in which such authors as B. F. Skinner, Philip Berrigan, Malcolm X, Che Guevara, Sigmund Freud, Paul Tillich, Albert Einstein, Leo Tolstoy, Spiro Agnew, Cardinal Newman, Rollo May, Pope Paul VI, The Supreme Court, Martin Luther King, Galileo, Erich Fromm, Ernest Hemingway, Carl Rogers, Mark Twain, John Donne, Mohandas Gandhi, Germaine Greer and St. Theresa of Avila express their views on such topics as loneliness, the family, sex, women's liberation, Zen, cosmic consciousness, the holocaust, evil, LSD, the Jesus movement, the rules of the Black Panther Party, suicide, ecology, the university, the new generation, birth control, the charter of the international military tribunal, the priesthood, and yoga. What is this field called 'philosophy' that brings together authors with such diverse backgrounds, writing on this wide variety of topics—does philosophy have any borderlines? Is this *grand menagerie* of readings the answer to the problems we face in teaching philosophy?

One's answer to the question "How ought philosophy to be taught?" will, of course, be influenced by one's answer to the question "What is Philosophy?" One who believes that philosophy is personally oriented and should lead the student to have some type of subjective insight would teach a philosophy course differently from one who believes that philosophy is oriented toward the study of language and logic, and should lead to the development of certain objective, analytic skills. The individual who believes that philosophy is socially oriented and should lead to passionate involvement in political action would also teach differently. New introductory philosophy anthologies reflect these divergent interests as a multitude of views promenade across their pages. What they do not reflect, however, is an important element that is common to the various 'schools' of philosophical thought, namely, the desire not only to introduce the student to differing points of view, but also to develop certain abilities and attitudes that will influence the way the student carries out his daily *activities*.

The role the anthology plays in presenting differing points of view is quite clear; the role it plays in developing abilities and attitudes is not so clear. Indeed, the role the *instructor* plays in developing abilities and attitudes is not at all clear. In this paper I shall explore this role, primarily as it arises in the teaching of a course concerned with what is often referred to as 'philosophical analysis.' Later I shall attempt to point out the relevance of my exploration to other philosophical 'schools.'

Teaching the Skill of Analysis

Primarily under the influence of Russell and the early Wittgenstein, much of western philosophy took its 'linguistic turn'; under the influence of the Vienna Circle, the Russell-Wittgenstein style of philosophy took its 'activist' turn. Philosophy was no longer declared to be a set of beliefs, but an activity—an activity focusing on the clarification of the language and logic of argument. The question 'What philosophical system do you believe in?' became *savage*; 'What sort of philosophy do you do?' was the fashionable question. Although the borderlines of 'Analytic Philosophy' are presently rather wide, with edges quite blurred, there is still a large group of philosophers who place a good deal of emphasis on the ability to analyze, or the 'skill' of analysis.

The teacher of analytic philosophy attempts to impart one of the most important skills that a student might acquire. For, how could an individual ever make sound decisions—whether it be about himself, his society or the world—if he is unable, or unwilling, to think about these matters clearly and to determine what counts as good evidence for or against taking a specific course of action? Surely the relevance of the attitude which one hopes accompanies this skill, namely, a penchant for clarifying one's beliefs and basing those beliefs on evidence.

If, however, the student is going to acquire a skill, it would seem that, at the very least, he must have practice in the skill to be acquired. Further, this practice must be supervised; the student must be provided with objectives, prompted, encouraged, given individualized feedback, and his correct responses must be reinforced. Also, if this skill is going to be conjoined with appropriate attitudes and transferred to the student's everyday life, the student must be helped to relate his course work to his normal daily activities.

The typical media utilized to teach the skills and attitudes of philosophical analysis are anthologies and lectures. Yet, anthologies often give practice only in reading. As a teaching medium, the lecture differs from the anthology only in that it sometimes has more potential for entertainment. Usually, however, this potential is not realized since the typical instructor has not been trained to entertain and, even if he has innate talent in this area, his competition in the form of television and movies is far superior. Further, the lecture, when compared to a readable essay, has many drawbacks. A student cannot follow a lecture at his own pace; he cannot review different points at will, in fact, he often cannot review them at all; he cannot give full attention to a lecture since he usually must take notes. Of course, the lecturer could simply make copies of his delivery and let the student read it, but most teachers would rather not do this because they would want to formulate their views more clearly before they put them in writing for public consumption. This points out another area in which the essay is superior to the lecture—the normal essay is usually more clearly formulated than the normal lecture. Perhaps the worst drawback of the lecture is that while it is being presented the lecturer is depriving his students of other kinds of very productive interactions he could be having with them.

Neither the anthology nor the lecture allow for practice, let alone supervised practice in which the student is prompted, encouraged, given individualized feedback and reinforced. Is it then surprising that the typical midterm paper is often an example of totally undisciplined and unskilled philosophical writing, especially given that it is one of the few times that the student actually has a chance to practice *doing* philosophy and that this practice is unsupervised?

The Guided Design Approach

Many alternatives have been put forth by innovative educators to correct the defects of the lecture, alternatives such as personalized instruction, competency based instruction, programmed instruction, computer assisted instruction, etc. In so far as these methods can more efficiently help the student acquire information, we believe they are laudatory. However, in so far as they are intended to teach *skills* and instill *attitudes* which will be transferred to the kinds of *decisions* students have to make in their everyday lives, we believe something more is needed, something like Guided Design.[1]

Guided Design is a new approach to teaching and learning which focuses on developing the student's decision-making skills as well as teaching specific concepts and principles. In a Guided Design class students work in small groups to solve meaningful, open-ended problems which require them to think logically, gather information, communicate ideas and work through certain decision-making steps. The students are guided through the solution of each problem by a series of printed "Instruction-Feedback" pages, by their discussion with other students in their group, and by the teacher, who acts as a consultant. The students do the thinking, they must make value judgments, and they play the role of the professional decision-maker.

In the Guided Design systems approach each open-ended problem establishes a need for a unit of subject matter which each student is expected to learn, on his own, outside of class. This approach helps the student learn that facts, concepts and principles are part of the background information required for the decision-making process. In addition, this organization establishes a pattern which will serve the student well after he leaves school, where continued independent learning is prerequisite to success. Although some class time is required to check on the student's progress, examine his homework for errors and give examinations, most of the class time can be freed for decision-making activities. In the Guided Design system the primary role of the teacher is that of guide, prompter, reinforcer, and consultant. During class the teacher moves from group to group listening, asking leading questions and encouraging the students to participate in the decision-making process.

An Example

Guided Design was developed by Dr. Charles Wales of West Virginia University and Dr. Robert Stager of the University of Windsor, who, being engineers, applied the concept of systems design, as it is used in engineering, to education. The most recent application of Guided Design has been to a multi-disciplinary philosophy of science course at West Virginia University entitled 'The Nature of Evidence.' The primary objective of The Nature of Evidence is to help the student learn about the similarities and differences that exist between the ways in which different professionals in the natural sciences, the social sciences, and the humanities gather evidence and use it to make decisions. The secondary objective is to instill in the student a certain attitude, namely a penchant for basing their beliefs on evidence and for opening those beliefs to criticism. At the same time it is hoped that the student can be introduced to some subject matter in the particular disciplines being compared and contrasted.

The first step in the development of The Nature of Evidence was to find interested faculty. A twelve member committee was selected which represented the fields of: Biology, Chemistry, Anthropology, English, Philosophy, Psychology, Geology, History, Physics, Drama, Engineering, Education, and Political Science. Each committee member had a history of scholarship and high quality teaching. The committee worked for over two years considering how it might meet the course objectives. They decided that the best way to present the evidential strategies of the various disciplines to the student was to demonstrate how each of these strategies might be applied to the solution of a simple, realistic problem. Desiring to maintain continuity among the problems, it was decided that all problems would arise in the context of an actual experimental village in Tanzania called Rwamkoma. One of the committee members had spent a year in Rwamkoma studying its political problems; the College of Agriculture had an experimental station in the village; the West Virginia University Library had one of the largest repositories of East African literature in the country.

The committee then endeavored to find problems or to create hypothetical problems in Rwamkoma which might be solved by the methods of their specialties. The basic constraints were that each problem typify the sort of problem any experimental village might be confronted with and that it would be a problem which a university student could relate to. Thus, for example, the Geologist was concerned with finding new sources of badly needed water; the Anthropologist had to overcome cultural beliefs which were limiting meat, egg, and milk consumption, leading to malnutrition; the specialist in English was grappling with the problem of whether or not a purported pornographic poem, which had created great concern in the village since it was written by one of the villagers, had any literary value.

The next task was to put these problems into the Guided Design format. To do this it was necessary to reconstruct the way each committee member, as a professional, would work through a problem, particularly as to how each would support the claim he made. The process would then be translated into a series of instructions which would guide the student through the problem in small steps. The student would discuss each instruction, arrive at a group conclusion, and then compare their decision with that of the professional as rendered in a written feedback. In this way, they would be using class time to model the behavior of the professional decision-maker, and hence would be getting practice in the skill of making decisions based on evidence. This skill would be reinforced in the feedback, and by the instructor who responds favorably to student decisions that are based on sound evidence. Since the problems being dealt with were realistic and since the students worked through the problems with their peers, we believed they would transfer the attitudes and skills they learned into their daily lives.

The course was offered for the first time in the Spring Semester of 1974. Because many faculty were involved in the development of this new multidisciplinary course, and because student interest was so great, two different classes were developed and taught. In each three-credit class the first week was devoted to a project on educational systems design which introduced the students to the Guided Design system. The next project used some basic techniques from philosophy to develop a set of questions about the methods, achievements, and attitudes of the scientist, questions such as "Does the scientist make predictions?," "Does his work lead to the discovery of novel facts?" and "Is he open to criticism?" These questions were used throughout the rest of the course to compare the work of professionals in different disciplines.

During the rest of the semester the students dealt with two projects from the natural sciences, two from the social sciences, and one from the humanities. At the end of each project, students were asked to use the questions developed in the philosophy project to examine the way in which the professional had operated. By doing this they learned about such things as the different types of explanatory models used in the natural and social sciences, the different types of ethical and operational constraints involved in testing hypotheses, and the different ways in which each professional opened his beliefs to criticism.

The Nature of Evidence has already had an impact at West Virginia University. Some committee members are producing articles based on the research they did to create their problems; some are further developing their material along different lines for use in other courses they teach; one faculty member developed supplementary audio-visual material for his project which will be made available to the actual inhabitants of Rwamkoma to help them learn about the geology of their area. Many faculty members in different colleges in the University have asked to be a part of the Nature of Evidence committee, while other faculty members have been stimulated by The Nature of Evidence to develop their own multi-disciplinary course on other topics.

New interest is being generated in the philosophy program, particularly in the area of philosophy of science. The Philosophy Department has already been asked by other departments to design three new courses which will be sequels to The Nature of Evidence: a course in the philosophy of the social sciences, a course in the philosophy of sociology and anthropology, and a course dealing with philosophical problems in political science.

Although it is desirable to have experienced faculty present class work, a thoroughly polished Guided Design project can be handled by a knowledgeable undergraduate assistant working under professional supervision. This is possible because the Guided Design materials develop the logic of the professional and the assistant does not have to create and present these—he simply manages the operation. This sort of arrangement has been used in other courses which utilize Guided Design and has been quite successful. Using this pattern we expect to expand the offering of this course to hundreds of students. Thus, for example, a historian might supervise ten teaching assistants as they guide 10 groups of 30 students each through a two- or three-week project. In this way, we believe we can achieve a high quality, well tested course which reaches a great many students at a low cost.

Because of the goals and design of the nature of Evidence, it could be offered in most institutions of higher learning, not only for the purpose of increasing interest in philosophy, but also as a humanistically oriented general education course. A junior college which does not have a complete spectrum of professional teaching resources could offer this course by using our book entitled *The Nature of Evidence*. Those institutions which have the required professional resources could either use the book in their classes or use our material as a model and prepare their own course.

Other Applications

The Guided Design teaching learning system is well suited to the teaching needs of the analytic philosopher. Since a problem is broken down into small steps, its logic is made clear for the purpose of analysis. Further, since all material is written in advance and discussed by student and instructor alike, it is possible to ascertain where the language of any of the individual steps is unclear and to improve on it. Of course, Guided Design is not the servant of analytic philosophy only. In so far as it is a format for developing attitudes and abilities it is useful to philosophers of all persuasion. In so far as it releases the instructor to interact with students on a more personal basis, it is useful to all teachers. Most importantly, since a problem is broken down into small steps, the instructor can observe the student working on each of these steps and determine whether or not the student is having any difficulties. Thus, the instructional system is testable; a teacher knows where he has made an instructional mistake, can learn from it, and make appropriate corrections.

Finally, the Guided Design approach can be of help to a philosophy department which, in order to survive, must increase its enrollment and teach larger numbers of students with fewer faculty members. One way to increase enrollment is by introducing team taught, multi-disciplinary courses. Because of their training, philosophers are in an excellent position to manage such courses. Further, such courses stimulate *faculty* interest in philosophy, as well as student interest, and therefore help increase the prominence of philosophy on the campus. The main problem with team taught courses is, however, that they often fail because the student is threatened when he is confronted with the numerous faculty members utilizing a wide variety of styles and teaching and grading. A multi-disciplinary course that utilizes Guided Design, however, makes teaching styles more uniform and requires the faculty to prepare their material in advance of delivery in order that it can be commented on and tested by other faculty involved before presentation. Also, as mentioned earlier, well prepared, well tested Guided Design material can be presented by non-professional personnel under the supervision of a professional and hence generate low cost student credit hours.

Notes

Originally published in *Metaphilosophy* 8 (1977).

1. A series of eight articles on the Guided Design concept were published in *Engineering Education* 62(5–8) (February to May 1972).

Using Computers to Make Logic Relevant

FREDERICK SUPPE

1. The Standard Conception of Logic Courses

Charles Peirce, in his architechtonic of philosophy, placed logic as a sub-branch of ethics: For did not logic tell us which arguments are good, hence instruct us in the virtues of argument? As two recent authors put the point starting in their logic text:

> Logic is concerned with arguments, good and bad. With the docile and the reasonable, arguments are sometimes useful in settling disputes. With the reasonable, this utility attaches only to good arguments. It is the logician's business to serve the reasonable. Therefore, in the realm of arguments, it is he who distinguishes good from bad.
>
> Virtue among arguments is known as validity.[1]

In principle I am willing to accede to such lofty claims—that it is the logician who distinguishes good from bad in argumentation. But principle is not practice, and practically speaking the logician has precious little to offer in evaluating genuinely problematic arguments.

Nevertheless, the typical logic-text authors pass off logic as a valuable practical means for evaluating arguments. For example, Irving Copi in his *Symbolic Logic* says,

> [t]he study of logic, especially symbolic logic, will tend to increase one's proficiency in reasoning. And ... the study of logic will give the student certain techniques for testing the validity of *all* arguments, including his own.[2]

Upon reading this the student thinks he is on the threshold of realizing Leibniz' dream, a *Calculus Ratiocinator*, which mechanically will enable him to determine when Nixon is cogent, and whether to be convinced by his Mother's pleas for chastity. But such hopes quickly fade as, instead of such important arguments, his attention is diverted to P's and Q's and the most exciting arguments he evaluates are at best as interesting as

[n]o student who fails some course that Rudolf teaches fails all the courses that Alfred teaches. Some student fails all the courses and also fails all the courses that Rudolf teaches. Therefore, if Rudolf teaches any courses, then there is a course that every student fails.[3]

And as the semester progresses he feels increasingly cheated.

Is our student wrong? Has he been cheated? Are the textbook authors, and the instructors who transmit their offerings, dealing in fraud? Or is our student just confused—the only failing of instructors in logic being that we haven't succeeded in convincing him that logic (the logic *we* transmit) is of inestimable practical value to him? My own opinion, which I will attempt to defend below, is that our student has the goods on us and on the authors we subsidize by teaching such a course.

If I am correct about this, then the insult to the student often is double. For not only do we present a fraudulently offered course, but often we sanctimoniously require that he take the course (at least if he is to use philosophy to satisfy his humanities liberal arts requirements): After all, is not correct reasoning essential to good philosophy? And how can he appreciate philosophy if he can't reason correctly? And how can he reason correctly if he doesn't know logic?

Before entering into a consideration whether the above charges are justified, let me make a crucial observation: whether the above student reaction is defensible or not, it is a fact of current academic life that this is a typical reaction to introductory logic courses—especially ones which concentrate on symbolic logic. And whether or not we think it a fair or rational reaction, it poses a problem for the teaching of elementary logic courses—namely, how do we make them relevant *in the eyes of our students*? Whether or not it is true that the content of elementary logic courses is in principle an aid to improving the rationality of practical argumentation, on a large scale our courses and the textbooks we use fail both to convince our students this is so and to give ours students any rational argumentative edge in practical disputes. If you don't believe this, just consult typical student evaluations of introductory logic courses taught on the above premise. As an example, I quote from summary student evaluations of such courses taught at the University of Illinois:

> Students were generally disappointed with this course. It is taught basically as a math course dealing entirely with manipulating symbols in a context-free language and proves to have little relevance. "This course was a waste of time except for the fact it fulfilled my LAS [humanities distribution] requirement. It was completely dull, boring, and irrelevant."[4]

Admitting all the above, it is possible for one to react as follows: the problem is not with logic—it's just the way it is taught. Most logic courses are mistaught and fail to realize their promise—which promise is aptly captured in the first two quotations above. My own response to this is that if you escape the above student objections while teaching introductory logic on the foregoing conception, you've done nothing to vindicate that conception of an introductory logic course: You've shown your own charisma, not the viability of such a logic course.

The problem here is not the teaching: it's that formal logic is not a practical means for evaluating genuinely problematic arguments. If you don't believe me, try the following experiment: Take an Agatha Christie short story and, using the techniques of an introductory logic course, try to figure out exactly what Poirot's argument is in solving the case. ("The Kidnapping of Johnny Waverly" is a particularly apt one; I once had a class do this and they understood less how Poirot solved the mystery after doing so than they did when they first read the story). But enough of polemics and examples. I think a kind of theoretical argument can be given which tends to show the practical uselessness of formal logic in evaluating arguments. To adapt an example from Benson Mates (whose skepticism on the practical value of logic is heartwarming but errs in the direction of optimism.),[5] consider the following genuinely problematic argument:

1) Socrates is human.
2) Human is human.
3) For every A, B, C: If A is C and B is C, then A resembles B with respect to being C.
4) Therefore, Socrates resembles Human with respect to being human.[6]

Is it sound? Since our students are aware (from our courses) that 'is' sometimes signifies identity and other times predication, they interpret 'is' in each instance in what seems the most natural way, using 'is' as identity in the second premise and 'is' predicatively in the other three sentences, and then mechanically determine the argument is invalid although the premises seem true. Does this settle the case? No. for might not the author have used 'is' systematically with just one of these two meanings? If he did, the 'is' of identity is ruled out as being implausible; and, so we take it as the 'is' of predication. Doing so we find the argument becomes valid, but that the second premise is false or meaningless. Well, we've exhausted the standard textbook moves, and so we conclude the argument is unsound. But, notice the following: if we interpret 'is' by the phrase 'is included in' it turns out that the premises are true and the argument is valid; so it *is* sound!

What do we make from this? The following, I think. The argument in question is genuinely problematic as to its soundness. To apply formal logic to evaluate even its validity, we have to resort to a fair degree of philosophical analysis. And depending on our analysis, the application of formalism would be question-begging. And, in this argument, at least, once the analysis has been made, no real question of the validity or soundness of the argument remains to be solved by resort to formalism.

This example makes, I think, the following two points: (1) if the argument is relatively simple (as the above is) yet genuinely problematical, any resort to formal logic will be question-begging unless the formalism is bolstered by an adequate prior philosophical analysis, and the analysis usually will render the formalism superfluous; (2) if the argument is not relatively simple, the formalism may help, but only when it is justified by an adequate prior philosophical analysis of the argument. Therefore (3), the legitimate recourse to logical formalism in the evaluation of genuinely problematic arguments requires a prior philosophical analysis. Moreover (4), formal logic cannot provide that prior philosophical analysis (else via (1) and (2) we get into a vicious infinite regress). From this I conclude that logic itself (at least as measured by the content of the typical introductory logic course) cannot provide an effective practical means for evaluating genuinely problematic arguments.

The argument just given leads to another argument displaying the limits of formal logic for evaluating genuinely problematic arguments. For any attempt to use logical formalism to evaluate *that* argument *ipso facto* will beg the very question!

Thus, our disgruntled student is not "too blind to see the value of what we are teaching" him; rather he has seen through our fraud. And this poses a genuine problem: Why are we teaching him logic under the above fraudulent conception?

2. Other Conceptions of Logic Courses

Instinctively feeling fraudulence in the standard conception of logic courses, some instructors have attempted other approaches to the subject matter.

One reaction to the argumentative irrelevance of standard logic courses is to blame the problems on symbolic logic—perhaps echoing Strawson on its deviation from the use of connectives and quantifiers in ordinary English.[7] typically this takes the form of retreating to the traditional logic of the syllogism and sorites. Not only does this seem to me intellectually dishonest (being akin to teaching only Aristotle's physics in a survey physics course), but it does nothing to save the above concept of logic. For to use a standard example, it demonstrably fails to be adequate for the evaluation of rational arguments, hence is inadequate for evaluating most arguments. It cannot even show sound the following argument; "All horses are animals. Therefore, all heads of horses are heads of animals." At best, traditional logic has an antiquarian interest which properly is relegated to a segment of a course in the history of (ancient and medieval) philosophy.

An obvious approach is to just teach symbolic logic in its full mathematical glory, disclaiming any relevance to it at all. Taken to its extreme, one teaches it as a kind of openly irrelevant intellectual puzzle; this is an approach I've often taken and find many students responsive to. As much merit as this approach has, it leaves unanswered the question of why we should require anyone to take it or make it the typically required portion of a philosophy liberal arts sequence. Moreover, it suffers most grievously by failing to make the course relevant in the way it could be, as I shall argue below. Closely related to this approach are the approaches of (1) exploiting the elegance and rigor of logic to make it an *aesthetics* course in the "beauty of mathematics" or else (2) an out-and-out high-powered course in the substance of mathematical logic. Against both it can be objected this is not the appropriate function of an introductory logic course in a philosophy liberal arts sequence. Against (1) it can also be said that few introductory logic instructors can successfully do it.

What I am suggesting is that it is a function of an elementary logic course to be relevant to the practical concerns of the average student, that the standard conception of logic courses intrinsically fails to be so relevant, and that none of the above alternatives does any better. If the relevance of introductory logic courses is to be teaching students to reason better, then I suggest we relegate our logic courses to the scrap heaps they belong in and replace them by "introduction to philosophy courses" which intensively teach one to do informal "philosophical analysis";[8] for if my argument above is sound, that is the essence of evaluating arguments, not formal logic.

3. Using Computers to Make Logic Relevant

An underlying bias in my preceding arguments is the idea that our elementary logic courses (as opposed to courses in mathematical logic required of majors[9] or advanced logic courses for those interested in mathematical logic) should enjoy a relevance appropriate to that of a humanities course satisfying a "liberal arts" requirement. What is the purpose of such liberal arts courses? This is a legitimate matter of debate, but I would suggest that a liberal arts course *minimally* should give the typical student some intellectual advantage in coping with the human environment he has to live in. The *promise* of the standard conception of logic courses clearly aims at satisfying this desideratum; unfortunately its *deliverance* does not.

Several years ago Professors Arthur Burks, Jaakko Hintikka, and I discussed this very issue: how do you make introductory logic courses relevant in the sense of the above conception of the purpose of a liberal arts sequence? Out of that conversation emerged a very interesting idea, which I wish to relate to you: At various times in human history there have been major technological innovations which have radically transformed the quality and nature of human existence. One need not go so far back as the Bronze Age for an example. In the Industrial Revolution of the 1760's onward, we find an example we can empathize with. But, to be more contemporary: since the ENIAC became operational in 1946, we have experienced an equally important example—the Computer Revolution. Today the computer is so persuasive in everyday life—the IRS audit of our taxes, the collation of credit and other personal information into computer files and other computer invasions of privacy, university records, industrial management decisions, bank statements, plotting war strategy, the manipulation of telephone switching, etc.—that in the last two decades the computer has radically changed the shape of human existence—especially in the technologically more advanced societies. Just as Henry Adams correctly found it necessary for the educated person to learn about, and come to grips with, the "Virgin and the Dynamo" if he was to adequately cope with his changed society,[10] so too the educated man today must have a clear understanding of computers—what their intrinsic limitations and capabilities are, and some clear idea how they do what they do.[11] For only with such understanding can we hope to cope with our computerized environment and realistically decide whether the likes of HAL of *2001* are more to be feared than our politicians.

How does one impart this important "humanistic" understanding of the non-human computer and its intrusions into human life? Learning to program a computer is little help—it only teaches you to talk with them, but gives you no insight into them except that they "speak" funny languages such as FORTRAN. And understanding the electrical engineering of micro-integrated circuits, thin-film or cryogenic memories, etc., is too much to expect of the average educated person. Out of that discussion with Burks and Hintikka emerged the following suggestion: There is a branch of logic, *automata theory* (the logic of computers) which—without getting involved in the engineering complexities of the actual construction of computers and without the ephemeral loss of touch with the actual internal operation of computers that comes from the study of programming languages—is ideal for efficiently imparting in fair logical detail a clear conceptual understanding of computers to the average college undergraduate: what their intrinsic capabilities and limitations are, and how they work. From such a study, a quite full conceptual understanding of computers can be gained. Granting that such an understanding of computers is of high humanistic priority, where is the best place to impart it in the college curriculum? Our answer was—in an elementary logic course. For on the basis of the minimal normal content of the typical elementary logic course, (propositional calculus, truth tables, disjunctive normal-forms, and a bit of naïve set theory—all of which I have found can be taught in 4-5 weeks), one can develop the substance of automata theory so as to impart such a conceptual understanding of computers.[12]

As an outgrowth of that germinal idea, the last several years I have been developing an experimental introductory logic course—first at the University of Illinois[13] and now at the University of Maryland—which minimally develops symbolic logic up through predicate calculus, then exploits the logic to develop automata theory—which in turn is used to impart a *conceptual* understanding of computers. The development of logic (including naïve set theory) and the automata theory are interspersed; and the automata theory developed includes the theories of switching nets, logical nets, Turing machines, Universal Turing machines, and a proof of the non-decidability of the halting problem. In the remaining time we consider modern prototypical computers; their esoteric applications in biological simulation, the computer compositions in music, artificial intelligence (including Samuel's Checker Playing Machine which learned to play tournament-caliber checkers); and finally the mind-machine problem ("Can Computers Think?"). In the course students learn the standard symbolic logic, though they spend less time on it and are much less proficient in using it to "evaluate" arguments in the usual question-begging ways. They do, however, come out knowing quite a bit about computers, can program the Universal Turing Machine, and have understood the philosophical significance of Church's Thesis and the non-decidability of the Halting Problem for Turing machines. And they have a healthy respect for computers, but have lost their awe of them. Most importantly, they react very favorably to the course, and feel they are getting something importantly relevant from the course (namely the understanding of computers), which is notably absent in their reactions to traditional logic courses. It is no wonder, then, that they are far more excited by and interested in this course than are students in traditional logic courses. And students who have studied computer programming since taking the course express the opinion that the course gave them an advantage over other students in learning the program. Thus student reactions vindicate this conception of using computers to make logic relevant.

4. Teaching A Computer-Related Logic Course

In arguing against the traditional conception of logic courses, and in pushing for the computer-related logic course, my motives obviously have not been merely to relate to you a novel and somewhat esoteric approach to teaching introductory logic. If my arguments and polemics against the standard conception of logic courses make their case, then either we must drop introductory logic from the curriculum (hopefully replacing it by courses in philosophical analysis), or else we must radically reconceive what we're trying to accomplish in such courses. And I have been urging a particular re-conception of introductory logic courses that I've found relevant in students' eyes and for which I think I can find reasonable academic justification. It should be obvious that my intention here is to convince the reader to attempt such a computer-oriented logic course, in the hopes that such courses eventually will become a standard part of the undergraduate philosophy curriculum.

There is, however, one practical problem facing the widespread incorporation of such a course into the undergraduate philosophy curriculum—namely that there does not presently exist a textbook suitable for the beginning undergraduate level course which comprehensibly develops the required automata theory out of the normal elementary symbolic logic. The problem is further complicated by the fact that existing automata theory textbooks[14] do not develop automata theory in a manner that easily can be adapted so as to be readily comprehended by typical undergraduates. Indeed, our experience in teaching the experimental course described above indicates that a nontraditional development of the material, unlike that found in existing automata textbooks, is a key element of its pedagogical success.[15]

Although this problem soon will be solved,[16] for the moment the instructor desiring to introduce the sort of computer-oriented logic course advocated here will have to teach it from duplicated notes he must prepare himself. By way of encouraging and aiding the introduction of such a course, I will briefly sketch the development of the course material which has proved successful in the experimental course outlined above.[17]

The logical apparatus required for developing the automata theory consists in rudiments of propositional calculus and naïve set theory. Any standard truth-table presentation of propositional calculus will suffice, though it is advisable to use '1' instead of 'T' and '0' instead of 'F'—as is standard in automata theory. In addition, the notion of a disjunctive normal form should be introduced, and an algorithm presented for obtaining disjunctive normal forms from truth tables.[18] The required set theory consists of the standard set operators, ordered n-tuples, and relations and functions.[19]

The first branch of automata theory to be developed is switching theory. This is done by introducing three basic switches—*not, or* and *and*. Their behaviors are defined by the truth tables for the corresponding sentential connectives, interpreting '1' as "on" and '0' as "off." Rules then are introduced for connecting these switches together to form switching nets.[20] The behavior of these switching nets can also be described by truth tables, which in turn allows wffs in propositional calculus to describe the behavior of these switching nets when net inputs are labeled by propositional variables. The truth-table algorithm for finding disjunctive normal forms (cf. above) is then adapted into a general procedure for constructing logical nets which realize net behaviors characterized by wffs of propositional calculus.[21]

Next the theory of switching nets is expanded into the theory of logical nets, which are constructed out of *and, or,* and *not* switches and a unit delay element which serves as a memory unit.[22] Then the Burks-Wang τ/λ techniques for describing the behavior of logical nets are introduced,[23] as are State diagrams.[24] Then Burks-Wang normal form logical nets[25] are introduced and exploited as a general procedure for constructing logical nets which realize behaviors specified via τ/λ techniques.

Turing machines are introduced by attaching tape read-write heads (having four inputs—"move right," "move left," "mark," "erase"—and one output which emits the contents of the cell under scan) to a logical net with one input and four outputs such that at most one output can ever be on.[26] It is observed, then, that all the logical net does in a Turing machine is to give the tape read-write head instructions to move its tape to the right or left, or mark a 1 or 0 on the tape, where the instruction given may depend upon the contents of the tapes. This means that the behavior of a Turing machine can be specified by a program of instructions to the tape read-write head. A variant of Wang's program-characterization of Turing machines[27] due to Thatcher[28] is then introduced, and subsequently used to work with Turing machines. Following Thatcher's development, it is shown how Turing machines can be used to compute functions. Then it is shown how to build a Universal Turing machine which, when suitably instructed, can compute any function which any Turing machine can compute.[29] Church's Thesis is then introduced and argued for,[30] from which discussion it is concluded that Turing machines can do anything any possible computer can do. Thus the capabilities of the Universal Turing Machine are exhaustive of the computational abilities of all possible computers. This establishes the intrinsic capabilities of computers. Next, the Halting Problem is introduced and show undecidable,[31] and it is shown how this establishes intrinsic limitations on what computers can do.

Having completed the automata theory, it next is shown how modern-day digital computers are realizations of automata,[32] and how the computational abilities of computers established in our study of Turing machines can be harnessed via numerical coding to perform a wide variety of practical tasks. For this part of the course I rely on the *Scientific American* reprints contained in Sections II and IV of Fenichel and Wizenbaum, *Computers and Computation*. This part of the course includes consideration of issues on artificial intelligence which, via a consideration of the parallels between logical nets and the human brain,[33] raises the mind-machine problem—Can machines think? Then the standard literature on this subject[34] can be considered; in dealing with this issue I find the approach taken by Arthur Burks in his APA Presidential Address[35] especially effective.

5. Summary

In this paper I have considered a number of standard conceptions of introductory logic courses and found them wanting. In Section 1, I argued the most common premise on which introductory logic courses rest—that formal logic provides an effective general means for evaluating arguments—was fraudulent, and that students recognize it as such. In Section 2, I considered various other frequently encountered conceptions of logic courses and found them unsatisfactory—at least if introductory logic courses are to function as part of required liberal arts general education sequences; for these approaches lack the relevance to the human situation essential to such courses. In Section 3, I suggested that there was a way to make introductory logic courses enjoy that relevance—namely by using the logic commonly taught in such courses to develop automata theory, and then use that automata theory to impart a thorough conceptual understanding of computers. Section 4 discussed the feasibility of such a course, pointing out a practical problem caused by the temporary unavailability of an adequate textbook for such a course—which requires that it be taught from notes prepared by the instructor. A somewhat detailed outline of such a course was presented, indicating the sources an instructor should consult in working-up such a set of notes. My experience has shown the course can be taught quite successfully from such notes distributed to the class. Working-up such a set of notes requires effort, but expending the effort is morally preferable to the easier practice of continuing to serve our students the academic fraud kown as the standard elementary logic course.

Notes

This is a revised version of part of an invited address given before the Western Conference on the Teaching of Philosophy in conjunction with the 1973 Western Division meetings of the American Philosophical Association. I am grateful to my former colleague at the University of Illinois, Professor Hugh Petrie, for comments on a draft of this paper. This paper is dedicated to Stephen Toulmin—who although trained as a mathematician, has developed a healthy disrespect for mathematical logic as a philosophical tool.

1. D. Kalish and R. Montague, *Logic: Techniques of Formal Reasoning* (New York: Harcourt, Brace, and World, 1964), 3. The spirit in which this passage obviously is intended in the overall context of the book should not be overlooked.

2. Copi, *Symbolic Logic*, 3rd edition (New York: Macmillan 1967), 1–2; emphasis added.

3. Kalish and Montague, *Logic*, 176.

4. *The Advisor* (Urbana: University of Illinois Press, 1969–1970), 239.

5. See especially chap. 5 of his *Elementary Logic* (New York: Oxford, 1965).

6. This argument is from B. Mates, "Synonymity," reprinted at L. Linsky, *Semantics and the Philosophy of Language* (Urbana: University of Illinois Press, 1952), 111–136; the discussion which follows is based on Section III of that paper.

7. See P. F. Strawson, *Introduction to Logical Theory* (London: Methuen, 1952).

8. From my own experience, such courses do a better job of improving reasoning ability than standard logic courses.

9. I'm not sure there is any rationale for requiring courses in mathematical logic of them, except the fact it is a kind of literacy now required to read portions of the philosophical literature. And for this a good twenty-five page set of mimeographed notes on logic is enough. In this vein, while I was teaching at the University of Illinois (Urbana) we revised our Ph.D. logic requirement there. After discussion, the committee drafting the new requirement agreed the ideal logic requirement for philosophers *qua* philosophers was to prohibit any knowledge of symbolic logic at all. Feeling this was unenforceable and unrealistic, it finally was decided that we would require at least as much logic as was contained in Vol. 1 of A. Church, *Introduction to Mathematical Logic* (Princeton: Princeton University Press, 1956). For in that case we could rightly hold them responsible for any misuse of logic they might make!

10. See his *The Education of Henry Adams* (New York: Modern Library, 1931).

11. The importance of this need is reflected by the fact that the Smithsonian Institution's Museum of Science and Technology devotes as much display space to computers

as it does to medicine and pharmacy, to petroleum, or to the origins of modern science. The emphasis in their displays is on understanding how computers work.

12. This is no accident; historically, the first computers were, from an engineering point-of-view, simply devices to do automata theory; and the first computers were designed by teams of logicians and engineers building machines to do logic. Since then, automata theory has emerged as an abstract field of computer design, though it has tended to supplant logic by its algebraic extensions in the field of automata theory.

13. In developing the course and trying it out on students at the University of Illinois, I was aided by Professor Thomas Nickles and my graduate assistants Mr. Michael Drummer and Mr. Richard Schubert.

14. For example, M. Davis, *Computability and Undecidability* (New York: McGraw-Hill, 1950), or M. Minsky, *Computation: Finite and Infinite Machines* (Englewood Cliffs: Prentice Hall, 1967).

15. The situation is not unlike that encountered in introducing symbolic logic into the undergraduate curriculum. So long as textbooks only developed symbolic logic axiomatically along the line of *Principia Mathematica*, there were extreme practical difficulties facing the introduction of symbolic logic into the undergraduate curriculum. However, once textbooks were introduced which presented non-standard developments of symbolic logic along Gentzen natural-deduction lines, symbolic logic courses became standard undergraduate offerings.

16. Namely by the textbook for such a course I am writing, *Introduction to the Logic of Computers*.

17. The version of this paper read before the Western Conference on the Teaching of Philosophy (cf. unnumbered note above) was approximately eight times longer than the present version, and contained a quite detailed development of the course material sketched below. Copies of the longer development can be obtained by writing the author.

18. Such an algorithm is presented at G. Massey, *Understanding Symbolic Logic* (New York: Harper and Row, 1970), 43–46.

19. A sufficient development can be found in R. Stoll, *Sets, Logic, and Axiomatic Theories* (San Francisco: Freeman, 1961), Sections 1.1–1.6, 1.8.

20. The rules are rules 1, 2, 4, and 5 of the definition of a logical net given in Section 4. of I. Copi, C. Elgot, and J. Wright, "Realization Events by Logical Nets," in E. F. Moore, *Sequential Machines* (Reading: Addison-Wesley, 1964), 175–192.

21. Various aspects of this development of the theory of switching nets can be found in Copi, Elgot, and Wright, "Realization Events by Logical Nets," and the works cited in Note 23 below, as well as in the longer version of this paper cited in note 17.

22. Cf. Copi, Elgot, and Wright, "Realization Events by Logical Nets," for the definition.

23. Cf. Section 2.2. of A. Burks and H. Wang, "The Logic of Automata," in H. Wang, *A Survey of Mathematical Logic* (Amsterdam: North Holland, 1962), 175–223.

24. Cf. Section 1. of R. McNaughton and H. Yamada, "Regular Expressions and State Graphs for Automata," Moore, *Sequential Machines*, 157–174.

25. Cf. Burks and Wang, "The Logic of Automata," Section 2.3.

26. For an intuitive description of Turing machines, see Wang's article in R. Fenichel and J. Weizenbaum, *Computers and Computation* (San Francisco: Freeman, 1971), 136–144 and Section 6.0 of Minsky, *Computation*.

27. Cf. H. Wang, "A Variant to Turing's Theory of Computing Machines," *Journal of the Association for Computing Machinery* 4 (1957): 63–92.

28. Cf. Section 1 of J. Thatcher, "Self-Describing Turing Machines and Self-Reproducing Cellular Automata," in A. W. Burks, *Essays on Cellular Automata* (Urbana: University of Illinois Press, 1970), 103–131.

29. This is done along the lines of Thatcher, ibid., Section 6, except that the Universal Turing Machine presented operated on a three-digit binary code. See the longer version of this paper noted in Note 17 for the details of this design.

30. Cf. A. Fraenkel and Y. Bar-Hillel, *Foundations of Set Theory* (Amsterdam: North Holland, 1958), 297–303; chaps 11–13 of S. Kleene, *Metamathematics* (Princeton: Van Nostrand, 1950); and chap. 5 of Minsky, *Computation*, for Church's Thesis (also known as Turing's Thesis) and the evidence in support of it.

31. The proof follows Thatcher, "Self-Describing Turing Machines," Section 4.

32. Cf. Section 1 of Fenichel and Weizenbaum, *Computers and Computation*.

33. Cf. W. McCulloch and W. Pitts, "A Logical Calculus of Ideas Immanent in Nervous Activity," *Bulletin of Mathematical Biophysics* 5 (1943): 115–133; and John von Neumann, *Computer and the Brain* (New Haven: Yale University Press, 1958) and *Theory of Self-Reproducing Automata* (Urbana: University of Illinois Press, 1966), Part 1.

34. Cf. A. R. Anderson, *Minds and Machines* (Englewood Cliffs: Prentice Hall, 1964).

35. Cf. his "Logic, Computers, and Men," in the *Proceedings and Addresses of the American Philosophical Association* 46 (1972–1973): 39–57.

PART IV:

RETURN TO THE TRADITION

Dare to Be Wise

Richard Taylor

Students of philosophy learn very early—usually the first day of their first course—that philosophy is the love of wisdom. This is often soon forgotten, however, and there are even men who earn their livelihood at philosophy who have not simply forgotten it, but who seem to positively scorn the idea. A philosopher who, disclaiming any philosophical knowledge, dedicates himself to wisdom is likely to be thought of as one who has missed his calling, who belongs in a pulpit, perhaps, or in some barren retreat for sages, but hardly in the halls of academia. For philosophy, it is supposed by vast numbers of students and teachers of the subject, has for its goal philosophical *knowledge*, and indeed even *certain* knowledge. It is presupposed, therefore, that there is such a thing as philosophical knowledge, and there are even men who think themselves the possessors of at least some of it.

I shall maintain that there simply is no such thing as philosophical knowledge, nor any philosophical way of knowing anything, and defend the humble point that philosophy is, indeed, the love of wisdom. I believe the philosopher's claim to philosophical knowledge is pretense. It is, moreover, precisely this pretense that has tended to make philosophers of today look ridiculous in the eyes of the world. With so much folly abounding, so much unhappiness even in the midst of riches, so many lives seemingly wasted in the pursuit of specious ideals, men have looked hopefully to the philosophers for light upon some of those things that have always been of deep concern to thoughtful men. They have been puzzled and somewhat dismayed at what they have found. The philosophers, in turn, have been surprised to find their work the subject of considerable and unflattering editorial comment, which they have for the most part swept under the rug and out of sight. It has been a matter of genuine concern to those "outside" philosophy to realize, when wise men are sought, that not only do the philosophers not resemble very closely what they would suppose were men of wisdom, but many do not even seem to profess a love for it. They are instead embarked upon the pursuit of philosophical knowledge – which of course no one wants to find fault with, provided there is any such thing. But what this philosophical knowledge more often than not turns out to be is either knowledge of the meanings of more or less ordinary words, facility in the techniques of logic, or felicity in saying what everyone already believes, and none of these is likely to seem to other men of mature judgment very promising of wisdom nor, indeed, even worthy of men of learning.

Knowledge vs. Wisdom

Socrates considered himself the wisest Athenian, precisely because he knew nothing, and was aware that he knew nothing. His advantage over his fellows was just this, that although they similarly knew nothing, they thought they knew much, while he was spared this conceit. A similar thought was expressed by Lao-tse: "To know and yet (think) that we do not know is the highest (attainment); not to know (and yet think) we do know is a disease."[1]

Now of course Socrates, in his profession of ignorance, was not disclaiming the kind of knowledge that is the common possession of men—the knowledge that water is wet, that fire burns, and snow melts, etc. But there is a vast realm about which men cannot know just by observing, which includes such things as the nature of man, the rational life, what is good for men, what is good for the state, and all those things that are so deeply important to religion and bear upon the meaning of life. It was about all these things that Socrates somewhat ironically professed ignorance. But he did not on this account deem them unimportant. On the contrary, he thought they are the only things that are really important at all. Though he *knew* nothing about them, though they could never be known in any way comparable to our knowledge that water is wet and fire burns, he never doubted that there is such a thing as wisdom concerning such things, and through his whole life he sought it. His searching expressed itself, not merely in his curiosity and his paradoxical dialectic, but in his whole manner of life. Indeed, it entirely determined his whole outer and inner life, and even his very death.

Except for the Cynics, the Stoics, and Epicureans, who were Socrates' true heirs, many of his successors even to this day have more or less substituted the ideal of philosophical knowledge for philosophical wisdom. They were largely guided to this by the example of mathematics and particularly geometry, which seemed to thinkers even as recently as Kant to be an existing proof of the possibility of purely rational knowledge. St. Thomas "proved" that God exists, and numberless things besides. He "answered" just about every question a thinking man might ask, setting out his philosophy as a seemingly endless series of questions and *answers*, and with a note of finality that seemed to leave no doubt. Very few today would concede that he really proved any of those things, in the sense of producing any knowledge of them at all. Yet who can deny that those who embraced this thinking were infinitely better off than those who scorned thought altogether, or embraced superstition? And the reason is sure that *thought itself*, even though it may yield no knowledge, is something to be prized. Descartes and Spinoza similarly "proved" that God exists, and a great deal more. Indeed, they both thought that we can achieve not only knowledge, but even certainty, concerning the soul, human motivation, free will, and virtually everything under the sun. It is significant that both philosophers, quite unlike Socrates, took geometry as their model. We know now that the profession of knowledge of all these things was a delusion, and that they possessed knowledge of none of the things they set forth with such imposing proof. And yet we know too that their writings are among the intellectual treasures of the world. Why? Because we recognize that profound thought, even when it seeks knowledge and yet gives us knowledge of nothing, may nevertheless help us towards something infinitely more precious, which is philosophical wisdom.

The Myth of Philosophical Knowledge

Philosophers of this generation do not appear to have disabused themselves of the idea that there is such a thing as philosophical knowledge, that the key to such knowledge is found within the discipline of philosophy itself, and indeed, that such knowledge is possessed by at least some of those—very often themselves—who have extensively pursued this inquiry. That this latter supposition is naïve should be obvious to anyone who merely looks at the externals of the situation. It is perfectly commonplace to find philosophers who meet and talk daily, customarily read and discuss each other's work, who have abundant time to acquaint each other with the fruits of their inquiries and the foundations upon which these rest, and who yet agree upon absolutely nothing of a philosophical nature. One believes, the other denies, that universals exist; one maintains, the other doubts, that the mind acts upon the body; one shows his students that the ontological argument is sound, and his colleague shows the same students that it is not; one affirms, the other rejects, the doctrine of free will—and so on to every philosophical question on which one may have an opinion. This is perfectly obvious even to philosophical beginners, and yet the pretense persists, even among philosophers, that there is such a thing as philosophical knowledge, and even that philosophers possess it. Now to be sure, there are differences of theory in every area of inquiry, but in the sciences, for example, it is not pretended that the truth is known in those areas of research and speculation where there is in fact controversy and deep division of opinion among those who are learned in the subject. There are differences of view even in physics, certainly. But what if there were a department of physics whose members held different opinions on virtually every area of physics? Suppose some affirmed and some denied the existence of phlogiston, some defended and others attacked the doctrine of the elasticity of air, and some upheld the atomic theory of matter while others preferred a theory of elemental qualities. Would not the suspicion arise that perhaps there was no real *knowledge* of physics in that department in the first place?

Now I am not, of course, denying that there is knowledge about philosophy, or that philosophers can be, and sometimes are, learned men. Some philosophical scholars have, in fact, a vast erudition, which is not only an enviable ornament to themselves but an inestimable credit to their culture. Such knowledge, then, is not denied; for just as there can be knowledge about music but not, strictly, musical knowledge, so also there can be knowledge about philosophy. Almost any philosopher knows, for example, that Socrates died in 399 B.C., that he taught Plato, believed in the immortality of his soul, and so on. Similarly, a philosopher can explain what pragmatism is, is likely to know Santayana's theories of essences, and can usually give some account of Kant's transcendental aesthetic. But none of this is philosophical knowledge; it is purely biographical and historical, and can for the most part be found in any schoolroom encyclopedia. From similar sources one can derive all sorts of information about music, composers and musicians, or about poets and their work; but just as such knowledge fails to make one a musician or a poet, so likewise the knowledge about philosophy, however great, does not make one a philosopher.

Philosophical Argument

One might be tempted to say, then, that philosophical inquiry is just very difficult in comparison, for example, to scientific inquiry, and its fruits of knowledge are therefore yielded more slowly and in small bits. Difficult it most certainly is, for one really must think even to understand it, to say nothing of contributing something of one's own. But is it really an *inquiry* at all? Is it a quest that yields knowledge, of anything? If so, what is its method? Not, evidently, observation and experiment, for there are no laboratories of philosophy; there are only libraries. And blackboards and chalk.

Well, there *is* alleged to be a method, a procedure for the attainment of philosophical knowledge, and the mention of blackboards suggests what it is. It is the method of the *philosophical argument*. This consists essentially of seeing what is implied by what, typically by writing things all down on paper or blackboard. By this method philosophical knowledge, sometimes even certainty, is supposed to be acquired by a rational mind, and while the device itself is not the unique possession of philosophy—it has always been useful in law, for instance—philosophy is nevertheless its original home, and philosophers the trained experts in the use of it. Now no doubt the latter is true. Philosophers are, in varying degrees, the trained experts in philosophical argument. But what I am maintaining is a pretense, is that any knowledge is obtained by this instrument. Probably no man ever wielded philosophical argument more skillfully than Socrates, or with more devastating effect, and philosophers today possess absolutely not one particle of knowledge that was not equally known to Socrates, excepting that vast knowledge which they, together with those who are not philosophers, have gleaned from *outside* philosophy—from history and science, and generally from seeing what goes on and reading of what others have seen. From philosophical argument itself philosophers have learned nothing that was not known to Socrates, and he honestly and rightly conceded that he had thereby learned nothing at all.

Philosophical argument takes a variety of forms, and I shall not attempt an inventory of them. The simplest conception of such argument is that we write down true statements—statements that are most often taken as true by ordinary commonsense, incidentally, and not by any special philosophical vision—and then see what they *entail*. We know that if the original statements (premises) are true, and the reasoning valid, then lo! the emerging conclusion will have to be true too, and therefore an item of knowledge. The "evidence" for it will be the very statements appearing above it. And it will therefore be an item of *philosophical* knowledge, since it was gained in a purely philosophical way, that is, by a philosophical argument.

But that nothing has ever been *learned* by such a performance is quite readily seen by considering that if the conclusion of such an argument is implausible, if it runs contrary to what jurists sometimes refer to as one's general "knowledge of the world," then there is not the slightest reason left for clinging to the premises. Indeed, if the conclusion appears the least doubtful, then at least one of the premises, indispensible for getting such a conclusion, is automatically infected with the same doubt. In short, unless the conclusion is something one already happens to believe, the argument accomplishes nothing at all. If the plausibility of the premises is supposed to be evidence for the plausibility of the conclusion, then by the same token, the implausibility of the conclusion is equally evidence for the implausibility of at least one of the premises. So far as gaining any knowledge is concerned, then, we end up exactly where we started, with what we already knew having the final say in the matter, and we have obviously *learned* nothing. Philosophical argument may indeed be the child of philosophy, but commonsense or the general, educated knowledge of what is so in the world most assuredly is not, and if the latter, with which we begin, is still what we are obliged to end up with, then the profession of philosophical knowledge is a pretense indeed.

Here it might be thought that we should simply be more fastidious in the choice of our premises. We should not pick them willy-nilly from the common knowledge of mankind. We should, guided by the example of Descartes, start with things known with certainty to be true, so that they will not later become infected with any doubt that may appear in the conclusion drawn from them. But here the difficulty is obvious: By virtue of what do we know those things to be true? Not, surely, by philosophical arguments, for we must first know these things to be true before we can even compose such an argument. By what is self-evident, then? But here again, what seemed self-evident ceases to seem so the moment it is seen to entail what is implausible. By the immediate testimony of our sense, then? But philosophers have no special gifts of the senses, and what they are able to infer from this testimony, others who have never heard of philosophy are able to infer just as well. From the sciences, then? But again, scientists themselves are quite as capable as any philosopher of seeing what is implied by their findings and drawing the proper inferences. So long as intelligence is the more or less common possession of men, we shall not need one group of observers to see what is so, and another group of thinkers to draw the appropriate inferences—though some persons unfamiliar with the subject seem to have the quaint notion that this latter role is to some extent filled by philosophers of science.

Philosophical Analysis

Another form of philosophical argument has for its goal the refinement of meanings, and this is much cultivated in philosophical seminars today. Here a typical procedure is to begin with certain words in more or less common use, express them in ordinary or interesting contexts, and then try to enunciate the connotations of those words in such contexts. This is sometimes done by listing, on blackboard or paper, what must be true, in case the given statements in which those words occur are assumed to be true. For instance, what does it *mean* to say that a given man *moved* his hand? That he did this *freely*? That he hereby *caused* a fire? That he is thus *responsible* for this? And so on. The manner in which this is discovered is quite interesting: It is done intuitively, through the consideration of imaginary cases. And the results obtained are then tested by what might be regarded as still another form of philosophical argument, namely, by the "counter-example." Thus, having listed what must be true in case the original statement is assumed to be true, the task is to try to invent some imaginary situation in which all the listed statements would be true, but the original is false! This having been done, the next step is to find still another condition to add to the list which will have the effect of ruling out the counter-example while preserving the assumed truth of that with which we began. This sometimes goes on for weeks.

This sort of exercise is highly invigorating. It also promotes what men have always found to be a most exhilarating pleasure, the pitting of wits one against another, and it is therefore in some ways ideally suited to the philosophical seminar. It does, moreover, produce intellectual benefits whose value I shall not for a moment diminish. It sharpens the mind to an unbelievably keen edge, and it was, in fact, by essentially this method (without blackboard) that Socrates so refined his own intellect and speech, to the rue and resentment of his victims. It is much cultivated today in England and America and fills a mountain of philosophical journals. The late J. L. Austin, from seminars at Oxford bearing such titles as "Puns and Riddles" (in which the only text was a dictionary) sent forth legions of young philosophers into the English-speaking colleges and universities, their minds honed to an edge capable of splitting out the most subtle distinctions of meaning imaginable and with the felicity of discourse that so agreeably reflects such a mind.

But my point surely remains, that through such a procedure no philosophical knowledge ever emerges, but only a type of wit and skill. The statements which are the data for such arguments are not even things that anyone for a moment supposes are true; such statements as, for example, that a certain man (usually "Jones") moved his hand, striking a match, causing the woods to burn down, and whatnot. The question is never whether any such thing actually happened; the question is only what things like that *mean*. And there is a perfectly plain sense in which an illiterate janitor knows quite well what they mean. He knows exactly what is being said if told that someone burned down the woods with a match, and he also knows quite exactly the circumstances under which such a thing would be true. He only lacks the wit and facility of language to spell it all out. A philosopher may not, therefore, on the basis of such exercises as this, pride himself on any knowledge that is denied to the vulgar, not even, I believed, on any additional power of good judgment or reason. His "knowledge" is only a knowledge of how to put what is known—or rather, generally believed—with fastidious precision.[2]

Ethics and Analysis

In contemporary ethics the method of argument is even simpler, and it is significant that here philosophers, with an air of modesty, sometimes seem to vie with each other in disclaiming philosophical wisdom with respect to things good and evil. The typical procedure is to set forth some fictitious situation—such as some professor's imagined neglect to return a borrowed book—and then consider "what we would say" concerning various features of this. Or sometimes questions having a semblance of ultimacy are put forth—such as, whether pleasure is a good, or the only good, whether there are right actions that exceed obligations, whether responsibility attaches to actions arising from ignorance of fact, and so on. But they are "answered" in the same way; namely, by eliciting "what we would say" about them. Now it is obvious that what we (whoever that is supposed to include) *would say* concerning anything under the sun is precisely what we happen already to believe about it. What turns out to be the final appeal here, then, is ordinary opinion, and opinion which was, moreover, settled before the inquiry even began. What this or that man would upon reflection *say* about this thing or that might, of course, be utterly foolish; but there is nothing in this type of procedure which would be likely to exhibit this, precisely because what "we would say," or in other words, what "we" happen rightly or wrongly to think, is itself the ultimate test of what ought to be said. The best that can be achieved by this approach is consistency; but of course the silliest discourse imaginable can be perfectly consistent throughout. It appears again, then, that by such argument no knowledge results, except the knowledge of what we already think, and the knowledge of how to put this clearly and consistently. It is almost too obvious to point out that no philosopher, by such a procedure, comes to know anything that is not just as well known by any decent civilized man, nor, even more obviously, does it make the heart any better—but of course it was never meant to do that.

Philosophical Refutation

While philosophical arguments evidently do not, then, lead to any knowledge of truth, it must nevertheless be conceded that there is one important use for them, and that is the refutation of error. They are thus used, and often used effectively and well, not only in philosophy but in science, law, and every area where reasoning occurs. If, for example, one shows that a given theory, principle or generalization of any sort—philosophical, legal, scientific or whatever—is inconsistent with itself, or with some generally accepted principle, or with some datum that is accepted as true, then the demonstration of this constitutes a philosophical argument. In a similar way it can sometimes be shown that certain positive (enacted) laws, for example, are inconsistent with each other, or with some superior law such as the Constitution, or that their effects are inconsistent with the purposes for which they were framed, and so on, and these demonstrations take the form of philosophical arguments. Again, philosophical arguments are sometimes applied to philosophical theories themselves, to show that such theories are inconsistent with themselves, or more commonly that their implications are inconsistent with certain facts that have been overlooked, and so on.

In this restricted sense, then, it cannot be denied that philosophical arguments sometimes do yield knowledge; namely, the knowledge of error. The discovery of error does not by itself, however, exhibit any positive truth. A man might know that ever so many things are false—and here again, Socrates comes to mind—and still not have the least idea what is the truth of things. And what I have been maintaining is that philosophical argument, so useful, sometimes, for the discovery of intellectual error, is by itself utterly useless for the discovery of truth; it can show what is *not* so, but never what is.[3]

Sapere Aude!

There remains, accordingly, wisdom. That not all philosophers possess it, or even love it, is a truism; but from another point of view a philosopher has surely failed, as a philosopher, if he utterly lacks it. The image of a philosopher who is at the same time a fool is in some ways droll, but from another point of view it is appalling.

There is nothing eternal about wisdom, though in a sense it is timeless. What was wisdom for the age of St. Thomas is perhaps not wisdom for us, but at the same time, the question whether this or that man's thought embodies philosophical wisdom is one in which time is usually no factor. Wisdom need not perish with the passage of time, nor does the succession of generations automatically add to it; one age can be as wise or as foolish as another, however far removed from each other they may be.

And what is it? What is this wisdom that philosophers, by their very name, are supposed to prize above every earthly honor or possession? It is, I think, what

Aristotle referred to as the exercise of *theoria*, which is a unique capacity of men and one which, alas! more or less slumbers throughout the lives of most of these, including even some who are learned. It is something that cannot be taught, cannot be conveyed even by fathers to sons, as Socrates repeatedly observed. It can therefore not be taught in a classroom, nor can one be certified in it by any examination or degree. Essentially it seems to me to be this: the power of seeing those things, great and small, needed for that kind of inner and outer life that Aristotle likened to the life of the gods, to which the eyes of most men seem closed. And philosophers, some of them, have certainly had this. It can, in fact, be claimed to be almost their unique possession, the one thing which they, more than any others, have really offered to the race of men. Story tellers, poets and artists have certainly possessed this perceptiveness, but in a very superficial way in comparison to philosophers. The truths that are embodied in philosophical wisdom cannot be proved, but only shown or displayed, the idea of evidence is out of place with respect to them, and such wisdom is therefore not ordinary knowledge. But it is something infinitely better, something far more precious than any fact or conclusion that one merely knows.

If one reads Descartes he is rewarded mainly by the instructiveness of his errors. Such works stand as a lasting reminder that an intellect so great can nevertheless get everything so terribly wrong, so utterly out of accordance with what actually exists, so fantastically unbelievable, in spite of the most elaborate precautions against error (immunity to doubt) that it is possible for one to erect. The same type of distortion runs through Spinoza, whose imposing demonstrations have not the strength of a feather. Yet between Spinoza's proofs—in the corollaries, notes and asides—there resides a priceless philosophical wisdom for anyone who can disregard the intellectual window dressing and see things as Spinoza saw them. Without this his philosophy would survive, if at all, only as a curiosity. His observations on self-love and the love of man, the bondage to the emotions, freedom, human nature, human well-being and so on, are so clearly independent of his ostensible "proofs" that the connections must be contrived; but they are nevertheless filled with reflections on what we see all the time, but their significance has so eluded us that it is as if we were without eyes. Some philosophers, recognizing the character of wisdom, have disclaimed any pretension to prove what they were saying. Epictetus addressed himself to his pupils in an epigrammatic, oracular style, enunciating how life, death, folly and moral virtue appeared to him, and illustrating with examples from the daily life that is familiar to everyone. Protagoras approached things in much the same way, and when Socrates asked him for an argument, Protagoras delivered a long speech, and a speech so wise, so perceptive of the ways of man and the world, that I believe it was partly lost even on Socrates. Protagoras denied, in fact, that there is any truth, and hence any proof of it; there is only better and worse, and it was his self-appointed mission to display what was better, drawing from what he saw going on around him. The same is found in the writings of William James, who similarly had a low view of truth as it is usually conceived in philosophy. He enjoyed jolting his readers by describing truth as "what works" and in terms of "cash value" and so on, and of course his critics found in him an easy target for refutation. It is difficult even now for students of philosophy to read his arguments without feeling pity for their inventor. Still, the thought of William James has endured while the refutations and even the names of his philosophical critics have been all but forgotten. The reason is that James's wisdom was genuine, and the knowledge of his critics was superficial. James looked at the same world we all look at, but he saw in it what most men go to their graves without seeing. He could describe the most commonplace situations, attitudes and feelings in a manner that the reader could see to be true, touching sometimes the deepest meanings of life, but it took the eye and mind of a James to see and record them. The special regard a man has for his own clothing, the act of will in climbing from a warm bed into a cold room, the delight one can derive from a smell that is bad, the concern a man has for the comforts of his home, the love of one's country, the simple sentiments of piety—things of this sort, some significant and some seemingly banal, were the grist of James's thought. In themselves they are neither rare, profound nor mysterious. We look at them without seeing much; James looked, and saw, and therein lies his incomparable worth as a philosopher.

Such philosophers are not exceptional, nor have I just picked out some few that I happen to admire. Most of the philosophers whose works have endured and have earned the title of "classics" have embodied wisdom in the sense that I have tried to adumbrate. Some philosophies, such as the paradoxes of Zeno, have gained fame primarily as intellectual curiosities and specimens of intriguing dialectic, to be sure, but this is what is exceptional. The greatest philosophical arguments that we still hold up to students to emulate have seldom made their way into posterity by their incisiveness alone. The dialectical acumen of a Hume or a Leibniz was an embellishment, almost a veneer, to the clearest and deepest knowledge of the world and could never have existed without it. The arguments of such thinkers—Hume's arguments for skepticism, for example—are sometimes hardly more than ingenious *tours de force*. They are not really studied with the purpose of deciding whether to embrace their conclusions, for men's opinions on things of importance are in fact never arrived at by that route. But Hume's reflections on morals, religious faith, human sentiments and passions exhibit truths that stand in need of no strained argumentation, and are in fact supported mostly by illustration drawn from the common experience of mankind.

Nor is wisdom just a thing of the past. One must be more than an acute thinker to be a wise man, but the two are not enemies. Wittgenstein's arguments, for instance, are sometimes so curious and puzzling that even his followers dispute what they are, and yet this great man intrigued his students, even wrought a "revolution in thought" according to some, largely by begging them to look at what it was they were saying instead of being obsessed with what followed from what they were saying. It was characteristic of him to say such things as "Don't think about it; *look* at it." *Theoria* of the very same kind is beautifully exhibited in the writings and talks of Gilbert Ryle, whose controversial fame is for this reason most assuredly well earned. Here is a man who adores puzzles, and one is hardly a philosopher who does not, but his thinking does not end in them, and he does not imagine that they settle anything. Indeed, when one occasionally runs across his papers of an earlier decade it is sometimes hard to believe their authorship, so far has he moved from the mere argument of then to the philosophical wisdom of now. The older things seem like curiosities hardly worth reading. His great work, *The Concept of Mind*, is an extensive description. Philosophical argument appears in it almost entirely destructively, intended to bury old prejudices, and is quite ancillary to the author's positive philosophical purpose. The great insights of the book, like those of James, are supported entirely by observations, mostly upon perfectly commonplace things, pile one upon another until the truth is virtually driven into the reader's skull—illustrating again the capacity of a wise man to see what fools, and even learned and subtle fools, can somehow only look at.

The enemy of wisdom is not so much ignorance as blindness and folly, and wisdom is nourished not by argument, but by curious wonder. It will never perish so long as there are perceptive minds that are deeply bewildered and honest, whatever may be the fates of the schools.

Notes

This article was composed at the request of students of the University of Rochester for circulation among themselves. The title is borrowed from McTaggart. Published in *Review of Metaphysics* 20 (1966).

1. *The Sacred Books of the East*, ed. F. Max Muller, vol. 39 (Oxford 1927), 113.

2. These remarks have been taken to mean that I think such philosophical activity is of trivial value, though in fact I assert the opposite. (The examples are drawn from my own writings, which I do not despise.)

3. The foregoing remarks altogether have been strangely taken by some to mean that I think, in agreement with some of its recent critics, that philosophy is a pretense. I have in fact claimed the opposite, that philosophy is the love of wisdom.

Philosophy Today

PAUL FEYERABEND

In a few words, the situation of philosophy today is as follows.
Philosophy has ceased to exist as an intellectual enterprise without limits that examines special professions, changes them, tames them, puts them in their place, and it has become a special profession itself. This profession may deal with some of the problems of its ancestor, it may analyze them in detail, and with considerable skill. What is missing is an overall purpose that connects the problems with the rest of knowledge and of human life, that defines their "location" in the kingdom of thought, their importance (or the lack of it), and that might lead to a reform of traditional procedures.

The absence of such a purpose is not surprising for the professors who are now running the business are not, and cannot be philosophers. They are illiterate, provincial, without a sense of perspective, too concerned with their reputation (and their salaries—a topic very dear to *my* heart) to be capable of arriving an an independent judgment.

Their pupils are not likely to reverse the trend, they have been trained to regard the shortcomings of their masters as virtues, and so they now confound narrowness with depth, illiteracy with professional excellence (just remember how proud a logician is when he can say "I do not understand this"), lack of perspective with either profound commitment or, if they belong to a different school, with an honest regard for (particulars and for) the truth.

Nor is there any hope that pseudosubjects such as "black philosophy," or "philosophy from the point of view of the liberated woman" are going to improve the situation. First of all, these subjects still have all the drawbacks of their orthodox rivals (illiteracy does not cease to be illiteracy when practiced by blacks, or by women, nor does a change of perspective compensate for the lack of it). Secondly, because they are so nicely "integrated" into the status quo that they are not likely to lead to decisive changes (the situation is here not different from the effects or, rather, the non-effects of "integration" on a larger scale).

A citizen interested in the revival of philosophy thus cannot rely on the existing institutions (which at any rate become more and more similar to business enterprises). Nor will he be so conceited to believe that he can change the world all by himself, that he has the imagination to invent the necessary ideas and the strength, and perseverance to make them real. To get his ideas, he will turn to the past. He will study the work of individuals such as Pherekydes, Hesiod, Plato down to Brecht and Ayn Rand and the anonymous myths of literate and illiterate societies. And to increase his strength, he will assemble, or will join a circle of friends of similar inclination whose minds are not paralyzed by professional standards and whose jobs leave them time to do anything they want. Such a circle should not be held together by intellectual interests alone, intellectual interests should play a minor part, just as they do in a complete life. They should appear and disappear as naturally as any topic appears and disappears in an animated conversation that ranges from the personal to the abstract, from the profound to the trivial to the ridiculous to the abstract, and back to the personal again. Not principles, but the free interplay of affection and interests (in food, movies, ideas) should be the binding force of such a group—or else we are back where we started from, we have another religion, another "school of thought," not the beginning of a new form of life. (It is better to be united by a liking for the Marx Brothers than by a "profound concern for justice.") I do not know of any such group today though I know some people who by casually drifting together might form one. Nor am I sure that these people will like what I am going to say. Still, I am talking to them, and not to the professionalist.

Philosophy was once concerned with *comprehensive views* of the world, the position of man in it, his physical makeup, his hopes, his possibilities, his obligations. Such views might be inherited and traditional, as were the views of the Greek Epic, or the views of the Dogon, or they might be invented and revolutionary like the views of the Presocratics, of Plato, of Brecht. Most of the time the distinction is just a matter of degree. The important point is that each particular enterprise, each profession, however powerful and advanced, each personal opinion, however attractive and self-evident, each individual *is compared with, and has to measure up to, something outside itself.*

This comparison is not a one way process. The rise of new classes, new forms of life, the physical, moral, intellectual results of wars, migrations, discoveries do not leave the general standards unchanged but lead to their most penetrating criticism. It is interesting to see how the heroic morality of the Greek Epic gradually gives way to a more humanitarian point of view and how this development influences, and is in turn influenced by, a conscious examination of the values of the heroic age. The examination ranges from the mockery of the "Milesian tales" to the broad surveys of the tragedians to the aggressive *intellectual* criticism of Xenophanes, and it creates a series of new and fascinating subjects. Tragedy, lyric poetry, the rationalism of Xenophanes, and of the Ionian philosophers of Nature, mathematics, astronomy are all the by-products of this interaction between *general standards* that *set examples* for the life of society and *concrete developments* that *constitute it.*

The interaction is recognized as a driving force by Plato, but Plato like all rationalists after him tries to *tame* the force by subjecting it to the jurisdiction of a debate between reasonable men. The debate is open, it admits any view, makes use of any method that seems appropriate through the discovery of the peculiar character of mathematical concepts (*Phaedo* 74aff) and the hypothesis that the concepts of justice and of the good might be structures in a similar way *temporarily* (*Statesman* 294b/c) restricts its scope. The debate is supposed to *direct* the fate of man in an orderly way rather than exposing him to the accidents of history, of talent, of the inventions of individuals. but it still contains the general side by side with the specific and permits either of the two components to influence the other.

A most interesting example of this interaction between general philosophical principles and methods of research in restricted fields is astronomy. Plato makes fun of the empirical astronomers of his time who "examine the proportions of day and night and their relation to the month, and that of the month to the year and of the other stars to these and to one another." He wants an abstract theory dealing with "the real speed and the real slowness, in their true measurements, and in all their true forms." "In fact," he says "we shall pursue astronomy just as we do geometry by making use of problems, *and we shall leave the phenomena of the heavens alone.*" The change is not suggested to adapt astronomy to the "professional standards" of geometry and thus to make it more "scientific." It is suggested "to make the right use of the inherent intelligence of the soul" that is, to make the right use of *man* and thus to *improve* him (*Rep.* 53aff; cf. *Lgg* 818c). This "humanitarian" suggestion played an essential role in the rise of a theoretical astronomy, it is responsible for the tremendous difference that exists between the highly developed "empirical" astronomy of the Babylonians and the astronomy of the Greeks, and it determined the path of astronomy for centuries to come (cf. Simplicius *de coelo* 451c).

"Humanitarian" influences in special fields are not restricted to antiquity. They occur wherever curious, critical, and imaginative individuals strike out on a new path and make new discoveries. *Ernst Mach* believed that Newtonian mechanics had ceased to be fruitful, he was convinced that it had started to become a hindrance of progress and he thought that it should be viewed as a temporary scheme for the ordering of data of a particular type rather than as a *conditio sine qua non* of rational understanding. The accepted forms of thought such as absolute space, absolute time, the boundary between "objective" matter and "subjective" sensations were not necessary for explaining its success and they were highly questionable in themselves. So he envisaged a science that would either yield them as a *result* of research rather than *presupposing* them in every single piece of research, or that would show them to be entirely *illusory*. Mach's science was very different from the science of the realists who rejected it (even Lenin did not realize its dialectical nature), from the science of the positivists who bowdlerized it and turned it into a series of slogans as well as from the day-to-day bread-and-butter science of the Newtonians. Mach was not unduly worried by this conflict between his ideal and the science of the day. "It appears" he writes in reply to a particularly violent attack "that physicists are on the way of founding a church; they are already using a church's traditional weapons. To this I answer simply: ... I decline with thanks the communion of the faithful. *I prefer freedom of thought.*" In the twentieth century Mach's Utopianism led to important developments and changed some sciences beyond recognition. And yet our philosophers of science fulminate against all Utopianism and insist on an analysis, or a "logical reconstruction" of the *status quo*. None of them would ever dream of changing science to preserve freedom of thought. Specialism overrules humanitarian considerations and prevents fundamental changes in the special professions themselves. For this is the paradox of professionalism: *fundamental* improvements are possible only if one is prepared to proceed in a thoroughly unprofessional way.

A most interesting feature of Plato's philosophy is his attention to *style*. It is fair to say that contemporary philosophers at their best have no style at all. At any rate—they never consider the matter, they unconsciously drift into some jargon which then pervades everything—their writings, their lectures, their conversations, their jokes. Plato for whom philosophy was an ever-changing enterprise, a continuous debate, was aware of the difficulties that arise when one "freezes" the process by putting it on paper. He experiments, he tries different methods to capture the *intellectual motion* that is essential to every interesting discussion. He is lighthearted, frivolous, loquacious in one dialogue, tightlipped, serious, controlled in another. He recognizes that some things cannot be said, not even in a debate, but must be insinuated with the help of images, and he uses fairytales, myths, to do the job. He changes his style from libretto to treatise back to libretto, and he does this consciously, for he comments on the changes, and he tries to explain them (*Phileb.* 23b; *Theait.* 143b). He abhors jargon and useless precision ("To use words and phrases in an easygoing way without scrutinizing them too curiously is not in general, a mark of ill breeding; on the contrary, there is something lowbred in being too precise"—*Theait.* 184c) and then he explains the shortcomings of a written account: "You know Phaedrus, that is the strange thing about writing, which makes it truly analogous to painting. The painter's products stand before us as though they were alive, but if you question them, they maintain a most majestic silence. It is the same with written words; they seem to talk to you as though they were intelligent, but if you ask them anything about what they say, from a desire to be instructed, they go on telling you just the same thing forever" (*Phaedrus* 275d—compare this with the attitude of our professors who read even when they are supposed to talk, for example, when explaining their "ideas" at a *conference*: burying their heads in voluminous manuscripts they mumble sentences and phrases no one in his right mind would ever think of using in a conversation.) He contrasts the "living speech" of a debate with the "dead discourse" of a book (276a) which offers not wisdom, "but only its semblance" (275a). For the writer there arises then the task to find a style that captures this "living speech" and makes the "semblance" approach reality. Here is the reason for the asides, the concrete details, the loose ends which are excellent and superbly used stage props for showing the transitory character of a vigorous exchange of opinions. (The only modern scientist who was aware of the problem, and who tried to solve it by a special, quasi-historical way of presenting the results of his research, was Niels Bohr.) Every subject can enter the debate and, entering it, it loses its definiteness, it becomes problematic, it dissolves before our very eyes.

If we want to find modern writers who come close to this manner of presenting things we must turn not to the philosophers but to the *poets*—we must turn to Goethe, Hoelderling and Kleist, to Kierkegaard and Tolstoy, to Ibsen and Brecht. Like Plato these writers move from reality to the page and back to reality. Like Plato they breath life into their written accounts by exploring the possibilities of language and by bending language to their purpose (Kleist spent about the same amount of time on the first sentence of his *Michael Kohlacs* as Plato is reported to have spent on the first sentence of the *Republic* which sets the scene and has nothing to do with the argument.) But there is one decisive difference which anticipates the later degeneration of philosophy. Plato puts all his efforts into the attempt to understand the world "rationally" which in his case means: through the medium of a *debate* while the poets are much less convinced of the power of reason and want to get some insight into its scope and its limitations. Plato saw the problem as is shown by his use of myths, fairytales, stories right in the center of a rigorous argument. He seems to have realized that the rationalist account and, for that matter, all ideologies have limitations and that they must be examined by examining the effect of concepts on material that is not yet obviously ordered with their help. He is not content with knowing how ideas look when contemplated in isolation, or when compared with other ideas, nor is he satisfied with knowing their function in abstract games (arguments, derivations, proofs) only. He wants to know the effect which an idea has when it is embedded into the real world with its loose ends, strange connections, whimsical inhabitants. And as he cannot impose, or withdraw ideas at will, he must construct *models* (plays, stories, myths) where the interaction between idea and "life" can be studied at leisure: the "aesthetic" elements in Plato, far from being mere embroideries, or unintended (and, perhaps, unwanted) side effects of his "poetic" temperament (Wilamowitz) have a most important *theoretical* function: they set the stage for an examination of the doctrine of rationalism and of other, and even more narrow doctrine.

The method of examining a set of abstract ideas, an ideology, by *embedding* it into a model of "real life" and studying the tensions that arise in the model is employed by the Ionian philosophers of nature, by early historians such as Hekataeus, it is developed into a marvelous art by the founders of tragedy who expand the models, make them complex and almost as rich as "life itself" (cf. von Fritz, *Antike und Moderne Tragoedie* [Berlin: De Gruyter, 1962]) and by later playwrights such as Ibsen and Ayn Rand, and it is refined by comedy writers from Aristophanes to Brecht (theory) and Kauffman and Hart (practice) until a *single line*, a well placed joke suffices to explode an entire world view. To my mind this is the highest achievement of the whole tradition. It criticizes, it enlightens, it prepares improvement not by laborious arguments and droning sermons but by entertaining one-liners and it never relies on a profundity that turns nice guys into raving maniacs and makes intelligent people look like bedwetting imbeciles (remember how much a person who has just gained some "deep insight" resembles a child who has just wet his bed). Yet this glorious achievement can no longer be claimed for philosophy. The reason is that philosophy after Plato moves in an entirely different direction. Let me enumerate some of the steps that lead from the vivid debates of the Platonic circle to the dreary papers of the school "philosophers" of today.

The first step is the elimination of mythology. A philosopher *thinks*; he does not tell stories. He pursues the Truth; he does not entertain. Rationalism ceases to be a special doctrine that is embedded in a wider context and it becomes a universal medium of discourse. Secondly, this medium is transformed from an open debate into an exchange of standardized arguments: myth and open debate were signs of the "impotence of thought" (*Hegel Geschichte der Philosophie* Vol. II [Glockner Vol. 18], 188) and *not* of a wider perspective. Thought is developed and takes over everything. There arise then the magnificent cathedrals of the scholastics which succeed in accommodating even the principles of faith. This is the third stage. Fourthly, these cathedrals break up into special subjects which follow rules of their own and resent any outside interference. Philosophy keeps its name, even its function, but it changes its scope. Next comes the transition to analysis (the stages overlap, there are other developments as well, and there are always irregular and original thinkers who do not fit into any historical scheme). Instead of *changing* and *improving* a subject, philosophy now just *comments* on it, "analyzes" it. This is due to a rise of science and the defeat of earlier constructive proposals; many subjects went their own way, and the philosophers wanted to be on the safe side: analysis is a philosophy of defeat dressed up as a revolutionary movement. The specialist ideology which is by now in full bloom demands that philosophy, in order to qualify as a subject, must have special methods and a special lingo. So special methods of analysis and special languages make their appearance. Removed from the control of history (history of philosophy is just another special subject that is only loosely connected with the rest of philosophy) and invented out of the blue (many "analytic" philosophers believe that philosophy proper started with Wittgenstein, or Quine, or Strawson, or with some other midget of twentieth century "thought") these methods are often quite infantile when compared with their predecessors, and so are the debates about them (Austin against Ayer on sense data)—but nobody realizes this, and so it becomes possible to use illiteracy as a weapon for threatening those who want to make things a little more interesting: analysis is also an illiterate philosophy dressed up as a universal measure-stick of sense and rigor. (The answer to the logician who says "I do not understand this, I do not comprehend that" is: "Well, get a better education!") Attention gradually moves from an analysis of special subjects (such as science) to an analysis of the instruments for the analysis of special subjects. The break between philosophy and the rest has become complete. Even those who oppose concept-pushing and who are convinced that something has been left out silently identify rationalism with articulate speech and thus see themselves forced to promote stammering and absurdity—many forms of "mysticism" (but *not* the mysticism of Meister Eckhard) and "existentialist" irrationalism (but *not* the irrationalism of Kierkegaard) are impossible without a firm but unrealized commitment to some principles of the despised ideology. Add to this the transformation of all subjects into professions which are run according to strict business standards, the increasing emphasis on "teaching" where teaching means: giving a jazzed-up account of third-hand versions of the results of someone else's effort without having an inkling of that effort itself as well as the resulting ignorance of us professors (most so-called "teachers" now "explain" and, of course, "criticize" the "Thought of Plato" without knowing a word of Greek and without having the faintest idea of the historical and social conditions of the time)—and you have the picture with which I started: Philosophy has ceased to exist as an intellectual enterprise without limits that examines special professions, changes them, tames them, puts them in their place, and it has become a special profession itself, even a business that is run by illiterate and provincial practitioners. Can it be revived? And how can it be revived?

I do not think it can be revived from the *inside*. Being well paid and respected by his profession, being encouraged by the institutions of which he is a part, being admired and/or feared by his students, being advanced when he plays the game, kept in the same place, or fired, when he does not—why should the contemporary dealer in philosophical goods mend his ways and learn new things? (I, for one, am much too lazy to do anything that drastic.) So, the revival must come from other quarters. For the children of white upper middle class parents it must come from small circles of friends who have the time, the energy, the motivation to either reject or, what is even better, to simply *bypass* the *status quo* (live and let die:) and who have also sufficient reserves of joy and good humor to escape the dangers of self-righteousness. Is there any advice that we can give to those heralds of the future? I think there is.

To my mind the first and most important step is to reverse the trend and to revive alternative traditions such as the tradition of Plato, of Aristophanes, of the wise men of illiterate societies, and so on. Ideas do not come out of the blue and those which do are hardly worth mentioning. Ideas are the results of long developments, they occur and have meaning only to those who belong to some *tradition*. The first step therefore demands that we familiarize ourselves with some alternatives of the scientifico-democratic rationalism of today. And "familiarizing oneself with a tradition" does not mean reading fifth-hand accounts written by busy and ignorant compilers of fourth-hand accounts, it means studying the *original sources* (documents, institutions, societies) and trying to restore in one's imagination the form of life that produced the sources and gave them content. For example, there is no way of making up one's mind about Plato outside the domain of classical scholarship and, indeed, the best, the most imaginative, the most "relevant" analyses of Greek Thought have been written by classical scholars such as Rhode, Wilamowitz, Murray, Cornford, Snell, von Fritz, and, of course, Nietzsche. Replacing Plato with a translation, or with a paraphrase is not very different from replacing human contact with television. One continues to breathe, one continues to speak, but one cannot be sure that one does so because one is still alive.

In other cases the situation is exactly the same. One must learn the language, one must study the institutions, one must, if possible, *participate* in the forms of life one wants to consider in order to be able to judge those effects on thought, will, emotion which do not occur in written accounts and which cannot occur in them, for "methodological" as well as for personal reasons. What we want, after all, are not alternative *descriptions*, or alternative *arguments*, what we want are alternative *experiments of living*—and here everyone must decide for himself. *Learning* must be given the widest possible scope, it must become part of one's existence rather than preparing a professional competence that is part of an otherwise empty life. It is no use proclaiming a "radical" or a "black" philosophy when all one has to offer is another course at a university. Ethnic groups have the tremendous advantage of being united by a common interest that is a much stronger binding force than the interests of even the most dedicated intellectuals. *But a common interest is not a culture.* Being without a culture, a common interest can neither conquer despair nor escape the "new opportunities" of an "integration" that takes it for granted that what everybody wants most is being white and upper middle class. Ethnic groups thus have to revive their traditions just as we must revive ours. If there is to be a "Black philosophy" then it must be developed from a knowledge of African languages, African institutions, one must be ready and willing to base one's life, *one's whole life* and not just a little part of it on myth and magic rather than on reason and science and not a single element of contemporary Western culture must be permitted to pass without the most painstaking examination. Science must lose its ideological preeminence and the separation of state and church must be supplemented with the separation of state and science which means that children should be able to choose between instruction in science and instruction in magic just as they can now choose between instruction in methodism, catholocism, or no religious instruction at all. "Integration" which prevents a full and genuine recovery of ethnic traditions must be circumvented, or changed. Such an activity that restores old forms of life, old languages, old ways of thinking, that restores their original shape rather than their modern reflections, uses all resources of mankind, thought, imagination, argument, dreams, hallucinatory events, playacting, science, magic will not only revive philosophy, it will also return to us a humanity which we lost when we permitted ourselves to be run by the professionals and when we started taking it for granted that aggressive concept-pushing is the peak of human achievement. We, the products of Western culture who did not have to look on when foreign invaders killed our traditions but who did this job ourselves have a rather simple task before us. All that is needed is a little curiosity, a little affection for one's fellow man and a sense of perspective. But the very simplicity of the task makes it also most difficult, for what intellectual is prepared to trade a three-volume systematic treatise for a one-liner "on the same subject"? Indeed, the task would be absolutely hopeless were it not for a few people who just *might* be interested in the exchange and whose good sense and laughter might one day put an end to that nightmare called "contemporary thought."

Note

This paper has not been published previously. [Note added 2012.]

A Way to Philosophy

EVA BRANN

1. The Enterprise

At the present time the word philosophy is used to name a discipline which is one among many and which has, as do the others, formulated results, pre-set problems and articulable methods. I think no one would question that philosophy so understood can be taught.

But there is also an old, original meaning which I would like to recall. The word philosophy literally means *the love of wisdom*. I would like to avoid here the burden of argument entailed by this recollection, which is: To show that there is such a passion and such an object for it. Instead I want to take the word in a way which is at once practical and appropriate to schools: As the desire to reflect while learning, as a wish to look behind, beyond, beneath the matter in hand; or, concisely and negatively, as an aversion to being unaware of one's ground. Note that I am not intending to describe curiosity (the avidity for novelties) or critique (the project of evaluating whatever has been proposed).

So interpreted, it goes without saying that philosophy is the kind of shadow enterprise, suffused over and hardly separable from other undertakings, which is not directly teachable. But philosophy can perhaps be elicited. I shall, then, in the context of this volume pose myself the project of setting out the sketch of a somewhat practical plan for eliciting philosophy in institutions of learning. I shall depend for the formulations of this project at least in part on my own experience in the program at St. John's College in Annapolis.

Now the question whether the attempt to elicit philosophy should be made at all is a prime consideration *within* a philosophical setting. But it is one which no convert to the cause would consent to discuss before that setting had come into being, especially if the answer is meant to have a practical consequence, for instance that of abandoning the undertaking. Therefore the beginning must be abrupt. Unless a favorable setting has already been established, the most practical procedure is, without publishing any plans or premises, resolutely to subvert some class to the enterprise. Almost any class is suitable, as long as it is not one in which students were promised instruction directed toward competence immediately connected with their livelihood. Most students have enough of a philosophical propensity so that, though they may be surprised at this use of their scheduled time, they will not be offended.

2. The Texts

The problem now becomes: What to do in this class. The way I have formulated the enterprise might suggest that a fresh and thoughtful spirit would engender philosophy on any subject matter and that no special matter is needed. This must be true in principle, for philosophical learning is at bottom nothing but live learning. But it fails in practice, for very mundane reasons. When people meet regularly at scheduled times, they will not often be able to find a good beginning unless they have a prepared matter in common. Furthermore, in view of the mediocrity of our intellect it is practically indispensable to have a guide in the effort of reflection. Some help is therefore needed to prevent the occasion from being casual and the conversation, which is its object, from turning in tedious circles. That help is to be found in good texts.

One particular misgiving concerning the use of texts deserves consideration. It is patent that the study of books, which means the appropriation of the opinion of others, respectable though they may be, is in several ways seriously at odds with the enterprise of reflection, the attempt to think for and upon oneself. But again this question, which concerns the relation of learning to tradition, is profitably raised only within the tradition, which is to say within a setting in which thought and study have some sort of *de facto* compatibility. The participants in this enterprise must first "take up and read," then question the value of reading.

It follows that the texts which are intended to be the instigators of thought and guides into otherwise inaccessible depths should be such that students will be compelled (perhaps after an initial period of aversion) to give them respect and even to impute superiority of intellect and imagination to their authors.

There is one apparently obvious criterion for choosing such texts which will not, in fact, turn out to work very well, namely that of "primary" against "secondary." The reason is that most books, whether written in a spirit of critique or, more rarely, of approval, are about previous books and therefore in an important sense commentaries. So, for instance, one might argue that *Northanger Abbey* is a commentary on *The Mysteries of Udolpho*, or, seriously, that Galileo's *Dialogue Concerning the Two Chief World Systems* is a commentary on Aristotle's *On the Heavens*, a book which is in fact almost a participant in the conversation.

There is, however, a criterion which is more usable because it is less external: The texts should be original, in the double sense of being the result of the author's own thought and of presenting the pursuit of a matter to its very origins. Texts of this underivative sort usually reveal themselves by the manner of their composition long before the student has gone very far in penetrating them: They are so subtly and artfully woven that the reader sees inexhaustibly many avenues to their meaning without losing faith that there *is* a meaning.

But by and large it must be an act of trust, of perfectly reasonable trust, in the opinions of literate mankind to find and establish a working list of such texts. That is to say, the teacher will begin by looking to that very accessible corpus of books of secular reputation often referred to as "the tradition." This does not mean that there might not be good texts that are practically unknown (for instance a colleague's unpublished work), but only that their existence is less likely and their discovery is very difficult.

Texts of the sort described differ from textbooks and other derivative works in one way essential to the enterprise. They most further the inquiry while least obtruding themselves upon it. They do this because, contrary to most textbooks, they do not present themselves as covering a pre-determined field or treating a pre-set problem. Good texts rarely prejudge the first questions concerning the division of knowledge, but come before the students simply as reputable writings. And because they do not take their subject matter as given, because they so often begin by distinguishing their realm of inquiry and justifying that distinction, they further original inquiry—this is only one of several ways in which the tradition proves to be the best antidote to indoctrination. To give examples: Is Newton's work called the *Mathematical Principles of Natural Philosophy* a work of "mathematics," of "philosophy," of "physics" or of "theology"? Is *War and Peace* a work of "literature" or of "history"? The cause of reflection requires that these questions should be allowed to arise, and with them the inquiry into the meaning of these words.

Now on the very hypothesis underlying our choice, which is that the authors chosen know how to begin their work and how to secure the reader's understanding (or to put it another way, that they are truly elementary), the order in which the books are read should not be of the essence. There are, to be sure, two naturally given serial orders even in the absence of any classification by subject matter, namely those determined by the order of their publication, taken either forwards or backwards.

If the readings are to begin with contemporary authors, the teacher will first face the difficulty of choosing a text, because of the recent proliferation of printed matter and because of the absence of an established, and perhaps even of a nascent tradition of mutually responsive books of high quality. In this situation it makes a certain sense to ask the students whether they think they know some appropriate book with which to begin. The discussion of this book is then very apt to consist of penetrating the shield of its seeming familiarity in order to reveal the assumptions on which the work rests. Students may well find that these premises, whether idly inherited or knowingly appropriated by the author, seem astonishingly uncongenial to them. The enterprise may then turn into that of following the spoor of these assumptions backward to their sources. In those frequent cases where a modern book takes the stance of resistance or liberation, these sources will often be found in those very earlier teachings which are being denied; such books carry on the tradition in the mode of deeply engaged contradiction. An example: among the truly admirable modern texts is one—not long ago there were always some students who knew it—by Camus, called "On Absurd Reasoning," which begins with these words: "There is but one truly serious philosophical problem and that is suicide." The work itself ensures that the reader will wonder how much absorption and rejection of tradition goes into the asking of this purportedly "primordial" question, and from this wonder immediately follows the back-tracking I have outlined. In Camus's case it can surely only end with the very beginnings of the philosophic tradition.

If, on the other hand, the order of reading begins with early texts, students will at first feel a probably salutary shock at the brusquely remote unfamiliarity of their utterances and concerns. Here the teacher will do most by displaying an uncompromising expectation that these works will be treated as if they were close to us. Sometimes it will help to show how their forbiddingly simple and staid language is peculiarly adequate to spirited and subtle depth. Sometimes it will help to draw attention to an apparent contradiction. For example, to students who first read Homer, he seems so remote that they respond by disoriented talk about "the Greeks" and "their gods," an opaque and indifferent lot. Here the teacher might draw attention to the tale of Ares and Aphrodite caught up in unwillingly public and prolonged embrace by the net of the lame husband, and ask why *human* affairs of this sort are always treated gravely and delicately, and only the gods' affairs hilariously and scurrilously. The discussion concerning the gods then often becomes perhaps no less inconclusive, but far more charged with human significance.

3. The Teacher

In a setting in which it cannot be the teacher's task to impart knowledge (not to speak of "information"), what will he do? His work is clearly that of a solicitous guide, and it seems to me to have two chief aspects.

The teacher must first of all have and creditably display trust in the enterprise. It must be clear that he is not a wraith wandering unwilling far from the realms of action, power, competence or wealth, but in some moderate and therefore reliable continuous way a lover of learning. This character alone can give him the authority to institute and continue the proceedings I am describing.

The second aspect complements the first. The teacher will have to accumulate a fund of discoveries, even a modest treasury of revelations, with which to back this trust and to mediate between difficult texts and willing students.

In brief: the teacher must be a learner-in-chief (so to speak) who has learned, is learning and will learn alongside as well as somewhat ahead of his students. Indeed it must always be somewhat ambiguous whom a teacher is ultimately serving, himself or them. This observation has special force in view of the horrid dangers facing the studentless scholar, chief of which is that of producing a stream of answers to which there are no questions.

This kind of teaching cannot help but raise a difficulty for the teacher as a member of the scholarly profession. Just as philosophy as a way is frequently at odds with philosophy as an established subject, so learning and learnedness, inquiry and research are often mutually exclusive. I think a teacher of the sort I am describing had best forego all plans for rising in his profession, merely maintaining himself within it by meeting its reasonable requirements. Nonetheless a teacher must write, and write to be read by his students and his friends and his friends' friends. For it is not only necessary to the teacher to articulate and circulate his thoughts and discoveries and to have a project which will carry intellectual satisfaction analogous to those of productive craftsmanship. It is also vital to the enterprise that the repudiation of exclusive competence, which is after all intended to promote greater thoroughness at the roots, should not degenerate into evanescent dilettantism.

Furthermore, it seems to me especially important for that teaching which rouses and guides a common inquiry that a teacher should articulate his thoughts. For once students have persuaded themselves that the search is serious and has a desirable object, the time will certainly come when they will round on the senior member to ask, "Now what do *you* think?" And again, that response is best and leaves the inquiry most alive, which is most straightforward. And that is for the teacher to say with candor and clarity what he does think, whether he has a "theory" to offer or a reasonable formulation of doubts and difficulties. But that he has, or is about to have, one or the other is a precondition of presuming to teach at all, for a defensible view of matters is the proof that anyone has completed some small part of his studies. Furthermore, just as questioning cannot be empty, so listening cannot be lax, or superior leaning-back. For the teacher must be intent on grasping the thought intended in the student's words and must listen—contrary, I believe, to current wisdom—to the student's reasonable speech, and not to the student himself. This means that the teacher must, except at some felicitous moments, assiduously suppress most observations concerning the origins, upbringing, sex, mood and capacities of members of the class. I think I know from experience that students would rather have their thoughts attentatively opposed than their persons indiscriminately cherished.

It would be an error, I think, to accept or dismiss this way as "Socratic." Socrates is displayed in the Platonic dialogues as being only ironically a philosopher, if a philosopher is one who loves wisdom as he lacks it; in comparison to those about him he is shown as a man already wise who asks questions in the light of very high, perhaps complete knowledge. Furthermore his conversation is appropriate to the true leisure of a free life rather than to the simulated leisure of a school. The way I am proposing—not a method, only a mode—is much less demanding and exceptional. It requires of the teacher only a certain readiness of disposition and a moderate keenness of intellect.

One first and last requirement: A teacher should try not to talk too much, and if that proves impossible, at least not dogmatically.

4. The Students

The central figures in the teacher's effort are the students and they are, happily, I think, the given of the enterprise; they are to be taken as they come, provided only that they can, in a narrow sense, read, write, and do algebra—and that they have come to school by their own desire.

In particular, it is no drawback to the class if some members are rather simple-minded, perhaps even apparently dense. There is often a positive profit to the class in invincible, and therefore incorruptible, intellectual innocence. Let me give an example, not untypical, from life.

A class has just completed a discussion of a corollary to Newton's laws of motion which implies the notion of the center of gravity of a system of bodies as that point at which the combined masses of its bodies can be considered to be located. A certain student, who does not have a reputation for cleverness to maintain, asks: Why then, if a bullet passes to the right of another to the left of me such that the point where both masses can be considered to be located passes right through my heart, don't I drop dead?—a question more easily ridiculed than answered, and in this instance the beginning of a worthwhile discussion concerning the objects of mathematical physics.

A certain necessary homogeneity should then arise in the class through self-selection, rather than by selection directed toward great similarity of preparation or even ability. So also the variety requisite to the conversation may come rather from the student's own natures than from any deliberate composition by age, sex, social class or race. In a classroom those differences of view which emerge among people (who might be externally quite similar) as a consequence of their different inner natures as a rule turn out to be, if more subtle, yet more deep-lying and persistent than those which stem from grossly apparent distinctions like sex and race. Nonetheless, that way is ever best which least prejudices the matter, and so a mixed group is very desirable, provided it can be gotten without yielding to the destructive strain of external pressure.

Now as candor is a teacher's obligation with respect to the intellect, so guile seems to me to be often required where pedagogy is concerned. So for instance with very young students a teacher must cultivate a sort of clear-eyed obtuseness, by which their personal animosities are resolutely misinterpreted as differences of opinion, obstreperousness as high-spiritedness, obtuseness as valuable simplicity. And, of course, it helps if a teacher knows how to, "look sadly when he means merrily," to use a phrase describing the irony of Thomas More, a great teacher.

But the chief occasion for a certain suppleness is that which is at the heart of this kind of teaching: the asking of good questions. Such questions will be most often of three kinds, all implicated with each other. The first will be addressed to the student: What do you mean?; the second to the text: What does it mean?; and the third to the beings in question: What, how, why are they? It goes without saying that questions well-asked are not merely disguised directives or solicitations of certain responses, though most students see that in order to ask well a teacher must have "something in mind." Consequently they see that it is a just response for them to turn on a question and after exposing it as a premise to substitute a truer question of their own.

If it does not matter so very much where students come from, it matters very much on what terms and whether they stay. There are many students, sometimes the finest, who wholly approve and respect the enterprise and are yet drawn away from it, not so often into other university studies as into "real life." In part they are simply possessed by a young, spirited and entirely sympathetic desire for adventure, for which the cure is to go and seek it, and come back the wiser. Unfortunately for everyone's peace of mind, this natural desire is often propounded in the language of "experiences," which are thought of as being a kind of vividly immediate counter-education, in competition with the remote book-learning of schools. Similarly, the restless but perfectly sound thirst for deeds is often represented as opposition between "abstract" theory, absorbing as it may be, and action which is considered urgent and obligatory.

It is not very likely that arguments will overcome such a disposition to leave, or listlessly to remain. Not only is it too much aided and abetted by current opinion, but the arguments themselves are difficult to make. Some will be based on untransferable experience with the "realness" of life and the "abstractness" of the theory or on notoriously unpersuasive prudential considerations. The better arguments will be too intricate for the immediate purpose, for they will consist of carefully demonstrating that these oppositions rest on assumptions which students themselves find unacceptable, and that the results of acting in accordance with them are often self-defeating. Nonetheless, these arguments ought to be patiently made, first for future reference, so that students may have them at hand when the time comes, and second, to convince them of the teacher's conviction. For the rest, it seems best to urge students not to go without completing the work in hand, and then to wish them well.

What is *both* feasible and important is to see that the enterprise is in no way compromised by this centrifugal disposition which the world fosters. Reflective learning should be accepted as an overwhelmingly absorbing way of life. It is in spirit compatible both with the hard and involuntary work that many students must do to support themselves and with voluntary service; it ought to be graced with frequent entertainment and invigorated by regular sports, and it certainly should have action as one end—true action which prevails. But I can imagine no practical project conceived as a part of this undertaking which would be anything but a camouflaged diversion. Students should study, first and last.

5. The Issues

In a setting which is intended to be such that nothing human is alien to it, students will naturally air their current preoccupations.

These "issues," pervasive and almost mandatory concerns, seem to me quite distinct from the perennial human questions such as: What is human, what is good, what is a world, what is being? It is with respect to these passing issues that students differ, if they differ at all, from decade to decade. It would be a work of supererogation to detail once again what these preoccupations currently are, so I will refer only to those aspects which have a special bearing on the enterprise under discussion.

To begin with, there is a sort of obligatory doubt, a disposition to use the forms of inquiry as modes of attack, and to transform the asking of questions into "questioning" (the positive complement to which is "creativity"). This riotous Cartesianism has for its chief object commonly accepted goods, which are for this purpose denominated "values." The chief datum, replacing nature and the political community, is "the system" or "society," which poses "problems" but resists necessary change.

To question values, become creative, fight the system, solve social problems and produce social change are the perfectly honest concerns which students bring to school out of the world. They are, unfortunately, singularly inept for radical inquiry.

This judgment is, at least to begin with, quite separate from questions of acquiescence or resistance to our condition. To be sure, students are quick to see and to point out to each other that the true questions "What is it?" or "Why do you think so?" have a preserving character in so far as they intend to honor the matter in question with attention. Furthermore, the trusting use of texts means that the possibility of authority is imputed to something out of the past. But neither of these factors is unequivocally either conservative or subversive. In fact, the enterprise carries with it no particular political persuasion except perhaps the admittedly powerful one that thought must precede action.

What is amiss is rather that these issues so put forth are overwhelmingly fraught with unrecognized academic presuppositions. To use an ugly word, the views of many students, often the brightest, are extremely "theoreticized." Their genuine and justified passions are expressed, or rather dissipated, in a vocabulary assumed uncritically, mostly from the disciplines of psychology and sociology. It would be an enormous propaedeutic labor to distinguish the student's own naïve intentions from the current conventions which envelop them.

Of course, it could be done. The group might, for instance, read Durkheim's *Rules of Sociological Method*, and then consider his principle that "the determining cause of a social fact should be sought among the social facts preceding it and not among the states of individual consciousness." A discussion of cause, hence of "system" would follow. Newton's laws of motion might be studied in order to make available the notion of the interactions in a system of bodies. The question of the assumption of mechanical models into the study of men will then be raised. Some students will now grow outraged at the very concept of "society"; others will point out the ineluctable facts which make the concept plausible. Some will want to take refuge from the mechanical constraints of social "behavior" in their "creativity." They will be asked to consider the text: "In the beginning God created the heaven and the earth" and asked whether they mean to undertake similar projects. Some will own that they do. It is a fascinating, but also a chaotic and infinite undertaking, this critique of "opinion," as Socrates calls such received thought.

Happily we are still in possession of a more originally common language and experience. A teacher may worry about the fate of such human experience in view of so much vicarious "exposure" and "experiencing" and about the possibility of much intensity in view of so much easy access. Nonetheless, the best thing is to assume that love and life go on much as they always have, and to impute to students those ardent, wholehearted and natural modes which have common names but often lead to recondite discourse.

It is therefore best to eschew current issues as guides for inquiry, though I think no one would be altogether plausible in doing it who was not also an avid watcher of the modern scene and a fascinated reader of contemporary works.

6. The Arts

If the inquiry cannot usually be guided by the current problems brought to it from the outside, it yet requires something which is antecedent and external to the desire to know oneself and the world: the ability to read. I mean the ability to read in the widest sense, namely the possession of tools for interpreting those texts of words, symbols and even things which bear on these matters. This ability to read is fostered by the arts traditionally called liberal, which are the "instruments and rudiments" of philosophy.

The reason for the name and the established number of these conditions for gratifying the desire to know are almost totally lost to students studying at the so-called liberal arts colleges. It therefore makes sense to take some opportunity to read with them sections of works which deal directly and familiarly with the roots, parts and uses of the free arts, such as Hugh of St. Victor's *Didascalicon* and John of Salisbury's *Metalogicon*. But it is far more immediately important that their terms, observances, rules and methods should be made explicit and used as much as possible, even while the philosophical enterprise is going on. Uneasy though this simultaneous combination of exercise and reflection may be, one can certainly not count on students becoming versed in these arts at any other time.

The best and most satisfying way for students to acquire these arts is, in my experience, for them to devote a definite part of their three or four years at college to a programmatic study of the trivium (the outer and inner form of speech), and the quadrivium (mathematics and its application to things in motion).

Here it is necessary to point out that if such a program is undertaken, a kind of university study which usually constitutes the bulk of students' courses will be reserved for special study groups or postponed to graduate school, partly on principle and partly from sheer lack of time. These are the studies which can never be elementary without intellectual shoddiness. I mean the disciplines which are by their very nature sophisticated, since their existence depends on the formation of complex and precarious concepts and the accumulation of large bodies of special methods and results. The paradigmatic study of this sort is the discipline of history (as opposed to what Hegel calls "original history," an "inquiry" written down in the spirit of an eyewitness for general edification and enjoyment; he names Herodotus, Thucydides and Xenophon as examples). Certainly no one who has ever grappled with the recovery and interpretation of the past can think of history as a viable beginning study.

But in most schools it is very unlikely that the professors of such studies will often give way to, or wait on the acquisition of, the first arts. At the same time a teacher simply cannot count on students to possess them. Therefore another expedient, however insufficient, must be found, in order that the group may have some practice in common.

One way would be to take up the relevant arts in short illustrative exercises as the texts under discussion direct. Here are some examples, mere indications, of what has sometimes worked.

When reading the Phaedrus, the Platonic dialogue implicating love and rhetoric, it might be possible to stop a week over a Shakespearean sonnet and, perhaps, the *Gettysburg Address*, to look at them minutely and keenly as collections of words, grammatical structures, rhetorical efforts, works of music. Everyone, most of all the teacher, will consult manuals and reference books and with the aid of these meticulously prepare exercises, which might include making metric analyses, parsing particularly opalescent sentences, revealing and naming implied and patent logical relations. The object will be both to practice the art of dealing with language and to confirm admiration for works which are at once inimitable and exemplary.

Or, when, as it must, the time has come to study the *Critique of Pure Reason* (or at least the *Prolegomena to Any Future Metaphysics*) where Kant asks and answers the question "How is pure mathematics possible?," that would be a good moment to study together the definitions, postulates and common notions given in the first book of Euclid's *Elements* and perhaps to go on to follow the elementary consequences of that denial of Euclid's parallel postulate which is presented in Lobachevsky's *Theory of Parallels*.

So also there will be numerous textual occasions for studying the rudiments of the apprehension of "nature" as having numerable dimensions and the bases of the geometric representation of sensible qualities and the elements of the mathematics of motion, in short, the foundations of mathematical physics.

The effects of such sporadic exercises will be small but not negligible for students will become somewhat better readers first of books and then of themselves and the world. If none of us has much hope of becoming master of the arts, the next best thing is surely to be a responsible amateur.

It is important to make it quickly clear to students that while pursuing the free arts they will perforce, for lack of time, have to neglect the productive or fine arts except as serious recreations; while engaged in liberal learning they will not directly learn to write poetry, paint pictures or play the flute. And, having chosen to put self-formation before self-expression, they must be ready to relinquish the expectation (odd in any case) of having their spontaneity fostered. The liberal arts are first and last skills of understanding.

7. The Community

It is of the essence that this enterprise should be uncompromisingly represented as being in some central respect for its own sake. There are two aspects to this claim.

First, it is *the* axiom of inquiry and is simply tantamount to the proposition that there *is* philosophy, the love of reflective learning, and free or self-determined, inquiry which serves no external end.

The claim is, secondly, also a shrewd representation to make to students. The older wisdom was, and the current wisdom is, that the axiom is idle and that schooling should be immediately related to success in worldly matters—in the past to training for a profession, in the present to the production of social change or services. The views coincide in discounting the life of learning. But students with spirit have never been much enchanted with the previous view, and are now ready to doubt the current one. This is partly because they cannot find a course of study which offers both convincing deliberations concerning ends and reliable methods for effecting them, perhaps because such an undertaking is impossible. Therefore the ancient, scandalous claim again has a chance to engage at least the fascinated resistance of students.

And yet the program I have described *will* have palpably practical effects. I am not now referring to the more remote though eventually evident influence of a reflective education on the practical judgment of citizens, but to a very immediate result: A community comes into being. People who undertake such a program of learning together become friends—not, as a rule, intimates, because their purpose is to look not to each other but rather to a common enterprise—yet nevertheless serious and steady companions.

The sturdiness of this natural outcome depends on this: that it should be cherished without being directly intended. Accordingly students should feel it right to think and talk together as they sit in their rooms, as they walk to their class, as they eat and as they play. So also students should be encouraged to study together and to help each other with paradigms, problems and other preparation. It goes without saying that the best students will have a private pride in their freely acknowledged reputation for excellence, but it is also obvious that nasty ranking which goes with competitiveness is entirely out of place here.

In exactly the same vein teachers will find themselves consorting with and caring for students, always (with such very rare exceptions as may prove justified in the outcome) keeping that decent distance which makes such friendship possible. The limits, however, of such relations are strictly set (and this is an evidently insuperable, but ever-chafing difficulty) by the time needed for institutional occasions, preparation, study, private life, recuperation—and one more activity.

This activity is the fostering of the community of teachers, an absolutely essential project if the way described here is to be anything more than just another episode in the institution. For, first, the enterprise of philosophy must have a world in which to flourish, a world which is stable even if it is small, and the fellowship of teachers is the foundation of that world. And second, it is only sensible that the leaders in learning should regularly and formally become co-students.

Practically, this can be done through study-groups which propose for themselves a difficult but elementary matter to be studied, not under expert direction, not for research and results, but for the sake of the naivest possible reflection.

It is not heard to find suitable texts which present a matter from the beginning but with depth. Here is a merest sampling of proven works: a chorus from Sophocles's *Antigone*, the twelfth book of Aristotle's *Metaphysics* on the source of motion and *energeia* and with it Leibniz's first *Essay on Dynamics* in which the dimensions of the modern term "energy" are originally established, a Donne song, Vico's *On the Study Methods of Our Time* which sets forth the original terms of our unhappy division of learning into the "sciences" and the "humanities." A group which has many such studies in common becomes mildly invincible.

And finally, not only must the leaders in this enterprise learn with and from each other in this way, but they must allow themselves to be seen to do it. For to be seen learning is, I think, as close as anyone can come to teaching philosophy.

Note

Originally published in *Metaphilosophy* 6 (1975).

PART V:

A VIEW FROM THE LEFT

Philosophy as a Profession

ALISON JAGGAR

One of the main achievements of contemporary "liberation" movements has been to reduce the discrimination which bars certain groups of people, such as ethnic or racial minorities, women and the gay, from entry into the professions. In working for this end, such movements seem implicitly to endorse the practice of professionalism. By contrast, I want to question this practice and especially to question the professionalization of philosophy.

I

A profession is a subclass of those occupations by which one may earn a living. In current sociological theory, the notion of a profession is vague, although there is some rough agreement that professions are distinguished from other occupations both by a comparatively long period of training in some abstract subject and by commitment to the service of humanity.[1] In the absence of an adequate definition of "profession," I want to propose the following set of conditions each of which is necessary and which are jointly sufficient for a paid occupation to be a profession.

1. A profession is a paid occupation whose practice requires some expert knowledge or skill and, consequently, a period of special education or training;

2. A professional occupation has social importance both because it is taken to fill a significant social need and because, if it is neglected or done improperly, danger to the public health, safety or welfare is thought to result;

3. Because of this, those who practice a profession must be certified or accredited; a person who is not accredited is considered incompetent and is legally barred from practicing the profession;

4. Competence and fitness for accreditation in each profession are determined by those who are already established in that profession.

A professional person, as I shall use the term, is someone who practices a profession as defined above. By restricting the term "professional" in this way, I am, of course, excluding many who are commonly described as professionals, by contrast with amateurs, simply in virtue of undertaking an activity for pay. I make this restriction because I am less concerned to criticize the fundamental practice of working for pay than I am to investigate the consequences of "professionalizing" some occupation in a social context where the notion of payment for service is taken for granted.

It is clear from my definition that professionals are more than just experts. They are experts who, through professionalization, have achieved a high degree of control over the conditions of their work.[2] Their power of accreditation allows them to control the number of new entrants into the profession and, often, to define just what constitutes the practice of the profession. In addition, professionals are entrusted with the maintenance of high standards of competence within the profession by the adoption of a code of professional ethics. Such a code, like the test of professional competence, is designed by the profession itself and enforced by the use of in-group sanctions. It attempts to regulate the conduct proper between professionals among themselves and between professionals and their clients. Thus it articulates certain moral obligations which the professional has and which may be distinguished from the obligations of purely personal morality or from general obligations to persons as such.[3] An example of such a professional obligation is the requirement that lawyers or psychiatrists should not divulge the confidence of their clients.

In our society, the term "professional" is a term of respect. Professionals are esteemed higher than other workers and higher than amateurs.[4] This respect stems in part from the fact that the work professionals do is taken to be socially valuable and to require special expertise. It also results from the widespread assumptions that professionals are dedicated to their work (a professional is serious, not a dabbler or a dilettante), that they adhere to high standards of competence ("a professional job") and to high moral standards in the practice of their profession and that they are motivated by a desire for the public welfare. (Compare Freidson and Lorber's preliminary definition of a profession, quoted above.) As we shall see, however, these assumptions are unfounded; indeed, there are substantial reasons why they are more likely than not to be false of professionals.

II

In explaining why the term "professional" has such favorable associations, I have already hinted at much of the rationale for the practice of professionalism. It can be summed up as follows. The complexity of a technological society and the so-called knowledge explosion have increased the need for specialized expertise. At the same time, they have increased the need for the lay public to be protected from incompetence, fraud and charlatanism. High standards for important social services must be maintained and they must be maintained by the specialists and experts who deliver those services: there is no one else competent to do it. Hence, the experts must organize themselves into self-regulating professions.

In the rest of this section, I shall argue that this rationale for professionalism fails, that professionalism in fact has results which are often precisely the opposite of those claimed for it. I shall not be concerned to criticize certain contingent features of many contemporary professions; instead, I shall criticize the whole institution of professionalism. My conclusion is not that we should, or even can, reform the professions but that we should do away with professions altogether.

There are two possible lines of criticism that I shall not take, however. I shall not question the whole notion of working for pay, although this can, of course, be done in a number of ways. Nor shall I attack the specialization which is a precondition of professionalism. Specialization is sometimes criticized on semi-aesthetic grounds as being in conflict with a certain ideal of what a person should be, namely, an all-rounder, capable of fulfilling a variety of social functions. A more substantial criticism is that specialization renders individuals helpless in many crucial respects as they become dependent on others to fulfill many vital needs; with the loss of self-sufficiency, they lose their power to control their own lives. While this is indeed a danger of specialization, I believe that it is a danger which must be faced as the price of achieving a certain standard of living with a minimum of time spent in labor. It is a danger, moreover, which could be reduced with a different organization of society. In what follows, therefore, I shall assume a society which resembles our own in that there exists a division of labor and in which services are offered for pay. It is in this social context that I shall criticize the institution of professionalism.

The first thing to notice is that, in such a social context, there is an inevitable conflict of interest between those who make their living by offering certain specialized services and the public which buys those services. The specialists want to keep the demand for and the price of their services high; the public wants to keep them low. Therefore, in any social system which allows them to profit from their expertise, experts have an interest in preserving a monopoly on that expertise. My chief criticism of professionalism is that it allows the experts to do this in a variety of ways, all of which have unfortunate social consequences.

One of the most obvious ways is by limiting the number of entrants to each profession, thus keeping the demand for professional services at a high level. A notorious example of this was the American Medical Association's effort in the 1930s to limit the number of places available in medical schools, an effort which was so successful that the resulting shortage of medical doctors is still with us. The practitioners of many other occupations have attempted to impose the same sort of limitations on entry, with varying success.[5] In these circumstances, it is not accidental that the professional tests of competence are often applied in such a way as to exclude members of minority groups and women nor that some of the tests may bear no relation to professional competence, as when they require a certain standard of dress, a certain sexual morality or even certain political beliefs.[6]

Not only do the professions seek to limit the number of those who may offer certain services for pay. They also seek to impose restrictions on those who wish to dispense with professional services. Thus, to engage in certain transactions, such as the disposition of an estate,[7] one must employ a lawyer, and one's freedom to self-medicate is sharply restricted by the need for a doctor's prescription to obtain many drugs and even vitamins. Some of these restrictions seem to be justified by the danger to public safety or welfare but often restrictive laws are passed as the result of pressure from professional groups who have a vested economic interest in establishing a monopoly in their areas. Many of these restrictions have only the most remote connection with public health, safety or welfare; for example, in 1939 the state of Wisconsin enacted legislation requiring examinations for house painters. Those who helped their friends to paint their houses without taking the examination were arrested and fined for failure to possess the requisite license.[8]

The public and their legislators are persuaded to acquiesce in such restrictions by the mystification which surrounds all professions. Professionals work hard to foster the lay public's belief in its need for professional services by stressing, through the use of jargon and other means, the difficult and esoteric nature of the skills which they command. A familiar example is the incomprehensible prescriptions for medicine which reinforce the professions both of medicine and of pharmacy.[9]

The same goal of maintaining a high demand for professional services is pursued by the restriction of substitution services[10] and by breaking up professions into specialties. These devices are further aspects of the kind of territorialism through which professionals seek to establish a monopoly in their particular area. Such territorialism is unfortunate not only for the obvious reason that it allows professionals to charge inflated prices for their services but because it makes professionals resist the incursions of new knowledge or of contributions from other fields. An example is the traditional (up to 1961) AMA opposition to osteopathy[11] and its current skeptical attitude towards acupuncture. Thus professionalism encourages a conservative and piecemeal approach to problem solving which is unlikely to be the most effective.

To professionals, however, this may not matter since all specialists who earn a living through the practice of their special skill have a certain interest in failing to complete the work to which they claim to be dedicated. Thus, to exist, the police need crime; lawyers need legal disputes; physicians need sickness; psychotherapists need unhappiness and deviance; teachers need people who believe they are ignorant. Each profession has an interest in perpetuating rather than eradicating its own set of problems.[12] This conflict of interest with the public is not itself the result of professionalism, but in this conflict professionalism gives the experts the advantage. The prestige of the professions and their lack of accountability enable professionals to work effectively *against* final solutions to the problems with which they deal. Thus lawyers oppose legal reform, physicians for many years fought health insurance and social workers often resist the rehabilitation of their clients, preferring instead to play "I'm Only Trying to Help You."[13] Long term solutions, such as community improvement programs, the establishment of genuine health education or of preventative medical measures, the criticism of the social norms and institutions which create "mental illness" or the dissemination of various kinds of specialized knowledge, are even less likely to be supported by professionals.

The consequences of professionalism that I have outlined are not compensated by the public protection that it is supposed to afford. Since professionals are free from external accountability, they are provided with a built-in defense if they should harm or injure others in the course of their work. So long as it can be claimed plausibly that the professional services rendered were roughly those which many other established members of the profession might have provided, professionals are immune to claims of damage from their clients. Presumably this, along with their wish for the prestige which accompanies professional status, is the reason why the police seek to become professionals: there will be no question of their being subjected to civilian review boards.[14] It is true that the internalization of a professional ethic does exert some influence on specialists.[15] But where this breaks down, the professional bodies entrusted with maintaining professional ethics are inevitably reluctant to bring their profession into disrepute by allowing unethical behavior to become known. Furthermore, when professionals depend on each other for specialized assistance, for social intercourse and for peer recognition, they are provided with additional reasons for loyalty to each other which are often stronger than their reasons for loyalty to society at large; this is shown very clearly both by the My-Lai cover-up and by the number of alcoholic or drug-addicted but still practicing physicians. The internal structure of professionalism is such that the self-regulation of the professions is bound to be inadequate to its stated aim of protecting the public.

In many ways, therefore, the organization of specialists into professions actually works to prevent the services offered being ultimately effective. Moreover, it allows those with specialized knowledge to become an elite which exploits the rest of society.[16] Thus, despite the rationale for their existence, professions are designed so that they work systematically to defeat their own proclaimed goals.

III

Professional philosophers are professionals in exactly the same way as lawyers or physicians. We are paid for our work, although our pay is less than that of many other professionals since our work is less highly valued, despite the lip service paid to its importance. We undergo a very rigorous training culminating in the attainment of an academic degree which is accepted so generally as a certificate of professional competence that it is a cliché to refer to the Ph.D. as our union card.[17] It is true that the American Philosophical Association, our professional body in this country, is not itself an accrediting organization, but the notoriously stringent criteria for entry into the profession are still administered by those already established in it, namely, members of the graduate faculties of the more prestigious universities. We even have our code of professional ethics, governing such matters as standards of scholarship and fair treatment of students. Thus, professional philosophers, like other professionals, are a relatively exclusive group whose primary activity, doing philosophy, is official, legitimate, in a way that the philosophy of amateurs is not.

Most professional philosophers are employed in institutions of higher education. This, together with the fact that our professional accreditation serves as a license to teach, might suggest that professional philosophers are no more than a sub-class of professional teachers. However, although most professional philosophers are indeed a sub-class of university professors, university faculty in general are professionals of a rather different kind from other teachers. We have a contractual responsibility for so-called research as well as for teaching; our professional rewards are based far more on our research or on our scholarship than on our success in teaching; occasionally we are awarded leaves from teaching in order to concentrate on the research side of our activities; and our code of professional ethics governs much more than our conduct with respect to our students.[18]

Many problems result from the professionalization of philosophy. Some of the most serious are linked with our role as professional teachers of philosophy, a role which contradicts the stated aims of philosophy and institutionalizes a conflict of interest with our students. However, I shall not be concerned primarily with those problems.[19] Instead, I shall focus on some of the problems which arise when the teaching role of professional philosophers is viewed as an offshoot of, and thus subsidiary to, our research role.

In one respect, professional philosophers differ from other professionals. Since our reputation is made largely by showing the inadequacy of other philosophers' contributions, and since the "adversary technique" is the accepted way of doing philosophy, we have no incentive to conceal our colleagues' mistakes. Rather we have a motive to expose them.[20] However, since we view ourselves as members of a group which does have common interests, we are reluctant to denounce another colleague's work as being totally trivial, as opposed to being wrongheaded, and professional loyalty may also lead us to conceal considerable irregularities of conduct by colleagues, even towards those students whom we are bound by our professional ethic to protect.

In the last few years, professional philosophers have behaved like all professions threatened by a decreasing demand for their services, sharply restricting the numbers of new entrants to the profession—and incidentally showing our disbelief in the rhetoric that the primary motive for undertaking advanced study in philosophy is the disinterested pursuit of truth. It is interesting that the criteria of competence used to limit the new entrants into the profession are often little less sexist than those used by other professions.[21] Like other professions, too, we have sought new employment opportunities, such as teaching philosophy in high schools and even elementary schools.

All professionals, and especially all academics, have an interest in impressing the public, and since professional philosophers can rarely do this through the publication of important discoveries, hailed as advances by the profession as a whole, we must do it by mystification. This mystification takes the form of using jargon, formal logical techniques, etc., in situations where these are not necessary. Not that we should refrain from creating a special technical terminology when required, for an undue reverence for so-called "ordinary language" has its own disadvantages. But such a terminology is often created quite gratuitously. For example, in a paper that I heard recently, the quite ordinary fact that it is conveniently inappropriate to attribute certain qualities to men and others to women was christened "normative genderization." Another recent article, worried whether we can talk sensibly about those who will not be born if various population control measures are adopted (a problem which could trouble only a professional philosopher), states that one advantage of a certain moral theory is that it gives us no need to worry about "quantification over" non-existent people. It is interesting to note that our professional interest, *qua* researchers, in mystification is in conflict with one aspect of our professional interest *qua* teachers, which is to elucidate and explain. Some philosophers have taken up the task of making professional philosophical concerns accessible to the lay public, but their efforts as popularizers are met, not with professional approval, but rather with professional disdain.[22] This is another indication that our teaching role is viewed, at least by us, as subsidiary to our role of "scholar."

Professional philosophers demonstrate a conservativism and a territorialism similar to other professionals. We favor certain problems (mostly the esoteric ones, for obvious reasons) and certain approaches to those problems. We reject much interesting work as "not being philosophy" and tend to scorn interdisciplinary projects. In particular, we disdain so-called "popular philosophy," the metaphysical systems and moral codes towards which so many people look to guide their lives. Within our dominant analytic tradition, professionalization has resulted in a sharp division between popular philosophy, which is invariably normative or is taken to have normative implications, and professional philosophy, which is critical in nature and which explicitly, and sometimes mistakenly, proclaims its moral neutrality.[23] The few professional philosophers, like Russell and Chomsky, who have sought to provide moral leadership, have not done so in a professional capacity but rather have compartmentalized their activities into the professional and the non-professional.[24]

Until recently, these generalizations were truisms. But now things are changing. Motivated at least in part by a desire to stem declining enrollments,[25] some professional philosophers are now beginning to include in their courses a consideration of some questions called, vaguely and often misleading, "relevant." These questions tend to be overtly normative, and their resolution requires that an explicit moral stand be taken.[26] It is true that consideration of such topics is still limited chiefly to introductory courses which are regarded as "potboilers," providing the wherewithal for professional philosophers to spend the rest of their time in more traditional concerns. Nevertheless, the discussion of more popular issues is starting gradually to gain a little professional respect. Such discussions are now sometimes heard at professional meetings and published in such professional journals as *Philosophy and Public Affairs*.

In some ways, this change might be viewed as a welcome reform of the profession.[27] But it carries with it a danger characteristic of professionalization. This is the danger that, by extending the philosophical empire from the realm of "meta-" discussion into the area of more explicit normative judgments, we may well undermine the confidence of ordinary people in their ability to make their own moral decisions and to develop their own philosophy of life. (As a professional philosopher, I have an almost overwhelming urge to enclose the last phrase in "shudder quotes.") Thus, the resolution of moral dilemmas may become another task handed over to the professionals.

This is not to say that the discussion of normative problems could not benefit enormously from the contribution of trained analytical minds. But, like foreign aid officials, when professionals enter an area their natural tendency is to take it over. And so the new professional focus on issues which are explicitly normative is likely to remove such issues from the domain of ordinary people, in the same way as the general public has been excluded already from the discussion of most other philosophical topics and much as the medical profession has removed the processes of childbirth and death from ordinary experiences or as the legal profession has made the law incomprehensible to most of those who are subject to it. Just as we now call on lawyers to interpret laws which, theoretically, have been made by and for us, accountants to work out how much of our taxes we need not pay, and marriage counselors to tell us how to make love, so the inclusion of explicitly normative issues into the sphere of professional philosophy seems likely to result in the professional philosopher's assumption of the role of moral authority. If this happens, the non-professionals will have lost what little remains of their autonomy and "their" philosophy will have become finally a set of dogmas whose justification is as mysterious to them as the pronouncements of their doctors and lawyers and accountants. They will accept these pronouncements, like the rest, not because they can evaluate their truth independently, but because they have to trust the officially certified competence of the professional philosopher.

To make the activity of philosophy into a profession is to suggest not only that some people are better at philosophy or know more about it than others (this is indisputable), but that those who are not professionals ought not really to do philosophy at all. Amateurs do not do "real" philosophy or do not do it properly.

Their efforts do not deserve to be treated with respect. Thus, to view philosophy as a professional pursuit is to discourage most people, the non-professionals, from taking seriously their own ability to engage in what should be the central project of every human life, deciding how they should live. To accept one's philosophy on the authority of another is the ultimate form of alienation. Consequently, the professionalization of philosophy poses a danger to human dignity which is perhaps greater than that posed by any other profession.

Like other professions, the profession of philosophy works systematically to defeat its own goals. It substitutes mystification for elucidation; instead of being open to all sources of argument, it ignores or mocks the contributions of those who are not professional philosophers;[28] and it replaces the authority of reason with the authority of institutional status, the combined authority of the official scholar and the official teacher. Because of all this, to speak of a "professional philosopher" though not, of course, of a "philosophical expert" is to utter an implicit contradiction.

IV

What can we, who are nonetheless known as professional philosophers, do about this situation? Reform of the profession clearly will not work, for the problem is the result of the very existence of the profession. It is equally ineffectual to "drop out," renounce our professional status and do philosophy only unofficially. For even if we are prepared to forego the privileges of being even minor professionals, others are waiting to take our places immediately; so long as there are privileges to be had, people will try to acquire them.

The social need for specialized expertise inevitably carries with it the problem of ensuring that the experts are responsive to that need. Professionalism is one attempt to solve this problem, but we have seen that it is unsatisfactory. Even more unsatisfactory, however, would be the establishment of "free" competition among the experts by the abolition of any kind of restriction.[29] It was partly in order to eliminate the abuses resulting from that sort of competition that professionalism was instituted. Are we forced, then, to the conclusion that the problem is insoluble, given the social parameters of division of labor and working for pay? Must we either live with the abuses resulting from the existence of professions or else return to a technologically primitive society? If so, we have no choice. Even if we were prepared to accept the reduction both in our material standard of living and in our possible leisure time consequent on the abandonment of technology, such a return is a mere utopian dream, never, bar some cataclysm, to be realized in this world.

There is one society which has attempted to resolve the problem of expert accountability without resorting to professionalism and without abandoning technology, at the same time, indeed, as carrying through a technological revolution, that society is the People's Republic of China. In China, with its desperate shortage of trained personnel, the possibility of eliminating specialization is even more remote than it is in the West, but the Chinese, especially during the cultural revolution, have made every attempt to prevent their specialists from becoming a professional elite. The cultural revolution in fact has been described exactly as "a revolution against the intelligentsia, the new class which aspires to become the ruling class by its ownership of the brain power."[30] One of their methods has been to attempt to eliminate the mystification of knowledge by forcing the experts to explain, both to clients and to non-expert aides, exactly what they were doing.[31] The demystification of technical skills naturally undermines any tendency towards professional exclusivity and the same trend has been encouraged by a conscious effort to spread special skills as widely as possible: the training of the "barefoot doctors" is an obvious example here. In medicine, along with demystification goes an emphasis on joint decision making, not only by all concerned in the care of patients but by the patients themselves and their families. This has done much to make the medical experts answerable for their activity. They are not bound only by some professional code, formulated and administered by their colleagues. Nor do the experts get special privileges nor maintain a different style of life from lay people. And to make doubly sure that elitism does not arise, administrators and people with special skills are required to spend a certain proportion of their time on non-specialized, what we would call "menial," duties. Thus, while specialization and experts remain, there are no longer professions nor a professional elite.

Naturally, the effect of all this on professional philosophy has been profound. While there are still departments of philosophy within the universities, the role of the philosopher has been redefined so completely that philosophers are no longer professionals in our sense. For philosophers are no longer the aloof experts debating about esoteric problems in order to further their own careers. Not only are their teaching duties now primary, but the responsibility for instructing courses is now undertaken collectively and the relationship between student and teacher is now that of comradeship.[32] More radical even than these changes is the abandonment of the assumption that those who are paid to do philosophy are the experts and from whom, in a single direction, knowledge flows to the lay public.[33] Not only is philosophy taught to "the masses,"[34] not only are the workers "encouraged to write philosophy and to sum up their experience in their own fields of work,"[35] but it is even suggested that "the masses are already doing better philosophy than professional philosophers and hence philosophers must go among the masses and learn from them."[36]

This startling statement obviously presupposes a conception of philosophy quite different from that current in our society. For the Chinese, philosophy is not just a body of theoretical knowledge but a practical activity: just as practice without theory is blind, so theory without practice is empty.[37] The Chinese anticipate the day when, in Marx's words, "philosophy as an independent branch of activity loses its medium of existence. At best, its place can be taken only by a summing up of the most general results, abstractions which arise from the observations of the historical development of man."[38]

This conception of philosophy may be outrageous or even ludicrous to professional Western philosophers. Many are also sure to find repugnant the social changes on which the Chinese have based not only their reform of the educational system and the profession of philosophy but their attempt to eliminate all professions. But it is doubtful whether the problem of making the experts accountable can ever be resolved completely in a society which has wide inequalities of income and encourages individuals to profit as much as possible from their possession of specialized expertise. Similarly, it is doubtful whether a way can be found to overcome the endemic tendency of professional philosophy towards estoricism, mystification and fragmentation without far-reaching changes in the context, both academic and social, within which philosophy is presently done. Perhaps all that we can finally do, then, as long as philosophy remains a profession and as long as we remain professional philosophers, is to try to make ourselves and our students aware of the advantages and disadvantages of the possible alternative conceptions of philosophy in case the day comes when we can finally make the choice.

Notes

Originally published in *Metaphilosophy* 5 (1975), this essay was stimulated by a panel on professionalism held by the Society for Women in Philosophy at a meeting in Pittsburgh, February, 1973. In particular, I was excited by Marilyn Frye's "Professionalism and Sexism" and by Connie Price's "Professionalism and Women in Philosophy." Frye's paper is forthcoming in *Feminist Studies*; Price's is still unpublished.

1. Eliot Friedson and Judith Lorber, *Medical Men and their Work* (Chicago: Aldine-Atherton, 1972), 1. This collection was brought to my attention by Robert Baker, who also made lengthy and extremely helpful comments on a late version of this paper.

2. Friedson and Lorber claim that "a true profession may be characterized more accurately and precisely by its autonomy than by anything else." *Medical Men and their Work*, 3.

3. This point is made by Dorothy Emmet in *Rules, Roles and Relations* (New York: St. Martin's Press, 1966), 159. It was brought to my attention by Peter Hare.

4. "The concept 'profession' in our society is not so much a descriptive term as one of value and prestige." Everett C. Hughes, *Men and their Work* (Glencoe, IL: 1958), 44. This fact helps to explain why some women's liberation groups urge women not to engage in "menial" or volunteer work but to get professional training and to demand pay for their services. This is Betty Friedan's recommendation in the last chapter of her now classic *The Feminine Mystique* (New York: Dell, 1964).

5. "There is probably no organized occupational group in the United States which has not tried at one time or another to break into the ranks of licensed professionals." Jethro K. Lieberman, *The Tyranny of the Experts* (New York: Walker and Co., 1970), 16.

This book is rich in examples of the abuse of professional power. It was brought to my attention by P. P. S. Rama Rao.

6. Lieberman gives numerous examples of such tests. *The Tyranny of the Experts*, 25 and 95ff.

7. Ibid., 86–87.

8. Ibid., 15

9. I owe this example to Robert Baker. It is interesting to note that the lack of confidence in their own powers felt by lay people is often complemented by an over-confidence among professionals:

> A recent study indicates that physicians who flew light planes were found to have a fatal accident rate four times that of other private pilots. The Federal Aviation Authority attributed the cause to the risk-taking attitudes with 'the feeling that they are omnipotent'. Carried away with their invincibility" doctors are falling from the sky to their deaths like so many Icaruses. (*Ms.* [August 1973]: 99).

10. For example, one of my friends, part of whose work is to train veterinarians' assistants, is under considerable pressure by the veterinary profession not to teach his students too much.

11. Elton Rayack, *Professional Power and American Medicine: The Economics of the American Medical Association* (Cleveland: World Pub. Co., 1967), 241–253.

12. This was made clear to me by Michael Goldman, to whom I am indebted for many other constructive suggestions in working on this topic.

13. Eric Berne, *Games People Play* (New York: Grove Press, 1967), 147–149, quoted by Lieberman, *The Tyranny of the Experts*, 122.

14. This point was suggested to me by Newton Garver, who also helped me to articulate the ideas in the first part of this paragraph.

15. One's physician may be less likely to bungle one's appendectomy than one's automobile mechanic may be to cheat on one's tune up. (Another observation I owe to Robert Baker.) Nevertheless, it is notorious that the number of appendectomies, hysterectomies and tonsillectomies performed is determined at least as much by the economic needs of the surgeons as by the medical needs of their patients.

16. "Most professional incomes have climbed more rapidly than the growth in the average national income. Highest among these are the doctors. Between 1949 and 1964, the median net income of non-salaried doctors (who account for eighty per cent of all M.D.s) rose from $8,744 to $28,380. During the same period, the median wage or salary income of managers, officials, and non-farm proprietors rose from $3,345 to $7,560. Since the advent of Medicare and Medicaid, the pressure has become even more intense. The consumer price index reflects an eleven per cent increase for the cost of all items between 1966 and 1969. The comparable rate for physicians was twenty-one per cent; for hospital service charges, fifty-two per cent." Lieberman, *The Tyranny of the Experts*, 155.

17. The official APA statement on the "Criteria for the Constituting of a Department of Philosophy," which demands that the competence of every member of a philosophy department should be certified at least by an M.A. degree (or the equivalent), is clearly based on this assumption. This APA statement is presently under revision, but it is unlikely that the emphasis on institutional criteria of competence will be changed. The statement is published in the *Proceedings and Addresses of the American Philosophical Association* 32 (1958–1959): 85–90.

18. A clear statement of how university faculty constitute a profession is given by K. L. Parkhurst in an article on "Collective Bargaining in Higher Education," *Ohio Academe* (May, 1974). "Unlike union workers in industry, university faculty organize as a community of scholars who control the education and certification of new entrants into their profession as well as educational policy. They often exert a strong influence in deciding questions of college and departmental structure, selections, retention and promotion of their colleagues. Supported by the double principle of freedom and job tenure, the individual faculty member has developed a traditionally high degree of professional courtesy and independence. Since the faculty largely controls the content of the curriculum, the scheduling of work, and the evaluation of performance, the administration depends for its influence primarily on financial controls and effective personal leadership. Professional ethics and self-discipline among faculty are two factors that administrators might ideally rely upon in the long run in the opinion of the author." Although even the author recognizes that "the above tends to be an ideal academic model," his sketch shows that university faculty still view themselves as professionals—although it may be true that our status as such is eroding.

19. A fuller discussion of them can be found in Michael Goldman's "Institutional Obstacles to the Teaching of Philosophy," originally read at the Pacific Division of the APA in March 1974, and later published in *Metaphilosophy* 6 (1975), and reprinted below on 181–187.

20. An interesting article by Janna L. Thompson suggests that this is one way in which the structure of the profession shapes our idea of what philosophy is. "Philosophy—Practice and Theory: A Venture into the Sociology of Philosophy," *Metaphilosophy* 3(4) (October 1972): 274–284.

21. For documentation of this claim, see Marilyn Frye's "Professionalism and Sexism."

22. This is another point which I owe to Michael Goldman.

23. For example, Hilary Putnam has an extremely interesting discussion of the hidden ideological implications of much recent philosophy of mind. His paper, "Reductionism, the Turing Machine Model and the Nature of Psychology" was read at the University of Cincinnati Philosophy Colloquium in November, 1971. I do not know whether a version of it has since been published.

24. This view of contemporary philosophy is not, of course, unusual. "[M]any professional philosophers share this popular view. They agree that the content of philosophy is far removed from common problems. If they take positions on some current issue, they do not do so as professional philosophers. As professionals they will take positions

on nominalism, material implication, analyticity, deontology; as professionals they will tell you about Quine's quarrel with Carnap over intentionalism, about Hume's arguments against induction and Harre's response to Hume. But, as professionals, they won't take a stand on the value of punishment, the war, religion, or even about rational belief. They will not, as professionals, point out the inconsistencies in current thoughts, about education, the vagueness in popular ethical discussion, the lack of good reason for some psychological advice." Ed Helbig, "Professional Philosophy and the Layman," *Metaphilosophy* 4(1) (January 1973): 8g. (See above.)

25. This motive is often made explicit. For example, Helbig says bluntly, "I want to keep my job." (Ibid., 88.)

26. Although the questions studied are normative, the ones chosen deal invariably with such apparently self-contained and "individual" matters as abortion, capital punishment or suicide. Little attempt is made to point out the normative presuppositions of much of our science, for example, especially our social science. Thus, even the discussion of normative issues is handled academically in such a way as not to threaten the political *status quo*—which, presumably, explains how it manages to survive in educational institutions dependent on public funds.

27. One good result might be that the resurgence of professional interest in questions that are explicitly normative could encourage those (and they are most of us) who have an excessive respect for professional expertise and institutional criteria of competence to take such questions more seriously. As things are, "value judgments" are often contrasted with "objective knowledge" and viewed as a matter of purely personal or psychological interest, insusceptible to rational refutation or even discussion. The general respect for professionalism may have engendered the belief that an area of intellectual enquiry which is ignored by professionals cannot yield genuine knowledge and hence may have contributed to the extreme subjectivism which has developed in the public mind (as well as in the minds of many philosophers) with regard to normative judgments.

28. That this occurs is not just speculation. I have seen it happen time and again; indeed, I catch myself doing it. It is interesting to consider whether it is the unusual readiness of philosophers of feminism to take serious notice of what lay people say which accounts, at least in part, for the liveliness of this area of philosophy in contrast with some others. But how long can this liveliness last when feminism becomes fully accepted as a legitimate subject of professional philosophical enquiry rather than a token, though profitable, gesture to our female students?

29. This is the solution suggested by Milton Friedman in his chapter on "Occupational Licensure" in *Capitalism and Freedom* (Chicago: University of Chicago Press, 1962).

30. K. T. Fann, "Mao and the Chinese Revolution in Philosophy," *Studies in Soviet Thought* 12 (1972): 112.

31. Examples of this are given in William Hinton, *Iron Oxen* (1971) and in Joshua S. Horn's description of Chinese medicine and surgery in *Away with all Pests* (1971).

32. K. T. Fann, "Philosophy in New China: An interview with Fung Yu-Lan, Peking University," *Social Praxis* 1(2): 135–136.

33. One who apparently assumed this was Chou Yang, the former head of the Propaganda Department of the Party who claimed that "Workers in philosophy and social sciences are spokesmen of the ideology of a class; they are an important force in creating intellectual values and influencing the minds of the people." Since this conception of the role of professional philosophers was quite contrary to Mao's mass line in philosophy, Chou Yang was denounced as a revisionist and removed from his post. K. T. Fann, "Mao and the Chinese Revolution in Philosophy."

34. Ibid., 115

35. Apparently "in 1965, innumerable philosophical essays by workers, peasants, and soldiers were published in newspapers and collected in anthologies. These are typical titles: 'The Dialectics of Bus Driving', written by a bus driver; 'Philosophy at the Counter', written by the manager of a department store; 'Unity of Opposites and leading a Brigade', by the commander of a brigade; 'Dialectics of the Blast Furnace', by a steel worker, 'The Contradiction between Offense and Defense in Ping-Pong', by the world championship ping-pong player. These essays are written in a lively style, devoid of footnotes and philosophical jargon. They are strikingly different from the professionalized writings of career philosophers." Ibid., 116. This quotation should not be taken to mean that, in Mao's China, *all* philosophy is of this homespun type. But it does indicate general recognition of the continuity between the concerns of ordinary people and the more specialized and presumably more systematic philosophy done in the university.

36. Ibid., 118.

37. Ibid., 117.

38. Karl Marx and Frederick Engels, *The German Ideology* (Moscow: Progress Publishers, 1964), 38, and quoted by Fann in "Mao and the Chinese Revolution in Philosophy."

Institutional Obstacles to the Teaching of Philosophy

MICHAEL GOLDMAN

There have been any number of incisive analyses of the way in which educational institutions in general and universities in particular manifest positions which are plausibly labeled "political," even more plausibly labeled "moral," and in any case are matters of some controversy. The sponsorship of programs designed to train and educate on one side of politically sensitive issues: ROTC programs, Asian studies programs, police training, government research projects, have all been rightly criticized as being inconsistent with most of the ideals of the university as well as with standards of morally acceptable behavior. More significantly, the frequent absence of certain areas of possible concern, such as Black studies, women studies, peace studies, political economy, "revisionist" history, etc., have also been noted as contributing to a distortion of educational ideals. Vocationally oriented programs and departments have been criticized for training people for certain kinds of employment but not for other kinds: business schools thrive but there are no programs in "alternative live styles," education schools are well supported but there is no training for teaching in "free schools"; home economics is taught, but there is no preparation for communal living, etc.

These criticisms may well be valid, but I want to insist that even should all of these deficiencies and imbalances be rectified, there will still be at least two ways in which educational institutions as we know them will manifest fundamental social, political, and moral values. The first of these will be recognized as itself a significant philosophical problem. I wish merely to point it out here, and will not pursue it. The second will be seen to seriously affect the way in which we teach philosophy.

1. All universities and departments insist upon staff who are "professionally credentialed." This hardly seems a commitment to a particular social value, but it almost always is. To become professionally credentialed in any area, it is necessary to have adopted criteria of professional relevance, standards of evidence, methodologies, and ways of conceptualizing reality. It is gradually becoming evident to philosophers in general and philosophers of science in particular, that these criteria embody in significant ways certain ideological commitments. The social sciences

offer the clearest, although not the only, examples. By insisting, as they have for many years, that measurable parameters are necessary for legitimate scientific study, the social scientists have effectively removed from consideration the Marxist theory of alienation, which is almost a purely qualitative (not quantitative) phenomenon. By defining, as Parsonian sociology does, all "non-conformity" as "deviance," the social scientist adopts a single conceptual category for mass murderers, juvenile delinquents, freedom riders, homosexuals, etc. This renders plausible a certain uniform social response to these people. By defining "political behavior" in terms of voting frequency, campaigning activity, etc., they render it conceptually impossible to consider the deep political significance of, say, the institution of the family. By denying the uniqueness of the human being (something which "must" be done if psychology is to become a science like physics) the psychologist makes it plausible to consider human beings as exclusively "resources" to be used as a means to externally defined ends.

Some of these are fairly obvious points. There are others, however. The adoption of methodological individualism as a guiding methodology in social science renders any historicist analysis (e.g., Hegel or Marx) incoherent, and also, more importantly, renders implausible any social policy aimed at restructuring major institutions rather than individual minds. Under this theory it is appropriate to see a psychiatrist about your inability to adjust; it is not appropriate to join a revolutionary movement whose goal is to provide a wider variety of life alternatives.

These assumptions about methodology, these ways of organizing data, are all part of what is learned in the process of becoming "professionally credentialed" and hence illustrate a second way the university commits itself to a certain political, social, and moral stance. Of course, nothing above is by way of proof of the claims made. I merely mention them as a fruitful avenue for further philosophical investigation. I wish now to turn to the central claim of this paper: That all teaching, and especially the teaching of philosophy at the introductory level, is made particularly difficult by the educational structures imposed on us as college and university teachers.

2. There are some who insist that in teaching philosophy and other subjects in which there are traditionally differences in opinion, the teacher is obligated to present a "balanced" view of controversial issues. Sometimes this is interpreted to mean merely that the instructor must not state his or her opinion for fear of influencing the class not by reason alone but by virtue of the authoritative position he or she possesses. Other times this is interpreted to mean that the arguments on all sides must be presented with equal vigor and persuasiveness. As against either of these views, however, there are those who insist that the teacher's job is to present the truth as he or she sees it, as long as the other positions are presented fairly and as strongly as their merit warrants, and as long as the conclusions are supported by reason and fair argument alone. To do otherwise, this argument insists is to play a disingenuous game with one's students: to misrepresent oneself in a way as to lose

credibility with people who know perfectly well that you do have an opinion and that you don't take them seriously enough to share it with them. (This conflict raises an interesting paradox: if you do state an opinion there is little doubt that, given the traditional authoritative position of the teacher, you will have undue influence. This creates an unhealthy student-teacher relationship. On the other hand, if you don't state an opinion, it will be clear to the students that you are unwilling to share something important with them. This too creates an unhealthy student-teacher relationship. Conclusion: a healthy student-teacher relationship is impossible given the traditional authoritative position of the teacher.)

My thesis is that there are epistemological, ontological, and most importantly, moral and political presuppositions embodied in the educational structures we teach in, which, if we are trying to give a "balanced" or "neutral" picture of things undermine our efforts at neutrality, and if we are trying to teach the "truth" are often at odds with it. In so far as we take the learning of philosophy to be a mere intellectual achievement, with little or not influence on the life or attitudes of the learner, this ought not overly concern us. We can speak our piece, and if we are persuasive enough, if our techniques are highly enough developed, our students will remember and be able to emulate our logical exhibitions. But they will do so only in the context best described as "this is what they do in philosophy, which has nothing very much to do with 'real life'." If on the other hand we are genuinely interested in developing in our students an attitude toward life, a critical stance embodied not merely in their minds when they think "philosophy" but embodied in their behavior when they respond in any and all situations, then these structures must be viewed as subversive of our efforts.

I will concentrate on those structures which embody moral and political ideals, since our failure to successfully develop a critical faculty with regard to them is of much greater significance than our failure to successfully develop a critical faculty with regard to epistemological or ontological matters. The grading system embodies several very profound social presuppositions. By rewarding educational "success" and punishing educational "failure," the system teaches by example rather than word that it is perfectly appropriate for one's life activity to be engaged in not for its own sake but for the sake of extrinsic rewards. From the ages of five to twenty-two the activity which dominates a person's life (or at least a college student's life) is school learning, and the student learns, despite all our efforts to tell him or her otherwise, that what "counts" in terms of prestige and success is the grade that they achieve, not the learning that they may have done. In response to a question from Glaucon, Socrates argued that it is better to be a perfectly just man who is perceived as unjust than a perfectly unjust man who is perceived as just. I fear, however, that there is little in the experience of our students to indicate that knowledge is intrinsically valuable or that learning is something to be engaged in for its own sake. What they learn, and it begins in the earliest grades, is that important activity, like learning, is important because of something else. Such activity is classically (although not in modern parlance) called alienated activity, and while it is certainly true that the philosophy teacher does not initiate such an approach to learning, the fact remains that it is in philosophy courses that the distinction between alienated and non-alienated activity is most frequently learned, if it is learned at all, so that the grading system works a special hardship on the teacher who wishes to portray non-alienated behavior as an ideal model. It might be claimed, and it is almost certainly true, that most human behavior in most modern societies is alienated in just this way; that virtually all of our labor is engaged in for the sake of a wage, so that schools ought to be considered training for life activity. Perhaps so, but because we, as teachers of philosophy, are required to reinforce this value, it becomes virtually impossible to offer "utopian" alternatives which might motivate persons to seek significant social change in the direction of altering this unhappy feature of modern life. In short, we are precluded from doing our job effectively. If we try to be effective, we are brought up short by the grading requirement. Inevitably, students will view our remarks with cynicism; often we will foster a disrespect for learning, or higher education, or the university, or philosophy, or ourselves. If even we as philosophers engage in and require others to engage in alienated activity, how can we expect our students to take seriously our remarks and ideals? The structure in which we are required to work fatally undermines our effectiveness, and in effect makes certain positions antecedently less plausible, or at least less teachable.

A second consequence of the grading system, logically, if not politically distinct from the first, is that learning, and again by extension the important elements of life activity, is made a competitive rather than a cooperative venture. As long as grades are awarded differentially on the basis of "superior performance," and as long as grades are viewed as the purpose or goal of study, it will be apparent even to the slowest students that it is desirable to know more than another person not to be able to help him or her learn, but to score better on an exam; that it is in your interest to help someone learn only if he or she can help you at least as much, and preferably more. Again, this is a feature of virtually all school learning and is not unique to philosophy class, but it is in philosophy class that one is most likely to encounter competing theoretical models of social organization. One will have to compare, say, Hobbes's concept of the social order as a war of all against all held in check by powerful political organization with an anarchist or Marxist model of total social cooperation with no or minimal political organization. Whatever efforts the teacher may make in favor of the latter, and certainly if he or she tries to present a "balanced" view, the structure in which the student operates and has operated for years clearly prejudices the case in favor of the Hobbesian model. He or she understands, if not in a consciously articulatable way, certainly in terms of appropriate behavior in specific situations, that school is a competitive arena where anything goes as long as there is no school regulation against it (e.g., cheating of various sorts) or as long as we don't get caught. Even if we can persuade the student of the possibility or desirability of an anarchist state, the continued structure of differential grading, which is imposed on us and in turn imposed by us on students, will effectively turn our success into a meaningless intellectual achievement with little or no effect on the behavior and response of our students in real situations. He or she may believe that it is philosophically desirable—that is, desirable in terms of the presuppositions and arguments one learns in philosophy class—to have one sort of social organization, but he or she knows perfectly well in terms of behavior in particular situations, that it is politically impossible to have it, since even the philosophy teacher does not live by it, and in learning it it is necessary to compete with our fellow students to achieve a higher grade!

There are other structural problems. By teaching as usually we must, in pre-arranged classrooms and at pre-arranged class times, we reinforce the notion that human activity must be role or function oriented rather than integrated. Learning philosophy is something that happens in schools, from 9–10 a.m. or 1–3 p.m., etc; playing is something that happens in other places and other times (and moreover is something one is supposed to enjoy); working is something you do during summer vacations or after school, and is neither learning nor playing (nor to be enjoyed). So much of our life is organized in this way that it might seem extraordinary to mention it as raising a special problem in the teaching of philosophy. Again, however, philosophers are charged with exposing and encouraging serious speculation about alternatives, especially social alternatives. If we are anxious to defend the value of an "integrated" life—one in which work, play, and learning are all embodied in the same activity—the structure in which we are forced to do it makes a mockery of the theory. Again, if all we care about is the verbal response of our students to appropriate questions, this is unimportant. But if we care about their carrying this response beyond classroom situations, then it is very important.

Two structural elements in the classroom combine to seriously undermine any theory of democracy, and especially participatory democracy. In the first place, the university is designed so that we teach "subjects," thereby, as other critics have noted, perpetuating the myth that the universe comes packaged in plausibly separable units (so that, for instance, it makes sense to study economics but not sociology or political science or history or philosophy, something that is inconceivable to the political economist), but even more importantly, and less noted, encouraging the relativization of knowledge. Something becomes "true for history" or "true for political science," etc.[1] What is "true for psychology" is sometimes "false for philosophy." The social consequences of this are enormous. Not only does it breed cynicism where the discrepancies are noted, but it breeds a fatal unwillingness to participate at a significant level in social and political affairs. Unless one is an "expert in politics" (or economics, or environmental science, or whatever) it is deemed inappropriate to act or sometimes even to have an opinion about such matters. General education makes us expert in nothing, and specialized education makes us expert in at most one thing. We must therefore let others make the decisions. (There is an important corollary to this: since morals are not taught at all—even philosophers prefer to teach metaethics and other clearly theoretical topics—no one is willing to take on the difficult issues at a moral level. Moral relativism thrives, and decisions fall by default to those who have the fewest scruples. Relativism serves an important though unfortunate therapeutic purpose: if people were taught to have a sense of right and wrong it is extremely unlikely that they could tolerate the consequences of most of the things their job requires them to do. Relativism frees them from the anxieties inherent in such a situation.)

Efforts to redress this problem—by for instance articulating the virtues of a Millean democracy in which truth and right social action is generated through (an admittedly mysterious) process of total social participation and interaction are thoroughly undermined by the concept of "subjects" and the concomitant concept of "expertise." The structure in which we teach embodies these concepts and dooms to failure our efforts to teach otherwise.

Secondly, virtually all school learning is designed for the transmission of information, not the generation of truth by cooperative effort. Even where other things are at least partially valued (originality, creativity, imagination) the very architecture of the classroom—with the teacher often necessarily in front, set apart, on a platform, with different, more comfortable furniture, with students forced to look only forward, at each other's backs, etc.—tends to diminish the possibility of those values being maximized. The grading system guarantees an aura of authority, even when illegitimate, to the instructor. In such situations, it is respect for authority, not reason, which is encouraged. Even when the instructor preaches the value of reason, the structure in which he or she does it belies the ultimate efficacy of reason. The creation of non-autonomous persons is the end result of all this: persons who do not insist upon or engage in direct and efficacious political activity. It is almost as if the university were designed to make a living reality out of Plato's philosopher-king: the expert who knows the truth and ought, therefore, to have the power not only to transmit it but to run society.

One might ask why this has happened. No doubt it is possible to recite historical and casual explanations of the structure of the university, but I think that in this case functional explanations are more appropriate. We live in a society which, for many reasons I cannot go into here, requires its citizens to be non-autonomous, non-cooperative, and alienated (in all of Marx's senses). Schools and universities are major social institutions; they will either serve this social purpose or they and society as we know it will die. The relationship is organic, and the schools serve their purpose in the organism. Although we, as teachers of philosophy, might be sensitive to alternatives, and even attempt to convince our students of their validity, we are compelled to do our teaching in a structure which undermines our message.

If there are alternatives or solutions they don't appear to be things we can do in the classroom, unless we look forward to explaining why we do not turn in grades, meet assigned times, etc. A possible model which springs to mind is the "foreign language house" in which persons interested in learning a language live together using only that language. If several conditions could be met, this might be possible in philosophy and could overcome many of the structural defects I have mentioned, as well as others which I have not: (1) That few enough people wish to be accommodated. It is, I believe, important not to turn people down, since to do so would encourage the same sort of competitiveness which is so objectionable in class. (2) That no grades or "credit" be given for the experience; (3) That no externally imposed limits be placed on the nature and extent of things studied and discussed; (4) That no conflicting or additional alienating obligations be placed on the participants. If this were not met, I fear that most persons involved would by necessity ignore, or fail to take seriously, the experiment. Such conditions, while much stricter than a person like Illich might propose, would nevertheless combine to create something more like a philosophy collective or commune than a university program. It is unlikely that such an arrangement would be possible within a university, but it might be possible outside of one. There is no way such an approach to learning could be universally extended (to all persons at all levels for all interests) without a total social change.

Notes

The considerations articulated in this paper, and many others like them, have been intensely discussed in and around the philosophy department of Miami University for the past four years. If there are any valuable insights in this paper, they are the result of this collective activity. Originally published in *Metaphilosophy* 6(3–4) (July-October 1975).

1. This way of putting the problem was suggested by Peter Schuller.

Beyond the Eleventh Thesis: Philosophy and Social Change

ROBERT ATKINS

Any discussion which treats the teaching of philosophy as a subject which can be analyzed by itself must suffer from abstraction. Philosophy, and even the teaching of philosophy have histories of their own, but their connections to other institutions and social developments cannot be ignored, if one wants to understand why certain trends have occurred, and how they might be changed. In particular, the rather simple fact has to be emphasized that philosophy departments are usually located within universities and are partially determined by and partially determine them. Universities are in a similar relation of mutual influence with the social environment of which they are a part.

The suggestion of mutual influence may hide the imbalance of determination in both cases. Clearly, general social forces in America have more influence on the university than the reverse. And a university has more determining power over any particular department than the department power over the university. So, we can view the interrelation onesidedly, and assert that much of what goes on in philosophy departments and classrooms in America reflects certain social conditions which can be identified and analyzed as to their effects.

I want to focus on a particular feature of philosophy in our society, to draw out its connections to the larger environment, and to argue the need for change—as a benefit to students and as a socially progressive development.

Philosophy, the origin and focal point of thinkers who have had profound impact on society—of Plato, Aquinas, Locke, Rousseau, Marx—has become in our society a profoundly depoliticized field with essentially no effect on social development. The technicalization of the area, and the de-emphasis on social and political philosophy,[1] has brought our field as far as it has ever been from the real lives of our students and the population in general.

I'm not denigrating the content of university philosophy courses; as a specialized field, philosophy does make contributions to technical progress which has value of its own, despite its being beyond the conception of the uninitiated. My concern is with what isn't being taught, with areas which are almost totally excluded despite their connection to obvious educational needs.

Depoliticization is not unique to philosophy. It is a central aspect of the American experience, which academia reflects. As the word implies, depoliticization is not a character but a process. It is a movement between a depoliticized population and institutions which are produced by and support it. The view is pervasive in the United States that politics have a place in only a select group of functions, that it does not belong in almost all institutions and activities which have the most direct influence on our lives—in schools, businesses, clubs, trade unions, families, entertainment facilities, churches.[2]

Americans obviously have political opinions. But they are discouraged from spending much time in political thought, discussion, or action so that their opinions tend to be based on ignorance and acceptance of authority. They do not see what are in fact political activities as being political, they do not think that politics belongs where it does belong, they have a very limited sense of how political opinions should be put into practice, and they have a tendency to believe that they are not as qualified as people in public office to hold political opinions or to act on them. These are the basic characteristics of a depoliticized people.

As a population of this character, Americans support the maintenance of power by a microscopic section of the population, and support institutions which mythologically view themselves as nonpolitical while often acting as agents of those in power and supporting the continued depoliticization of the citizenry.

Universities are such institutions. Whether private or public, they are controlled by the economic elite, and are staffed by an administration and faculty who act out their American socialization in their offices and classrooms. So universities have cooperated in the development of tools essential to American business and government, while upholding the supposedly sacred academic principle of value neutrality, and disallowing political advocacy in the shrine of objective education.

Philosophy hasn't turned out to be of great importance to national defense or business administration, so it hasn't had much of a direct role in the furthering of ruling class interests. But it has fallen into the rest of the model, supporting the view that politics is a separate business from education.

In the last few years, many of the consumers of our teaching have undergone a change. This isn't the place for an analysis of the student movement, but the political activities of a large number of the students—in the civil rights movement of the early sixties and in the university-oriented and anti-war movements of the late sixties—have influenced their views of their education.

The interests and activities of political students have been met with hostility by the power brokers of academia despite the fact that these students are in need of a specific education which could be delivered in the university and without which their activities have suffered.

It is important to detail these educational needs to show how the classroom experience could relate to them.

1. Values and Political Goals

For various reasons, students are more willing at present than all other segments of the population to become involved in direct response to social events of which they disapprove. Although this response is a valuable and important aspect of their lives, and has produced activities for which we all should be grateful, it often doesn't have enough perspective. The immediate feeling of moral revulsion which has led to protest has been trustworthy, and I don't mean to be critical of it. But feelings alone don't provide either ethical or political analysis.

We[3] need to understand why certain actions should be opposed, and to gain this understanding requires a conception of how our values relate to each other and to the social world. It requires empirical analysis to provide an explanatory model for the otherwise arbitrarily interpreted empirical data. In short, we need to gain a perspective on our own sense of justice and on the historical and social context for our political activities.

What I'm saying isn't new. In fact, people have opposed student activism precisely on the grounds that it lacks this perspective, that is has been "mindless." My difference with these people is that I see the necessity for social action based on whatever information and analysis is available, but also realize some weaknesses which need to be worked on, whereas these opponents of political action, true to American depoliticalization, urge non-action as if it were neutral to prevailing conditions, and as if it were itself not a choice to be made from available knowledge.[4]

Some members of the academic community might argue that the university already has within its curriculum the means for gaining these two kinds of understanding. The combination of certain courses in ethics, government, political theory, and sociology might be seen as providing the needed information. To an extent, this is correct. If one had the time to take enough courses in all these fields to be able to extrapolate from the bulk of the material the few oases of relevancy, at least part of the road would have been passed. But it really is a long way from teaching on R. M. Hare and Stephen Toulmin to the war in IndoChina, and general surveys of political thought are useful only when they can be obviously applied to the immediate social context.

It is evident that this need for value and political analysis is most inefficiently and insufficiently met by the present curriculum.

2. Social Analysis

I have seen political people develop responses to particular incidents in a purely emotional way. A gut reaction strategy is common in these instances.

"Those bastards! Let's blow up a draft board!" An understandable reaction, but not one enlightened in how to attain political objectives.

The point of course is that the best strategy for social change is not the one which first hits you in the apex of anger, but that which most effectively can achieve its goal.[5] This strategy is equally unlikely to be found by the kind of speculation which also goes on in tactical discussions, based on little knowledge of how society functions.

The formation of strategy and tactics is really a process of social prediction. The most rational process for devising them then is the developing of a clear sense of the goal, an understanding of the present state of things, and a correct analysis of how society operates, and the use of deductive abilities. That is, one must operate as a practical social scientist, generating predictions about the effects of alternative courses of action.

I still insist on the necessity and value of action in the absence of social science training. I still insist that nonaction is a form of action, the results of which are as predictable (or non-predictable) as any other course. But the majority of people involved in political action, who have no training in social methodology, nor even a sense of the importance of such training for the devising of tactics, cannot move as effectively toward their goals as a result.

Again, it may be argued that the means of gaining this knowledge exists in present curricula, especially in sociology methodology courses and in certain branches of political science and the philosophy of social sciences. But beyond certain general considerations, there is little in the content of these fields as presently taught which is relevant to anti-war work or community organizing. It is at best inefficient to train yourself in tactical development by studying the effect of housing projects on tuberculin rates.

These educational needs were simply out of the picture as the relation developed in the sixties between political students and the university. Instead of concerning themselves with how higher education could adapt itself to the new interests of many students, administrators and faculty on the whole placed themselves in immediate opposition to the activities of the student movement and created thereby a spirit of antagonism which has determined much of the mood of the campuses to this day.

Organizations were repressed, meetings were outlawed, students suspended, and police called onto campus. Every means the scholars thought consistent with academic discipline as well as a few they weren't sure of were used to "quiet" the campus, and if their intellectual training was insufficient for them to draw the relatively simple prediction that these actions would have an effect opposite to the intended one, then this points to weaknesses stemming from their own political non-education. It should have been obvious that when freedom of speech and organization is dramatically restricted in an atmosphere which is filled with the illusions of a self-disciplined democracy, and when the repression is directed against students who have included themselves in a struggle to increase freedom, then the effect of the repression has to be the building of the student movement in opposition to the restrictive powers.[6]

This antagonism of the university toward the student movement then led as a natural consequence to its inversion. Where before their energies were focused on civil rights struggles, students now began to see their educational workplace as a significant target for their attacks. To a degree, this was a matter of survival, since they were organizing as students, and needed the facilities of their own community. But it developed into more than this. The issues of depersonalization, of irrelevant education, of autocratic university government came in, and beyond these internal matters, it was found that significant connections existed between the university and forces outside the academic setting against whom the student movement had been fighting. So the university became a local target for action, more visible and vulnerable than the external enemies had been.

In the context of this often violent struggle, the possibility of a more positive response to the educational needs of radicalized students was unthinkable. The few members of the academic community who supported some of the off-campus actions of the student movement still tended to see these as extracurricular, with no specific relation to college study, other than taking up time which might have been better spent in the library. So they made no attempt to incorporate the actions of political students into the academic boundaries of the institution.

Perhaps the atmosphere is different now. The student movement is in a stage of relative inactivity, and perhaps our community can study the situation with a bit more calm and rationality. Also, out of the troubled waters have come some specifically political programs, especially in ethnic studies, and the university, having not disintegrated in their presence, may be more open to alternative programs. It is in this hope that I write this essay, and the proposal which it carries.

The educational needs which I have indicated can be fulfilled only by specific programs which are directed to that end. These would be interdisciplinary of necessity, and could exist in specially created departments or could be spread out by coordination among several fields. Here, we shall consider only philosophy's potential contribution. But it will become apparent that the limits presently binding university philosophy courses will have to be transgressed.

1. Ethics—Students usually become politicized because of opposition to some action, institution or state of affairs. They need to understand how this moral feeling relates to other feelings they have, perhaps to a system of values. They need to place themselves in their personal and social context, appreciating the social and psychological factors behind their own positions. Since other people, perhaps even the majority of Americans, oppose their views, they must study socializing influences in our society as they affect different segments of the population. This opposition brings forward the importance of learning about moral and political persuasion, in its rational and non-rational forms.

2. Political theory and practice—The particularities of the society which faces us need to be put into a perspective which aids explanation and provides longer ranged goals for social transformation. So, alternative models for setting our social problems in a larger context need to be evaluated. This evaluation should include explanatory efficacy, non-utopian goal generation, and tactical usefulness.

3. Social Change as a Social Science—Philosophy can have value for political activists similar to its value for social scientists. This would involve courses relevant

to the formation of tactics and strategy, discussing methodology in general. Analysis of problems in causal and predictive analysis, as they arise for people concerned with social change, could be of enormous importance to political students, if there were a successful merging of theoretical and practical aspects.

Other courses come to mind—science and society, aesthetics and politics, politics and the law, for example—but they need not be described in detail. The point is to provide a philosophy curriculum devoted to the significant portion of the campus population who are involved in social action, and such a curriculum could be worked out without much difficulty.

The argument to this point has been that members of the student movement have needs for education which could be filled by the academic community and specifically by philosophy departments. With this, I would expect no disagreement, for the two propositions are evidently true. But the key question has yet to be answered—should the university or any part of it take on this task?

I am going to speak to this issue only briefly at this point, as several of the arguments also apply to the more radical proposal I will introduce shortly.

We all recognize the important role of the university in preparing students for their working life. This is normally interpreted as training for a profession, and is undeniably central to the functioning of higher education. But what of those students who wish to make social change their profession—i.e., their skilled primary labor—or those who wish to use their profession for social change?

If this were a small group, too insignificant to call for a redirection of university funds and energies, it might be justifiable to ignore their minority interests. But this is not the case in most of the major universities today. Too many radical caucuses exist in professional organizations to argue for insufficient interest. Too many students are engaged in political protest to argue that there wouldn't be enough involvement.

Philosophy, in particular, has attracted political students in unusually large numbers. For example, during the days of the free speech movement at the University of California at Berkeley, the major spokesman was an undergraduate philosophy major. The heads of some of the movement committees came from the graduate department of philosophy. Shortly afterwards, a graduate student organization and then a trade union for employed graduate students were formed. Several of the leaders of both groups came from philosophy, including the president of the union, and two members of the executive board.

Perhaps it was coincidental that philosophy students played such a major role, since the department certainly didn't relate academically to these interests, but we might also speculate that people who have the character to lead them to theoretical analysis also often have desires to move the theory into practice. At least this appeared to be the case for the graduate student who became an editor of *Ramparts* magazine, the student who became a leading member of Asian Information Service, the student who became one of the editors of the *Socialist Revolution* journal, or the student later arrested as part of the "Seattle Eight."

In general, we have a large group of students, with specific educational needs, directed toward their future professional life, clearly related to traditional academic concerns, but calling for a new emphasis in content. As long as higher education makes the political decision to ignore these needs, it is violating one of its essential functions.

But I want to take the issue beyond this position, which could be viewed as a matter solely of university reform. The politics of the issue haven't yet been fully developed, and in doing that, we move to a suggestion for more radical change in higher education.

It has been clear I trust that my concern has been with students who are interested in social change in America, as opposed to those who act politically to maintain things as they are. More particularly, I have referred to the student movement, which, while encompassing a wide spectrum of political positions, seeks changes which can be characterized vaguely as being left-oriented.

The professional training argument might apply to students of other political persuasions, but the further aspects of my proposal argue for left-oriented curricular changes only. This has to be understood in a very broad sense, but it is exclusionary nonetheless.

In this context, I mean by "left," a political perspective which strives to free our society from poverty, racism, expansionist wars, economic exploitation, sexism, tendencies toward a police state, environmental destruction, plastic culture, and miseducation, and to build a society based on a non-exploitative system which is supportive of the furthering of human capabilities—creative intelligent labor—something which nearly all of us are capable of, but which our society neither encourages nor develops in most individuals.

With this general description of the left position, my proposal is that the interests and needs of left students should be served in our universities, in an educational and political sense.

The argument for this is not complex. First, the complex of positions I have referred to as "left" are correct, from a moral and political point of view. Secondly, it is the responsibility of the university to become involved in political affairs, by supporting movements which represent a correct moral and political perspective.

This isn't the place to argue for the justice of the left position. Most of the points aren't particularly controversial in the intellectual community, and those which are, probably involve differences of interpretation. What is more controversial is the road from here to there, and I specifically did not categorize any particular strategies in my view of the left, although I have some rather specific views on this question. But my object is not to impose my particular politics on academia. Rather, it is to urge certain general political assumptions on that community.

So I will leave the matter of the moral and political correctness of the left position to other places, and pass to the more substantial question from the point of view of university functioning. Should higher education maintain a political stance in its functioning?

It needs to be repeated at the outset that American universities are not now non-political institutions. They train students to fit into professional molds which are supportive of the American socio-economic system and its political activities. They provide research which benefits businesses and the military. University funds are invested in business, often in highly controversial sectors.

Classroom teaching is not value free either. It tends to be supportive of basic political positions: in the texts, in curricular design, and in the analyses given by the faculty. It is interesting to note that these activities aren't usually seen as political, because they seem to follow assumptions which are so deeply ingrained that they aren't noticed as choices. But when challenges are made to these assumptions in university courses, they are immediately and correctly characterized as bringing politics into the classroom.

This overt politicizing of teaching is growing, as younger faculty, themselves schooled in the student movement of the sixties, join the ranks of their often disapproving seniors. So we find more and more faculty taking actions as faculty, resulting in public pressure on the University to drive political elements out—that is, to maintain the old institutions which are supportive of the established system, and to remove the thorny challengers.

In fact, it is impossible for a curriculum to be neutral. The distinction between fact and value isn't precise enough. The complexity of the relations between content and politics is far from obvious. And the depoliticized nature of academia makes it difficult to view curriculum politically, even for the purpose of weeding out politics.

To take a relatively obvious case, there is no question but that the teaching of evolution has political consequences, and has become once again a question of high political concern in many sections of the country. Evolution is in fact a theory which weakens the credibility of organized religion, and has had enormous historical impact on social life in America.

Whether evolutionary theory is true or not is a question of fact, not of value, but it is also true that the teaching of certain truths has consequences which have to be evaluated from a political perspective, so that the choice of which truths to teach is itself a political question, and one which cannot be neutralized. Surely, most faculty would judge a course on the construction of bombs from a value laden position.

Somewhat less obvious is the political nature of the development of social science curriculum in American universities. Without going into any depth on this question, it need only be mentioned that most areas in the social sciences ignore the relations between the phenomena they analyze and the social-economic system as a whole. The effect of this is to support acceptance of the system, since problems are viewed only from the perspective of apparent immediate causes and potential reformist solutions.

I have already discussed the political aspects of philosophy, which primarily involve the exclusion of certain areas from the curriculum, and the depoliticized style of philosophical analysis.

Several detailed studies of the political role of the university have been given, and it isn't my intent to rehearse them fully here. But that higher education is infused with politics doesn't mean that it should be. As difficult as the job may be, we might make a more conscientious effort to rid the university of its attachments to government and business and to neutralize the curriculum. I have suggested that this is an impossible goal to attain, but we might initiate a process which moves in that direction.[7]

This would be the wrong emphasis to take in educational change, not simply because of its futility, but because it would ignore a political responsibility of the university community.[8]

The depoliticized character of our society leaves enormous power in the hands of the rulers, and provides few channels for change stemming from other segments of the population. The people aren't organized into political units, so that even when we feel a need for political change, we have no means for collective expression or action. We are isolated, separated from power, impotent. So we tend to remain silent, even when we have overcome other aspects of depoliticization and have something to say.[9]

This has been less true for students and oppressed minorities, who retain communities more than other groups, and who have moved to protest, overcoming some of the stifling aspects of our social life. So we have had an era of protest, which has created a new meaning for those who remain silent.

The phrase "silence is consent" has undoubtedly been used since the beginning of social struggles. It has meant simply that affirmation is assumed unless one specifically voices opposition. The argument is not obvious, as it appears that silence leaves the question of judgment open. What is more to the point perhaps is that silence isn't opposition, and that it is wrong when opposition is called for.

But the era of protest has given new truth to this old aphorism. It has produced an environment in which support is assumed from those who don't join the actions.[10]

When President Nixon in 1972 announced his mining of the harbors of North Vietnam and the increased bombing of the Vietnamese people, he asked in a television address for the American people to support that escalation of genocide. This request didn't mean to send your letters of support, and take to the streets to show that you approve of my actions. Of course Nixon would have been overjoyed to see mass signs of overt support. But he knew that that wasn't a likely prospect, so his request for support was really a negative one. It meant to remain silent; don't demonstrate or cause social disorder in the face of my action.

And indeed, the media—the major interpreter of news events for the American public—did gauge support on the basis of the degree of protest at that time. This illustrates the fact that especially in a period of protest, lack of protest is judged as signifying agreement. So the silence of the major portion of the isolated depoliticized citizenry is used by those in power as an expression of support for their policies.

Depoliticization nourishes itself in many ways. For example, the lack of political organization for the masses of American people supports their detachment from politics, and this detachment prevents the development of more groupings for political purposes. There are many external elements which affect this mutual development, but one explicit way to break out of the cycle is for existing organizations, regardless of their principal purpose, to involve themselves in political expression.

To wait for political organization to form, to argue that politics isn't the business of an institution, is to submit to the blanket of impotence which pervades America. It becomes another form of non-action which at best is neutral when it shouldn't be, and more often is supportive of injustices which should be opposed. Not only for individuals, but also for businesses, unions, softball teams, cooperatives, for universities—silence is consent.

The university has the responsibility to move into the political focus; indeed, it has a special responsibility because of the power of learning behind its evaluations. But it also has a special task, pertaining to its principal functioning.

The easiest response for the academic community to make is one which has already been seen in many instances—resolutions of protest to particular situations. Even though tangible results seldom follow from such actions, they are still important. In the short run, they become part of the total response which occasionally has affected policy. But of more importance, they serve to establish the connection of educational institutions to the political scene.

Still, the declaration of opposition isn't the essential business of the university. Preparing young people for taking their place in our society is more to the point. How absurd it is for a faculty to vote for a resolution opposing American warmaking, while doing nothing to help train themselves and their students to more effectively struggle against the war. Along with the obligation to stand in protest then, higher education also has the responsibility to provide the necessary education for those who take on the job of trying to change America. It also is responsible for building the ranks of political students, for breaking the hold of depoliticization on the people who come for education.

If this is the task, the program I suggested for political education must be made more specific. General discussions of values and strategy may be valuable for people who aren't clear about how their feelings relate to the social world, but certain political principles need to be settled early on, to set the basis for the training of agents of social change. The statement on page 196 represents the kind of principles which could found this education.

Beyond the political correctness of these positions, there is a pedagogical reason for establishing first principles. As in any field, one cannot spend all of his or her time deciding on basics, but must move from basics to their consequences. Any program devoted to the training of political activists must then provide opportunities for different analyses to be fully developed.

For example, the general left position as I have defined it has room for both reformists and revolutionaries. Providing opportunities for working out analyses means that there would be a place for the debate as to whether it is necessary to overthrow capitalism to create a human society, but that there would also be sufficient space to move from either of the positions on the question.

It should be clear that the search for "objective" truth isn't violated by this program. Starting from particular premises doesn't lead to subjectivity. The conclusions which follow in the development of the system are true if and only if the premises are true. Students need to be aware of that, and they need opportunity to think out those premises. But they also need to move from them—carefully and with the best possible training.

Such a program would also bring political practice into higher education, as a counterpoint to the learning of theory. From an educational point of view, political action is as essential to the training of social change agents as laboratory work is to a student of chemistry. From a political point of view, the activities of students and faculty are part of the fulfillment of the responsibility the university shares to react with other elements of society to create social change.

Philosophy's role in a social change program would be essentially an extension of what was suggested earlier. The political theory, value orientation, and tactical methodology would be applied to the discussion of basic principles and the movement from them. Among other things, the study of Marxism would find a more central place than currently exists. But it is of no practical use to work out the details of philosophy's input, in the absence of such programs.

As we approach the end of this essay, it is time to come back to earth, or at least that part of it which makes up the United States of America. The kind of program I have argued for isn't about to become a feature of American higher education, because American higher education reflects the American reality in general. So I intend it as a principle for struggle in the university community, which itself is reflected outward into the struggles for progressive change in our society.

As in other struggles, it would occur in many communities, constituting in total a national movement. Victories in those places where conditions make it more possible would perhaps change the situation at the larger universities where such an idea is almost unthinkable today.[11] However it might occur, one thing is clear. Persuasion alone won't bring the suggested changes.

Still, persuasion is an element, especially at a time when there isn't yet any struggle over this question. My purpose has been to introduce the development of social change programs as an educational and political responsibility of higher education, and therefore of philosophy departments in particular. It is a persuasive argument, I think, but hardly destined by itself to change the university.

Notes

1. At the date of this writing (May 1973) there is some evidence of changes in this regard. Several introductory texts have become popular on the basis of including social and political essays, and there appears to be a growing demand for faculty members

whose competencies lie in these fields. Perhaps this will turn into a development which brings these branches of philosophy back onto center stage of our activity.

2. Of course our outlook toward these activities is not completely apolitical. But in each case, the degree to which politics explicitly enters is well below what it should be, and the degree to which covert politics affects each is not recognized.

3. Although the major interest of this essay is with how we can provide a better education for our students, it is quite clear that this particular education is something which we all need to a far greater extent than we receive it.

4. Many academics have spoken of the revolt against rationality among the young. This has been true to an extent among politically active students as well and it is unfortunate. But much of the blame for this must fall on the model presented by the "rational" faculty who speak of rationality as contradictory with activism. If they are concerned with irrationalism, the forces of academia should put their rationalism to work in consort with political activity. For, as long as the purveyors of rationality condemn political activists as mindless youth, the politically active youth will reject the academics and their rationality as representatives of submissive complicity.

5. One would normally emphasize not only the effectiveness of a strategy but also its relation to ethical principles applied to it as a means. But I think that this separation of means and ends is confusing, and intend by my use of the term 'goal', not only the final social state one would like to achieve, but all the consequences of the actions which are taken to that end.

6. It has been argued that the relative inactivity of the student movement at present is a consequence of the more hardnosed policies taken by such administrators as S. I. Hayakawa at San Francisco State University. But I think that this particular period is much more a consequence of larger social features, and that changes in social development will produce an active movement again, however repressive university policies may be.

7. It is not only a logical impossibility because of the politics behind determining what to teach, but it is also a practical impossibility. The university could not survive in the current social context if it attempted to end its training of students for positions in the business world, for example. Nor would this be a commendable action, in any political system.

8. Although this would be the wrong emphasis, certain parts of it would not be incorrect, but they would be done, not in a context of depoliticizing the university, but on the basis of certain political judgments.

9. The "silent majority" are a majority, not in holding a particular politics, as Nixon would have us believe, but rather in remaining silent.

10. This was of course the purpose of Nixon's raising of the silent majority concept.

11. There are already, in a few private colleges such as Antioch College and Goddard College, programs devoted to social change training. They do not represent every aspect of what my proposal calls for, but they are steps in that direction. These institutions are, however, traditionally experimental, and because of their trustee structure, they do not fall under the kinds of political influences which act on the larger universities.

Teaching Alienation

Richard Schmitt

Philosophers say that they 'teach Aristotle' or 'teach logic' when they talk about these topics in their classes. In that sense alienation is not often taught in America today. But we perpetuate alienation in this society, teach alienation to successive generations, precisely by not talking.

Even if we do talk about alienation in classes, that often merely reflects and thereby perpetuates existing alienation. We tend to teach alienation, even if we do make it a topic in our classes.

Alienation is maintained by all our institutions. Even if they did not come to us to be educated, our students would end up alienated. Our teaching does no more than contribute to the pervasive social milieu. But it helps.

I shall argue these claims in the pages that follow. They are necessarily general claims and will not apply to the same extent to all individuals. But they apply to a sufficient extent to a sufficient number of people to be warranted. Each reader must judge for him or herself to what extent they apply in their own case.

I

We must begin by talking about the concept of alienation.

The word "alienation," once an esoteric bit of philosophical jargon, has lately passed into the general vocabulary. But the concept still awaits clarification. Here are some major features of alienation:

> What constitutes the alienation of labor? First that the work is external to the worker, that it is not part of his nature; and that, consequently, he does not fulfill himself in his work . . . [he] has a feeling of misery rather than well-being . . . his work is not voluntary . . . .[1]

This passage from Marx, however familiar, still stands out for its richness.

We must pay particular attention to Marx' insistence that we should speak of the alienation of *labor*, to the fact that the alienated worker's unhappiness is only one element of his or her alienation with lack of fulfillment and to labor being forced, i.e., involuntary.

There is a widespread tendency among contemporary writers to psychologize the notion of alienation. The term "alienation" is thought to describe an 'inner' state of persons. People are said to be alienated because they have certain beliefs, for instance, that they have little or no political influence,[2] or because they have certain feelings about their actions.[3] Alienation, viewed in this way, can be overcome by changing peoples' beliefs or emotions. The remedies proposed therefore range from drugs, to psychotherapy to religion, or the more old fashioned nostrums like finding a hobby, taking a trip or getting married. Social change is not considered a cure for alienation, except in the minimal sense in which it may change peoples' beliefs or feelings, or as a very extreme measure. Beliefs and emotions can usually be changed without genuine social change by public relations experts and experts in industrial relations, by religion, psychological palliatives and the diversions of a rising standard of living.

Marx, by contrast, insists that alienation is both a social and a psychological condition. Alienated persons are unhappy. But unhappiness is neither a sufficient nor a necessary condition for being alienated. A person may sincerely deny that they are alienated and be no less alienated for all that.[4] My feelings are neither proof nor disproof of my alienation. For to be alienated means that one's "work is not part of this nature" and that may well be the case even if one is not aware of it. In fact, we shall soon see that being unaware of one's alienation is just one particular form of it.

If alienation is not exclusively and not necessarily a psychological condition, it is a social condition. But what is more, it is a social condition not merely in the attenuated sense in which my social circumstances cause me to have certain feelings or beliefs. The sense in which alienation of labor is a social condition is a stronger sense. The nexus between social conditions and alienation is not a causal one. Having one's work "external to one," i.e., having no control over one's work, does not *cause* the unhappiness which we call "alienation." It is instead of the essence of alienation, precisely because unhappiness is a relatively peripheral feature of it. Marx does not argue that point. If we were to provide the requisite arguments we would have to show that social conditions do not *cause* alienation under suitable conditions. For if that were the case we could remove alienation either by giving workers control over their work or by removing the conditions under which lack of control caused alienation, perhaps by raising the standard of living or reducing the standard work week. But such moves do not abolish alienation, but only mask and, therefore, aggravate it.[5] For there are no initial conditions under which lack of control over one's work is not alienating. One prevents explosions in the powder house either by removing the cause of explosions, open flames, or by making conditions unfavorable to explosions, e.g., by wetting the powder. There are no analogous favorable conditions which can be manipulated to forestall alienation where work is "external to the worker."

What are these social conditions that constitute alienation? Labor is alienated, Marx tells us, if "work is not voluntary." But can we make sense of that? That may have applied, we might say, to the impoverished industrial workers of Marx's day, who worked 16 hours a day, six days a week, under barely human conditions. Poverty forced them to continue to work although they hated their work fiercely. But working conditions in our time have become much less burdensome. People move, besides, from job to job, and if they are tired of one, they are always financially able to move to another and tide themselves over in the interim. For those who do not want to work at all, and are not independently wealthy, there is always welfare. Not a comfortable life to be sure, but a real option. Even if this description does not apply to everyone in this society, the majority of people working in this society, do so voluntarily in all of these senses: They choose to work rather than not to work, they choose the work that suits them best among the jobs available. If they do not like the job they have, they can always get another one.

There are other questions that need to be raised about Marx' notion of alienation as applied to present conditions:

What is the connection between work being voluntary, or not, and it's being fulfilling? Can one not find completely unexpected fulfillment in work that one did not choose, or conversely, don't persons again and again abandon chosen careers because the fulfillment they hoped for in that work eludes them? Fulfillment and working voluntarily seem only fortuitously connected.

Similar questions need to be raised with regard to the claim that work, in an alienated society, is not part of the worker's 'nature'. Ours, we want to say, is a highly mobile society. We have developed elaborate ways of fitting persons to the jobs that they are most suited for. Thus to say that work, in our society, is not a part of the working person's nature seems clearly false. We have large numbers of tests, educational tracks, counsellors, personnel officers whose sole function is to provide everyone with an occupation that suits their abilities.

Thus Marx' claim about alienation does not seem to apply to our society, for work here is voluntary: it is, at least sometimes, fulfilling, and there is no reason to think that people are not matched correctly to available jobs for a good deal of the time. We seem to be blocked at the very beginning of our reflections: it makes little sense to say that we perpetuate alienation in our teaching, unless the society in which we teach is an alienated one. But if we take Marx' suggestions seriously, it would seem that our society is not, on the whole, alienated. In order to move forward with the argument, we need either a different description of alienation or a different reading of the passage quoted from Marx. I shall try the latter avenue.

Philosophers have thought much about the difference between voluntary and involuntary acts. The most frequently discussed obstacles to acting voluntarily are either brute physical coercion or inner impediments, either extraordinary ones like madness or drunkenness or the ordinary workings of psychological causes, like the wounds of childhood that affect our actions as adults. Actions are said to be voluntary if neither physical or psychological forces would have prevented one from making a different choice from the one they are making. But in that sense, the person who must choose between hanging and drowning chooses voluntarily for neither physical nor psychological forces constrain them to choose one alternative over the other. This seems however an unduly broad interpretation of the word "voluntary." Choosing the lesser of two evils may well be a genuine choice, without being a voluntary one. Being given the choice between hanging and drowning, I may end up being hung since that was my choice, but should I say that I went to the gallows voluntarily? In a more stringent sense, actions are voluntary only if they are not coerced by physical or psychological means and if, in addition, the actions are attractive to the agent. Actions are genuinely voluntary, where the choice that precedes it chooses not the lesser of two evils but the greater of two goods.

Given this more stringent sense of "voluntary," most of the job choices people make in this society are not voluntary precisely because work is, on the whole, not fulfilling. The choice that any person makes is from among existing jobs. What jobs exist is not determined by the needs of the members of the society for work that fulfills, but by the needs of a huge, competitive productive machine. New technologies, say, in agriculture drastically reduce certain kinds of jobs. Such technological changes alter the options from which any individual makes their choice. New jobs come into being in the same way. Jobs are neither abolished nor new jobs introduced because they would fulfill the life of the workers that do them.

In this way, Marx' explication of the notion of alienation still applies to our society. People do not work voluntarily precisely because their work does not fulfill, except accidentally. The society is certainly not organized to arrange work in ways that promise fulfillment to as many of its members as possible. For the same reasons work, in this society, is only accidentally part of the worker's nature. The elaborate counseling and placements mechanisms that exist seek to place individuals in *existing* jobs that may be suitable for them, but that fact tells us nothing whatsoever about the worker's nature. For the job is shaped not by reference to the worker's needs but by the needs of his or her employer.[6]

Thus Marx' notion of alienation is still useful for us. But as it stands now, it is not at all clear because the notions of "fulfillment" and "being part of the worker's nature," while not unintelligible, are not very precise. Philosophers are of little use here. They have talked much about pleasures and pains, but notions like fulfillment have not been discussed since the British Hegelians talked about "self-realization" and Dewey made 'growth' the central goal for human conduct.

An adequate explication of the notion of 'fulfillment' is very complex. But it is not needed for the present purposes. In order to say what I have to say, it is sufficient to draw on the ordinary understanding of the notion of fulfillment, which functions in the context where we think of human beings as possessed of many capacities.

They find fulfillment to the extent that their capacities are fully developed and exercised. This requires, among other things, that individuals know or learn what they can do. Such knowledge does not come to one through introspection, but through experience. Thus fulfillment is available for many only in a society that makes it its primary goal to provide opportunities for people to get to know their capacities and to develop them. In such a society, for instance, jobs are shaped not only by the demands of production but primarily by the needs of the workers. To the extent that a society does not make the growth of the individual its primary concern that society is alienated and the alienation of its members is a social condition.

II

Our society does not make the individual growth of its members its primary concern. What is more, it tends to conceal that fact from people. This concealment is practiced primarily by teachers, philosophers among them. We do not, as we just noted, talk much about the notions of self-realization and of growth. We do not talk about alienation, and thereby, perpetuate it. We teach our students to be alienated by not talking about alienation in our classes. This is true in a large number of cases. Alienation is, of course, discussed in philosophy courses, particularly in courses on Existentialism or on Marx. I shall give some reasons below for thinking that that does more harm than good.

Much is said in courses about Ethics and Political Philosophy about the happiness of individuals or of groups, but alienation as a major source of unhappiness is not often mentioned. One may try to explain that by saying that alienation is a proper subject for sociologists or psychologists, but does not belong in the scope of philosophy. It is true that many psychologists have a good deal to say about alienation, and that alienation is being studied and degrees of it measured by sociologists and political scientists. But philosophers have never yet been deterred from discussing a subject by the fact that it is discussed in one of the other sciences. There is, after all, philosophy of the social sciences and of psychology. The question, for instance, whether the sorts of explanations of behavior offered by Freudians is scientific is widely argued in philosophic journals. Nor do philosophers limit their inquiry to the methodology and standards of evidence of these various disciplines. One field of philosophy, the philosophy of mind, systematically explores psychological concepts. So does epistemology and even metaphysics. Social philosophy does the same for concepts in the social sciences.

Philosophers frequently discuss a number of concepts that are central to any detailed discussion of alienation. These are the notions of personal identity, the concept of the self, and of agency. But these notions are not discussed in ways that are helpful in any attempt to clarify the concept of alienation. For we talk about criteria of personal identity in a sense of "identity" in which to have an identity is a necessary feature of a person, and we ask what constitutes a self on the assumption that every human being has a self, by definition. We talk about agency in the sense in which to call someone an agent with respect to a particular action is to say that that action is *his* action. These usages make it impossible to ask, let alone illumine, the sorts of things we find ourselves saying about alienation, where we want to say that someone lacks identity, or is not in touch with his self, and where we want to say that an alienated person is not the cause of his own actions.[7] Philosophers are, on the whole, oblivious to problems of alienation, not just in general, but insofar as they completely pass over usages of terms like "identity," "self," "agent" that are relevant to a discussion of alienation. But since the terms are in the philosophic repertory, the refusal to think about alienation cannot be ascribed to a reluctance to stray across the boundaries between academic disciplines.

"An oversight," you say. "Philosophers cannot discuss all problems at once. Let us clear up what we are working on now and then we can come back and take care of the concept of alienation." Such a response is disingenuous.

It has been one of the rare points of agreement between philosophers, at least since Kant, that the point of reflecting about conduct is not to discover what we should do, and even less, what our problems of conduct are. The purpose of moral philosophy, Kant thought, is to keep one from muddying the waters of one's native moral certainties, when one is tempted to do what one knows to be morally reprehensible. In ordinary situations, Kant thought, the normal person knows what to do. The temptation to engage in subtle argument and, thereby, to confuse one's clear sense of duty, arises only in case of conflict between one's moral duty and what one would like to do. The clear awareness of one's duties is incontrovertible. We know how we should act. We know what needs to be done and what needs to be avoided. The philosopher's task is merely to strengthen this native certainty by formulating clear arguments in its support, which are proof against any attempts to escape one's duty through casuistry. Philosophers, since Kant, have perhaps been less suspicious of the motivations behind invalid moral arguments. But their general sense of their project has always remained the same: We know what needs to be done. The path is clear. All that a philosopher can supply is a set of arguments to form our original moral knowledge into a coherent, logically defensible theory.

Philosophers thus do not pay attention to problems of alienation. In addition, they claim that the facts of the moral life are well known to every normal adult. If alienation is not among the givens of the moral life, which are known to everyone, well, then it just is not a problem. Thus, in effect, philosophers not only ignore alienation and its constitutive concepts, but they declare that the problem does not exist.

But is there not a rather extensive literature on the subject? How can professional scholars claim that there is no problem of alienation in the face of so much writing on the subject? It is safe to say that a large number of philosophers have concluded that most of this literature is irretrievably unclear and thus does not merit the attention of professional philosophers. This is not to say, of course, that they have not read Fromm, or Maslow, or May, or, for that matter, Kierkegaard, Heidegger, or Sartre, but that they have concluded, on more or less cursory reading, that this whole literature is not worth careful study. For it is clear that the widespread rejection of writing about alienation, on the grounds that one cannot understand it, does not arise from the sort of exhaustive examination that is usually accorded to the works of philosophers in the official canon of respectable philosophy. One of Descartes' contemporaries, for instance, accused Descartes of arguing in a circle in his *Meditations*. The question whether that accusation must stand is still earnestly being discussed by professional philosophers. No one has been as cautious about accusing writers about alienation of committing logical errors. The claim that writers about alienation are unclear, and that, therefore, there is no genuine philosophical problem about alienation, is not a judgment backed by exhaustive scholarly inquiry. It is an informal judgment backed by rather cursory acquaintance with the literature.

Philosophers' deliberate refusal to deal with alienation, their insistence, that there is no problem, serves to perpetuate the students alienation in several ways.

1. As teachers we materially serve to block peoples' attempts to deal with their own alienation by suggesting to them, by our silence on the topic, as well as by our explicit disapproval of certain literature, that there is no problem of alienation. For one cannot begin to deal with a problem before one is sure that it exists. To the extent that we manage to persuade our students that the problem they sense, the problem of alienation, is unreal, we make it impossible for them to begin to resolve it.

(This is just one more instance of our society dealing with problems by denying that they exist. Until recently, problems of racism and sexism were treated in the same way. Universities have always been influential in the attempts to bury social problems. Remember the discussions about the virtual absence of blacks and women on the faculty!)

2. If one wants to tackle a problem, one must begin by thinking about it, but one can only do that, if a suitable vocabulary is available in which the problem can be formulated and clarified. A practical problem is stated clearly, if one can begin to entertain suggestions for solutions. The large literature on alienation provides some sort of vocabulary for talking about alienation. But the professionals' claim that that vocabulary is not adequate is, I think, correct. It is not adequate, for instance, to say that the alienated person is estranged from himself or has problems about finding his identity. For, these diagnoses are so general that we have no idea what sorts of remedies we might suggest, let alone, what remedies could suitably be tested in practice.

By failing to clarify the necessary vocabulary, philosophers have deprived their students of any possibility of even beginning to articulate their problems with respect to alienation, and have thus worked to perpetuate alienation in a second way. They give explicit and vocal support to the vocabulary and modes of thinking in which ordinary persons cannot even express their dissatisfactions. An example may make this clearer:

A central feature of alienation is the failure to find genuine fulfillment. But what is meant by "fulfillment"? As we noted earlier, little is said about this in the philosophical literature, even though "self-realization ethics" is one of the classes of ethical views discussed in ethics texts. But if terms are not discussed explicitly we cannot help but take their current uses to be clear and adequate. In the current sense of "fulfillment," a person is thought to find fulfillment if they find an occupation, among those available in this society, that fits their abilities or satisfies a reasonable fraction of their desires. The possibility that the existing society no longer offers occupations that are fulfilling is not usually taken seriously. To find fulfillment is to find one among the existing occupations that is most suited to one's aptitudes. Since our society makes considerable efforts to fit people to the available jobs in systematic ways, and since there is considerable mobility, the person who claims not to find fulfillment, *in the current sense*, appears to be either confused or incurably malcontent and, what is more, we can prove it to him.

By thus taking words in the senses in which they fit existing society, and by insisting that "ordinary language is alright," philosophers give valiant support to the society as it is and perpetuate alienation by blocking people even from saying with useful clarity that they are unable to find fulfillment under present conditions.

It should be clear by now that, if alienation is perpetuated by our refusal to take alienation seriously as a philosophic topic, it also does not help an awful lot to talk about alienation in very general and abstract terms, as is frequently done in discussions of Existentialism and Marxism. Much of what the classics of Existentialism tell us about alienation is extremely suggestive. The same is true of Marx. But most of it is also, as it stands, too general to help anyone think about alienation as they, as individual persons, experience it. Teaching Existentialism or Marx, has the virtue of recognizing the existence of the problem, but in most cases leaves people with the mistaken and utterly debilitating notion that they have understood the problem. Once the Existentialism course is over, once they have taken their exam on Marx, the students are left with nothing but a few general slogans. But in a society that vigorously denies, for instance, through the mouths of its philosophers, that there is a problem of alienation, connecting the general slogans with one's own experience is a difficult task. It requires skills that need to be learned. They are skills which, at present, we do not teach. Thus, what we pride ourselves on doing, as philosophers, namely to help people to think clearly, has not been done in this case. Our students do not emerge from our courses on Existentialism or Marxism with the ability to think clearly about alienation. They are not clear about the conceptual issues, nor articulate about the application of the concepts to their own experience. Each disability obviously reinforces the other. They owe that disability to what they, and we, call their "education."

3. This brings us to the third way in which we teach alienation by not talking about it. We deprive people of an awareness that there is a problem, and of the vocabulary in which to be clear about the problem. But alienation is, in the end, the problem of individuals. My alienation is different from yours, because my circumstances are different from yours. If I am to be clear either about the concepts or about individual cases, I must be able to state carefully and reasonably, the forms in which I experience alienation. I must be able to be lucid and articulate about my experience, particularly in those areas which are not frequently discussed (unlike, say, moral problems about returning borrowed books) and which are even mystified by official attempts to reinterpret the data.

To do this requires special skills, namely the skill to articulate one's experience, to be very clear about what one's situation and one's problems are. But philosophers have not only not taught such a skill to their students. They have, at least implicitly, denied that such a skill exists or that we need it. Remember Kant! The problems of the moral life, and the actions called for, are not in question. There may be genuine, and touching, moral conflict. There may be cases where rules are applied only after prolonged moral struggle. But there is no problem about knowing what one's situation is, what one's needs, what one's feelings are, or one's dissatisfactions.

The facts, of course, are different. It is difficult to be clear and sensible about one's situation. By implicitly denying that rationality extends to one's understanding of one's own situation, philosophers deprive their students of a skill essential to dealing with alienation. Thereby they work in a further way to perpetuate alienation.

4. They do more than that, however. They discredit reason. Professional philosophers pride themselves on being very rational while they are at work. They are clear. They argue carefully and they do not make many mistakes. The current philosophic production constitutes a powerful manifestation of real intelligence. That much is not in question and our students know it.

But they also know that we reject the literature on alienation out of hand. They also know that while we argue superbly, our account of the world and of our situation in it is often quite naïve. They sense, moreover, the gap not only between the content of what we say, and our claims to being rational human beings, but also between our claims to rationality and the form in which we present that rationality. For there is much that is not open to rational argument in the classroom: the content of the course, the way it is conducted, the ways in which students are evaluated and graded, the teachers' likes and dislikes, are, on the whole, not open to argument. It is impossible to persuade people to be rational when the advocate of reason does not dare to entrust himself to reason.

Confronted with that situation, it is not surprising, even if not warranted logically, that our students carry away from their philosophy classes a profound distrust of reason (other than as a set of technical manipulations) and turn, instead, to mysticism, astrology and pure foods. It is we who have misrepresented what it means to be rational and who have persuaded them of the impotence of reason.

Thus there are at least four ways in which our ignoring and belittling the problem of alienation perpetuates everyone's alienation (including, of course, our own as teachers): by denying that there is a problem, by failing to provide and teach the conceptual framework needed to discuss alienation, by ignoring the special skills needed to articulate one's own experience, and, finally, by depreciating reason in speech and example. What I have said was said explicitly about teachers of philosophy. But it is clearly true in many ways also of teachers in a variety of other fields.

Notes

1. Karl Marx, "Alienated Labor," in *Early Writings*, ed. T. B. Bottomore (New York: McGraw-Hill, 1963), 124–125.
2. See for instance M. Aiken, L. A. Ferman, and M. L. Sheppard, *Economic Failure, Alienation, and Extremism* (Ann Arbor: University of Michigan Press, 1968).
3. See for instance Erich Fromm, *The Sane Society* (Greenwich, CT: Fawcett Publications, 1955), 111.
4. This does not commit one, necessarily, to references to 'the unconscious' or worse, to talk about unfelt feelings. For a person may be unaware of felt alienation because they have always been alienated and because they have been told constantly that their life is, by and large, as good as one could reasonably expect it to be. One often becomes explicitly aware of one's psychological states by contrast to different states. As long as people do not experience approximation to being unalienated, they are not fully aware of being alienated.
5. Marx, "Alienated Labor," 132.
6. We can see that criticizing existing institutions on the grounds that they are alienated (and alienating) is to criticize them in view of an ideal. It is possible to argue for the adoption of ideals by examining present dissatisfactions together with limitations of what alternative ways of life are possible for us. But such arguments are extremely long and cannot be given here.
7. See note 3 above.

www.ingramcontent.com/pod-product-compliance
Lightning Source LLC
Chambersburg PA
CBHW051051160426
43193CB00010B/1146